THE BOOK OF
REVELATION
EXPLAINED AND PROCLAIMED

Abstract
The point and purpose of the book of Revelation is to introduce the Word (Jesus), and to wake up the loveless, compromised, corrupt, sleepily, dying, lukewarm churches, by issuing a warning and a window to repent. Repent, or else you will wake up in the Great Tribulation. For those finding themselves in the Great Tribulation, the message does not change, repent and worship the one true God, or else you will be cast into the eternal lake of fire.

MARC R. WHEWAY Ph.D.

www.kingdomseekers.com.au

Ark House Press
PO Box 1722, Port Orchard, WA 98366 USA
PO Box 1321, Mona Vale NSW 1660 Australia
PO Box 318 334, West Harbour, Auckland 0661 New Zealand
arkhousepress.com

© Marc R. Wheway Ph.D. 2021

Scripture quotations are from The ESV® Bible (The Holy Bible, English Standard Version®), copyright © 2001 by Crossway, a publishing ministry of Good News Publishers. Used by permission. All rights reserved.

Cataloguing in Publication Data:
Title: The Revelation Explained And Proclaimed
ISBN: 978-0-6451835-0-4 (pbk)
Subjects: End times; Revelation; Biblical Resource;
Other Authors/Contributors: Wheway, Marc R

Design by initiateagency.com

CONTENTS

CHAPTER ONE – THE INTRODUCTION OF JESUS 1
CHAPTER TWO – THE SEVEN CHURCHES 4
CHAPTER THREE – THE SEVEN CHURCHES 18
CHAPTER FOUR – THE RAPTURE 32
CHAPTER FIVE – THE SCROLL 46
CHAPTER SIX – THE SEALS 55
CHAPTER SEVEN – THE 144,000 SEALED JEWISH EVANGELISTS 87
CHAPTER EIGHT – THE SEVENTH SEAL 93
CHAPTER TEN – THE LITTLE SCROLL 139
CHAPTER ELEVEN – THE TWO WITNESSES 144
CHAPTER TWELVE – THE SEVEN PERSONAGES 155
CHAPTER THIRTEEN – THE SEVEN PERSONAGES 160
CHAPTER FOURTEEN – BRINGING HEAVEN DOWN TO EARTH 172
CHAPTER FIFTEEN – THE WRATH OF GOD IS FINISHED 183
CHAPTER SIXTEEN – THE BOWLS 191
CHAPTER SEVENTEEN – THE WOMAN WHO RIDES THE BEAST 197
CHAPTER EIGHTEEN – COME OUT OF HER MY PEOPLE 204
CHAPTER NINETEEN – AFTER THIS 211
CHAPTER TWENTY – ONE THOUSAND YEARS 234
CHAPTER TWENTY-ONE – THE NEW HEAVEN, EARTH, AND JERUSALEM 259
CHAPTER TWENTY-TWO – I AM COMING SOON 277

PROLOGUE

The purpose of this work is to characterize the book of Revelation in a positive light. While most believe it to be a book of judgment (which it is), or too controversial, the point is missed, and therefore the blessing (Rev. 1:3); that is, "the Revelation of Jesus Christ" (Rev. 1:1–2; 19:10). As such, throughout the twenty-two prophetic chapters (Rev. 1:3; 22:7, 10, 18-19, cf. 10:11), we view God revealing Himself in a way unprecedented for one last attempt to reach humankind (Rev. 6:14–16).

Within the seven-year period as described throughout this book, God appoints the greatest evangelistic force, with events never before seen since time began, to save the multitudes who would otherwise perish (Rev. 7:4–8; 9:20–21; 11:3, 7; 13:8–10; 14:9–10; 16:9b, 11b, 21b; 18:4). The result of such is the most significant revival known to man (Rev. 7:9, 14), yet acting somewhat as bookends to the church age, beginning with what took place in Acts 2. Effectively, Revelation 7 reveals the completion of the prophecy, which was partially fulfilled at Pentecost (Acts 2), as predicted by the prophet Joel (Joel 2).

INTRODUCTION

The book of Revelation is the most misunderstood—and feared—book within the entire Bible. Most believe that it is a book about Satan, the antichrist, the false prophet, judgment, doom, and gloom. Those who do spend time in it are usually tagged as unbalanced or doomsday preachers.

The author of the work disagrees on the ground of the opening verse, "Blessed is he who reads and those who hear the words of this prophecy and keep those things which are written in it; for the time is near." Preceding this statement, John reveals that the book of Revelation is a book of prophecy that specifically testifies of Jesus Christ (Rev. 1:1–2; cf. 19:10), not the devil or his demons.

The book of Revelation is not one of mere judgment but of blessing; it is the only book within the entire Bible that promises a blessing to those who read, hear, and keep what is written. The blessing is, as stated, "The revelation of Jesus Christ," revealed and unveiled throughout the Old and New Testament combined and gained through the study of this prophecy. Adding to the blessing in chapter one, six more blessings are contained within the book. These blessings are otherwise known as the seven beatitudes of Revelation (Rev. 1:3; 14:13; 16:15; 19:9; 20:6; 22:7, 14).

Once more, the one who reads gains revelation of the Son when combined with the keeping of His Word. "Blessed is he… who 'keep[s]' those things which are written." The idea of keeping is underlined with belief and obedience, which are our spiritual responsibilities, expressed throughout the Bible from Genesis to Revelation. The introductory 'keeping' of this book concludes in chapter twenty-two (vv. 7, 9), to avoid what lies in between.

Suffice it to say that obedient believers will not go through the Tribulation (Rev. 3:10), which is reserved for the rebels (Acts 17:30–31), Israel (Dan 9:24), and the unrepentant apostate church alone (2 Thess. 2:3; Rev. 2:22). For this, the apostle Paul provides support, indicating that the church will escape the "wrath to come" (Rom. 5:9; 1 Thess. 1:10; 4:13–18; 5:9). Additional evidence that the church will not go through the Tribulation is in the absence of scriptural reference to it after chapter three. Up until verse twenty-two of chapter three, the church is mentioned nineteen times, and afterward, it is 'missing,' from the earth, at least.

Alongside the reading and keeping of this prophecy comes the prediction that "the 'time' is near" (Rev. 1:3)." Therefore with the revelation of the Son, through the keeping of His Word, comes the announcement of His appearing as indicated in the latter part of verse three, thereby adding to the blessing. A priority is placed on reading, hearing, and keeping the prophecy of this book.

The announcement of Christ's return serves as a bookend for the twenty-two chapters given, seen again in chapter twenty-two (v. 10): "Do not seal the words of the prophecy of this book, for the time is at hand." Here, the words of Jesus are the opposite of the instructions given to Daniel, where Daniel was told to shut up the words and seal the book until the end of time (Dan. 12:4).

Revelation chapter one (v. 3, & 22:10) should not, however, be confused with chapter three (v. 11), which says, "I am coming soon," or chapter twenty-two (v. 7), which reads, "Behold, I am coming quickly." Here, Jesus is not saying that He is coming soon but suddenly. The apostle Paul presents the same idea by saying, "in the twinkling of an eye" (1 Cor. 15:52). Still, several authors have penned verses elsewhere supporting the nearness of Christ's return, as seen in the book of Revelation (Rev. 1:3; 22:10). For example, James writes, "The Judge is at the door" (Ja. 5:9); Paul writes, "He is at hand" (Phil. 4:5; 1 Cor. 16:22); and the author of Hebrews says, "The day is drawing near, and He will not delay" (Heb. 10:25b, 37).

CHAPTER ONE

The Introduction of Jesus

In the introduction to the book of Revelation, we see that the book's revelation is Jesus and that the mystery has been made known to the church (v. 1). We also see that Jesus is God (vv. 5-8, 18) and that He loves us (v. 5). Verses 5-7 capture the heartbeat of the book, and every other within the Bible, presenting the gospel, which is an expression of God's great love for us. Furthermore, we see the book is written to the church - therefore the church (vv. 12-13, 16, 20) should read it, and understand it, live it and proclaim it, and will, in fact, receive a blessing when they do (v. 3). The blessing is a greater revelation of Jesus. In that, we see the urgency of the book with three references indicating the nearing of Jesus' return (vv. 1, 3, 7), and what His return will look like for those caught in unrepentant sin (vv. 12-16). So terrifying was the image of Christ in His return, John fell at Jesus' feet as a man dead (v. 17). Remember, this letter is written to the church, warning of the things to come… The following two chapters address the churches, warning 5/7 unless they repent, they will suffer judgment. The literal application for our generation is, the unrepentant will go through the tribulation.

Jesus is the revelation with a message to the churches, which includes every church from every time since written (95 A.D.), up until His return (see 1:4, 1:11, 2:7, 11, 17, 29, 3:6, 12, 22, 23, 22:17-21).

The book is about Jesus with a message to the church, about judgment, with a warning, make right (repent), or else... And, "Hold fast until I (Jesus) come."

In this, we saw that God would judge some that are in rebellion, even within the church (2:23), that all the churches will know, He is God, alone (and, not of the cute and fluffy kind - see Exodus 19 & Heb. 12:18-29, 2 Thess. 1:7b-9, Rev. 1:12-17, 6:14-17, 19:11-21).

The purpose of striking the rebellious (even within the church) is to bring back holy 'fear.' (cf. Acts 5:11).

Leading up until Jesus' return, the church is going to be tested or sifted to see whether confessing Christians are real or not (1 Pet. 4:17, Heb. 12:3-17, 2 Tim. 2:1-13).

Those not living and walking according to 1 Peter 1:13-24 (for example) will find themselves on the wrong side of judgment, which is precisely the situation for 5 of 7 churches in chapters 2-3 of the book (Revelation).

The above-mentioned reminds us, none can stand before a Holy God in their own strength (1:17, 6:17, cf. Heb. 10:31). Therefore we must fully trust and surrender to Jesus, who is our only hope.

Due to God's great love and amazing grace, the failing churches are given a pre-examination with a chance to change or make right what is missing/lacking.

At the completion of the book, the same invitation is extended to all, whether of the church or not... COME! (Rev. 22:16-21, cf. 3:18, Isa. 55).

In sum, the letter is written to the churches - therefore the church needs to read it, hear it, and obey it (1:3). The church needs to also warn others of the things to come and the need to repent, alongside offering an invitation to COME and 'buy' from Jesus (22:17, 3:18), alone!

The message to the churches comes with a sense of urgency, for the time is near or at hand (1:1b, 3b, 7, 22:7, 12, 20. Therefore THIS message should be our priority!

The meaning of the names of each church addressed is important as they relate to the issues.

- Ephesus ("desirable") - Meaning provided by "Hitchcock's New and Complete Analysis of the Holy Bible" (published in the late 1800s)
- Smyrna ("myrrh") - from the Greek word smurna, meaning myrrh
- Pergamum ("married") - from the Greek word pergamos, a combination of two Greek words: pergos and gamos. These words combine to mean either "citadel" or "united by marriage."
- Thyatira ("sacrifice") - a Greek word meaning "the castle of Thya." An alternative meaning of "sacrifice offering" was suggested by "Hitchcock's New and Complete Analysis of the Holy Bible" and by Dr. Arnold Fruchtenbaum in his book "Footsteps of the Messiah."
- Sardis ("escaping") - Three meanings have been proposed: "prince of joy," "that which remains," and "those escaping." We relied on Dr. Fruchtenbaum's scholarship, which supports "escaping."
- Philadelphia ("brotherly love") - From the Greek word philadelphos, meaning "brotherly love."
- Laodecia ("people ruling") - From the Greek word laodikeia, which is a combination of two Greeks words: laos (meaning peoples) and dike (meaning justice or judgment).

CHAPTER TWO

The Seven Churches

The first of the seven churches from the book of Revelation, the church of Ephesus (Rev. 2:1-7). To understand the letter, we need to start by considering the history of that church, in particular, what they were dealing with. From there, we learn that this was a church plagued with false teachers, as described in John's letter, yet more so in Paul's letter to Timothy (1 Timothy). However, John's letter narrows in specifically on the Nicolaitans, of which both the church and Jesus hated their works (2:6).

The word Nicolaitan means 'to conquer' and relates to conquering others by 'lording over them.' The outworking of this is seen through the mentality of 'clergy over laity.' In other words, The Nicolaitans were 'false apostles' (2:2) attempting to control others by dominating through the religious rule. The Nicolaitans are also mentioned in the letter to Pergamum; they were accused of teaching false doctrine (3:15).

If these Nicolaitans were the same false teachers as mentioned in 1 Timothy, their false doctrine revolved around two errors: 1). Misuse of the Law (1:3-7, 4:1-3), and 2). Prosperity preaching (6:3-10). In both instances, they were accused of being void of understanding (1:7, 9, 6:4), replaced with speculations (1:4), and imagination (6:5).

When considering the above-mentioned, there is further reason to believe the Nicolaitans were controlling, legalistic, prosperity preachers when considering the link with 1 Timothy and the church of Pergamum. In the letter to the church of Pergamum, the Nicolaitans are mentioned directly after the teaching of Balaam. Balaam was also a false prophet who had gone astray, now prophesying for profit. In other words, offering 'ministry for money.'

When considering the mentioned concerns that were plaguing the church of Ephesus, it is easy to assume, amidst all this evil and false activity, within the church, those testing and recognizing it, even hating it and enduing against it, and not growing weary, should 'only' be commended… And they were commended (vv. 2-3). But there was a very serious problem (v. 4). They had abandoned their first love (v. 4), they had fallen (v. 5), and were failing to do the works they first did (v. 5). While they hated the works of the Nicolaitans, their own works were now lacking. This situation came as a result of falling away from their original position, resulting in abandonment.

The word 'abandoned' is also translated, 'left' or departed' which suggests that in all their testing, resisting, and rebuking, it had led them away from God and were operating independently of God. Their focus had shifted from being devoted to Jesus to doctrine alone. It meant: While the church of Ephesus 'hated' the works of the Nicolaitans, they loved hating their works more than they loved Jesus (see Jn.12:25-26). Jesus no longer held first place in their heart and mind. And, as a result, Jesus told them to Repent, or else…

On every occasion (Rev. 2-3), the 'or else,' or consequence of failing to repent is always significant for salvation. For the church of Ephesus, if they failed to repent, there was the threat of losing their lampstand. In other words, their testimony (cf. Rev. 1:2, 9, 12:11, 17, 19:10, 20:4). And, without their lampstand or testimony, they could not access Paradise. Therefore they could not eat from the tree of life (v. 7), and consequently, they would not be saved. Besides here (Rev. 2:7), the tree of life is mentioned in Genesis 3:22, and Revelation 22:2, and 14. Again, by preventing access to Paradise and the tree of life, Jesus was saying TO THE CHURCH, unless repentance comes first, you will lose your salvation!

In summary: The warning to the church of Ephesus is a warning to all of us (v. 7). It extends to every church and every believer of every age until Christ returns. The letter highlights the danger of being derailed by placing a greater emphasis on doctrine over devotion. While the doctrine is important, it must not take priority over Jesus. Yet, despite the church of Ephesus' great failure, God was merciful to them, and also to us! In the same way, the church of Ephesus received a 'pre-examination' with a warning: 'In your current condition, you won't make it...' We do too! By reading and meditating on the text, and by having an ear to hear what the Spirit is saying, and through examining ourselves (2 Cor, 13:5, 1 Tim. 4:16), we too receive the opportunity to repent and return...

"He that has an ear let him hear what the Spirit says to the churches..."

Smyrna

The name Smyrna comes from the Greek word, Smurna and derives from the Hebrew root word 'Myrrh,' meaning death. When myrrh is crushed, it releases a sweet fragrance, which applied to the church of Smyrna. Because Smyrna is the persecuted church, and although persecuted by remaining faithful while being 'crushed' their faithfulness releases a sweet fragrance unto God's nostrils (cf. 2 Cor. 2:15).

The church of Smyrna was suffering persecution based on three things. 1). Committing to the literal resurrection of Christ. 2). Not compromising, and 3). Resisting worldly riches. This is evident because Polycarp, the first bishop of Smyrna, was burned alive at the stake for preaching against prosperity and preaching on the resurrection of Jesus. The church of Smyrna was not pursuing riches (2:9) as the church of Laodicea was (3:17), but rather following Jesus alone. And in doing so, they fully put their confidence in Him, on His resurrection (2:8), thus on their resurrection (v. 10), and His return.

This was the reason the church was persecuted from both within and without. Both the professing Jews and Romans sort to kill the faithful due to their unwavering commitment to Jesus. So bad was the persecution, those in opposition, calling themselves believers, were actually referred to by God as the synagogue of Satan (v. 9). Simply put, while believing they were 'saved', they were actually and, in reality, serving Satan (v. 10).

When considering the church of Satan, if the church of Smyrna was commended and deemed to be faithful based on the above three points, then the church (synagogue) of Satan was condemned on the basis of the same three points: 1). Denying the literal resurrection of Jesus, thus His return, 2). Compromising, and, 3). Loving money.

Despite the church of Smyrna's commitment to Jesus, the absence of any rebuke such as the other churches received, bar Philadelphia, they were still charged to remain faithful (v. 10). In doing so, they would receive the crown of life (v. 11). The reverse is just as true. Further to receiving the crown of life, they would not be hurt by the second death (the lake of fire). Again, failing to remain faithful would not only cost them the crown, but it would result in being cast into the lake of fire.

A further reason for the charge was, they were about to be persecuted by the devil himself, through the false church and the Romans. Remember, this is the true church being oppressed by the devil! While some today say, the church has all authority over the devil, this verse (v. 10) states the devil can have authority over the church, somewhat like Job, for a season. The reason for the persecution to come is to 'test' or 'sift' the remnant. The testing will sift one from the other. In other words, those remaining faithful in easy times may not remain faithful in difficult times, hence the words: "Be faithful unto death" (v. 10).

In sum, in this life, as a believer in Jesus, you will be persecuted, and that persecution will mostly come from within the church. The testing is to see whether or not you remain faithful to Jesus, alone, during the persecution, thus releasing a sweet aroma unto God. Although the test may be intense, it is temporary (v. 10). Being temporary, however, does not necessarily mean short lasting here and now, but instead limited to this life alone. Those who conquer by remaining faithful to Jesus receive the crown of life, and they (alone) are delivered from the second death, the lake of fire. The reverse is just as true for the faithless, being those who fall away. Those faithless ones who lose their crown will be cast into the lake of fire. Again, this letter is addressed to the church, which includes you and me:

> "He who has an ear to hear let him hear what the Spirit is saying to the churches."

Pergamum

The church of Pergamum is also known as the compromising church. Prophetically, this church falls into the timeline of Constantine who was known for mixing his pagan beliefs with Christianity. Mixing pagan beliefs with Christian is otherwise known as Gnosticism and is seen today in the religious rituals of the Catholic Church, among many others. In fact, the Catholic Church finds its roots in Constantine and evidently, never departed from them.

Like the fulfilled prophetic and the allegoric problem of Pergamum, the natural problem was rooted in the literal church of Pergamum, which stems from its location. The church was located where Satan's throne was, and where Satan dwells (Rev. 2:13). The phrase referring to Satan implies the city of Pergamum was the hub of false teaching and false teachers, therefore the epicentre of deception. The city of Pergamum was likened to a 'Pick and Pay' supermarket, only instead of groceries, gods and goods/gifts from those gods were on offer, for a price, of course! Everything and anything you wanted and needed was available for the asking and for a fee. If you wanted money, there was a god for that. If health, there was also a god for that. Wisdom, education, power, position… whatever you desired, there was a god you could go to, to make a plea and a payment, with a 'promise' of whatever you wanted, it could be yours… (Sound familiar?).

The above mentioned is the historic and prophetic account of the problem, also brought out by the text (2:12-17) with the reference to Balaam, Balak (2:14), and the Nicolaitans (2:15). The history of Balak was, he offered to pay Balaam to curse Israel (Num. 22-25). Put another way, Balak was 'offering a gift' to Balaam in exchange for his desire to be met and fulfilled over his enemy. And, Balaam entertained the idea easily enough, accepting money for 'ministry.' You could say Balaam was, a prophet for hire, profiting from prophesying. The story of Balaam is not so dissimilar to that of Simon the sorcerer who also wanted to profit from ministry. Simon wanted to buy the power of the Holy Spirit so he could perform more extraordinary magic, for a fee, than he already did through the power of demons (Acts 8:18-19). In doing so, he received a threat of winding up in Hell unless he repented (Acts 8:20-22).

Within the text, when connecting the works of Balaam with the doctrine of the Nicolaitans we see more. The Nicolaitans were narcissists practicing neopaganism. Simplified, they were control freaks, lording it over others while indoctrinating their victims with combined pagan/Christian beliefs. On both accounts, Balaam and the Nicolaitans were successfully 'ministering' for profit while promoting false doctrine revolving around misuse of the Law, and hyper-grace. And, like Balaam of old (Num. 22-25), the false teachers in the church of Pergamum taught a twisted gospel designed to do the same thing… get God's people off track and out of favour with God. And, it worked! The evidence of their success is that members of the church were 'holding onto it' (2:14, 15). And, at the same time, these same members were also holding onto Jesus and their confession of Him (2:13). Sadly, however, the latter (vv. 14-15) discounts and disqualifies the former (v. 13).

By now, you should see a pattern, and you should be able to identify something similar in today's Christian culture… The problem then is just as much the problem now, if not worse! We were warned it would be worse and increasing as the day draws near (2 Tim. 4:3-4; 2 Pet. 3:14-18; 1 Jn. 4:1-6).

False teaching in the church today is the very thing preparing the way and leading up to the greatest false teacher of them all, the Antichrist (2 Thess. 2, 1 Jn. 2:18-19), who will operate with and by the power of Satan himself (2 Thess. 2:9-10). This is why Jesus forewarned, false teaching is the greatest of the end times signs, deceiving many (Matt. 24. 4, 5, 11, 24).

So serious was the problem, then and now, Jesus warned the false teachers and any holding onto their false teaching, to "Repent, or else. The following threat was that Jesus would soon come and war against them with the sword of His Mouth" (2:16).

The sword Jesus speaks of was first introduced in chapter one, and so frightening was the image John fell as a man dead at Jesus' feet (1:14-17). The opening line to the letter of Pergamum also offers the same introduction (2:12) as in chapter one. And, the consequence of failing to heed and respond to the threat (2:16) through repentance is revealed later in chapter nineteen of the book of Revelation (vv. 15, 21). These verses and passage offer such a substantial threat and imagery, there can be no mistaking the seriousness of it and the eternal consequences for failing to respond, like that of Simeon the sorcerer (Acts 8:20-22). And, remember, the threat Jesus made is to the church!

In sum: The problem for Pergamum, then, is the same problem for us today, seen mainly through prosperity 'preachers' presenting and promoting a twisted version of the gospel for 'their own' greedy gain. Although originally seen through the Catholic Church, in offering forgiveness of sin for a fee to avoid or spend less time in purgatory, we now see it in and through the Word of Faith movement, incorporating hyper-grace teaching. More recently, the New Apostolic Reformation (NAR) movement has taken first place and centre stage. Central to the teaching of the said movements and denominations is the 'promise' of pick/plead and pay (give your best offering today) that whatever you desire, declare, and decree, it will be given to thee. And that is the attraction of these movements. They use the same method Satan did to deceive Eve within the garden and tried to tempt Jesus within the wilderness, and later Judas. By using the same method, they, and those accepting it, 'hold fast' to the teaching of Satan, as delivered through Balaam, and the Nicolaitans (2:14-15), even while confessing Jesus (Rev. 2:13). Nothing has changed!

But, there have been, and always will be false teachers within the church. There will also always be a remnant who remains faithful, such as Antipas. And, for this, Antipas 'paid with his life' (2:13) at the hand of his 'believing brothers', who were 'paying for prosperity' to gain a better life. The name Antipas means 'against all' which implies, he was against all that was false, holding fast only to the teachings of Christ; and we should be too, at any price.

"He who has an ear let him hear what the Spirit says to the churches."

Thyatira

The church of Thyatira shared similar concerns to that of Pergamum. While the church of Pergamum is known as the compromising church, Thyatira is known as the corrupt church. Both were contaminated with false doctrine. For Pergamum, the problem was that some were holding onto the teaching of Balaam and the Nicolaitans. For Thyatira, most were tolerating and holding onto the teachings of Jezebel. The name 'Jezebel' means 'unhusbanded,' which implies, unsubmitted against legitimate authority, being God and God's established authority. Jezebel was primarily known for having no regard for God's Law, evident by introducing pagan worship to Israel. See 1 Kings 16:31 (the sin), 21:23 (the prophecy), 2 Kings 9:10 (the prophecy), and 32-37 (the prophecy fulfilled).

Although Jezebel was killed by Jehu, the spirit of Jezebel is very much alive and well today. The evidence of this is seen where the spirit murdered John the Baptist, who was likened to Elijah (Lu. 1:17). John preached repentance and confronted the false prophets, like Elijah, and would have fulfilled Malachi's 'Elijah, prophecy' (Mal. 4:5), as revealed by Jesus (Matt. 11:13-14) if his message had been received. Instead, the prophecy remains to be fulfilled and will be during the coming tribulation through one of the two witnesses (Rev. 11). Further evidence for the spirit of Jezebel being alive and well today is seen with her mention in the letter to the church of Thyatira. Chapter 17 of the book of Revelation should also be considered, revealing the Harlot (church), which is the coming one-world religious system operating during the great tribulation. Today, the Harlot is identified as the Roman Catholic Church, evident through the description of Revelation 17:4-6. Compare the said verses with the attire of catholic cardinals and their murderous history.

Further evidence is seen in their idolatrous worship of Mary, the 'Queen of Heaven'. Linking the worship of Mary to Jezebel is where the people of Phoenicia worshipped Baal. Baalism included the worship of Molech with fiery sacrifices of children and the worship of Astarte, the Phoenician Ishtar Queen of Heaven. The Phoenician princess Jezebel, who became the wife of King Ahab of the northern Kingdom of Israel, influenced him to fully establish Baal worship in his realm (1 Kg. 16:29-33; 21:25-26). This move entangled the people of Israel in Queen-of-Heaven worship, and it continues within Catholicism today.

In defence of Catholicism, some might at this point argue there are many Catholic institutions doing good works. Yet the church of Thyatira, holding onto the teachings of Jezebel also had 'good works' (love, faith, service, and patient endurance), which were increasing. But the works were 'their works' (v. 19). The difference is seen with the faithful few resisting Jezebel, who Jesus told to keep 'My (His) works' (v. 26). While religion can produce good works and even supernatural works, works void of a relationship with Jesus are worthless. And, although many will rely on their works on the day of judgement (Matt. 7:22), it will be in vain. Remember, Jesus is the one who will search the mind and heart and give according to what each person's works deserve (v. 23). When a person's works are 'their works,' being void of Jesus, judgement will surely follow (vv. 22-23a). When the person's works are 'His (Jesus) works,' on the condition that they continue until the end, that person will receive their reward (v. 27). The reward, in this case, is having authority over the nations, which refers to the millennium. Luke 19 picks up on the same with the parable of the minas (vv. 11-27).

Having authority over the nations in the millennium, runs contrary to having authority here and now as Catholics have enforced for centuries. This ideology is also seen through seven-mountain dominionists, who teach 'kingdom now theology.' Kingdom now theology is also found in the Word of Faith movement, which incorporates hyper-grace teaching, implying: 'You can do whatever you like, and it will be alright.' The thinking behind this deception is rooted in hyper-Calvinistic 'once saved always saved' rhetoric. The 'theology' supporting that nonsense argues because we are the elect of God, nothing can separate us from Him, not even our wilful, continual, habitual sin, whether it be sexual sin or even idolatry (v. 20). This line of thinking runs hand in hand with the teaching of Jezebel, which is also known as antinomianism, meaning 'against the law.' Antinomianism is applied where 'Christians' state they are saved by grace alone; therefore, there is no need for the Law or the NT commandments. However, Jesus states something entirely different! Unless Jezebel and those holding onto this teaching repent (vv. 21, 22), she will be thrown into a sickbed, and those with her will be thrown into the great tribulation (v. 22).

Furthermore (in the great tribulation), her children (followers) will be struck dead (v. 23a). The purpose of the judgement is to bring godly fear back into the remaining (tribulation) 'left-behind church' (v. 23b), similar to Acts 5:11. Godly fear will come over the left-behind church through knowing that God searches the heart and mind to determine the spirit behind a person's works and then judges accordingly. Which is to say, God will not be fooled by worthless, worldly works, such that religion produces, as good as those works may appear (v. 19).

Cleary, a lack of godly fear, is the root cause of the problem for those holding onto idolatry and false hyper-grace doctrine, which has no regard for Jesus' commands or God's Law. Moreover, not only is the church of Thyatira accused of holding onto false doctrine, they have gone a step further by learning the 'deep things of Satan' (v. 24). The deep things of Satan relate to learning and practicing the occult and even promoting it through the church. It is seen today where 'Christians' promote and practice angel, or destiny card readings, mirroring something of what the false prophets did in Jeremiah's day (Jer. 27:9). This practice involves consulting with demons to get 'words of knowledge', which is strictly forbidden (Lev. 19:31, 20:6, Deut. 18:9-13, 1 Chron. 10:13-14). Consulting with demons is witchcraft, practiced through tarot card reading, Crystal balls, and Ouija boards. Some partitioners are now even claiming to be 'Christian' witches, stating that the Holy Spirit, or 'Christ-Spirit,' sometimes also referred to as the 'Gift-Giver,' is leading and directing them in their reading. They are very wrong! As mentioned above, the spirit they are interacting with is a demon, such as seen with the young girl in Acts 16:16-24, who, by a spirit of divination, was fortune-telling (v. 16). The demon operating through the young girl even went as far as to disguise itself by proclaiming Jesus as the means of salvation (v. 17). In doing so, she would deceive many, just like today, with the primary aim to draw away from the true and pure worship of Christ alone.

As stated above, despite the church of Thyatira being so far off track, God is merciful, offering an opportunity to repent (vv. 21-22) after pointing out the problem (v. 20). And, He does so in the most confronting and frightening manner (v. 18). The imagery seen in verse 18 is the same as what John saw in chapter one (vv. 15-16), which caused him to fall as a man dead (1:17). The same response is required of us today - we must die to sin that we may live for Christ (Rom. 6:8). For those who do and hold fast until Jesus comes (v. 25), conquering and keeping His works until the end (v. 26), that one is guaranteed to be removed from the earth before the tribulation commences (3:10). The removal will take place via the pre-tribulation rapture (Lu. 21:33-36, Rom. 5:9, 11:25, 1 Cor. 15:51-52, 1 Thess. 1:10, 5:9, 4:13-18, Rev. 3:10, 4:1). Those who have compromised will go through the tribulation (Rev. 2:22). On the return of Jesus, seven years later, the raptured saints will accompany Him, and they will receive their reward of ruling over the nations (v. 26) during the millennium, under Christ (v. 27). Moreover, not only will they rule with Christ, they will HAVE Christ (v. 29), and every religious practice thereafter will be holy and without corruption (v. 27, Zech. 14:20-21).

"He who has an ear let him hear what the Spirit is saying to the churches."

CHAPTER THREE

The Seven Churches Continued

Sardis

The fifth church Jesus addressed in the book of Revelation is Sardis. The word Sardis means Escaping, which is quite appropriate when considering verse four in particular, where only a few within the church had not soiled their garments. They had not defiled their garments due to not succumbing to corruption - therefore they alone were counted worthy and would remain worthy on the condition that they continued (v. 5). As for the rest, they were in grave danger of being left behind to endure the great tribulation (v. 3), consequently they would not escape what was/is coming upon the whole world (v. 10). Jesus made this very clear with the phrase: "I will come like a thief in the night, and you will not know what hour I will come against you," (v. 3). Notice how Jesus makes the threat, TO THE CHURCH, I will come against you!

The phrase from verse three (I will come like a thief in the night, and you will not know what hour I will come against you) is also found elsewhere in scripture (Matt. 24:43, 1 Thess. 5:1-2, 2 Pet. 3:10). The saying in each account always refers to the return of Jesus, and implies, that on His return there will be a separation of sheep and goats. One group (the sheep) is to go to heaven, and the other group (the goats) to hell (Matt. 25:31-46). Both groups, up until Jesus returns, mingle together and can even be difficult to tell apart. And this is precisely what is seen in the church of Sardis, two types mixing together, professing Christ, yet having two very different theological positions and practices. The difference qualifies one group to be alive, and the other is near dead, spiritually speaking.

The church of Sardis is known as the Dead church, albeit lively in reputation; it was lifeless in Christ. It was due to what was once received and heard, but is now dying (v. 2). It was dying because it was replaced with a 'different' gospel. The different gospel is made up of two parts: 1). Prosperity preaching, and, 2). Paganism. These two issues have been intertwined, resulting in a departure from foundational truth (v. 3), that is, the pure unabated gospel of Jesus Christ.

Due to departing from the truth, they had soiled their garments (v. 4), which is essential for salvation (Rev. 3:5, 18, 4:4, 6:11, 7:9, 13, 14, 19:8, 14, see Eph. 5:27). As a result of having soiled garments, unless repentance came first, their names were in danger of being blotted out of the book of Life, and consequently not confessed before the Father (v. 5).

The book of Life is mentioned six times within the book of Revelation (3:5, 13:8, 17:8, 20:12, 15, 21:27), always making the distinction between those who will enter into eternal life and those who are damned to eternal hellfire.

As mentioned above, the garments were soiled due to departing from the true gospel of Jesus Christ, which was done through false prosperity preaching intermingled with pagan practices. We know this to be the case by the history and reputation of the church and its location. The location was in a wealthy city, and the church was located right next to a pagan temple. Like many churches today, the church of Sardis incorporated worldly wealth and worship into their own doctrine and works, hence their reputation of being alive, yet were dying.

The works of the church (v. 2) refers to salvation through a lifestyle of repentance and reverential fear of God. Supporting verses are found in Matthew 3:7-12, Luke 3:7-18, and Acts 26:19b-20. Luke's account is particularly interesting, linking repentance (v. 8) and good work (vv. 11, 13, 14) with the consequence of failure (vv. 9, 17). Paul's account also links obedience to the heavenly vision (calling) with repentance and performing deeds in keeping with repentance. This combination was clearly lacking within the church of Sardis, where their works were found incomplete (Rev. 3:2). The reason is they had fallen asleep, spiritually. Satan had sung the church to sleep with a lying lullaby, deceiving the congregation into thinking they are: 1). Alive in God, and 2). Their worship was acceptable and worthy in God's sight. Jesus, on the other hand, states the opposite: "You are dying, you are soiled, and you are not worthy."

To reconcile the problem, Jesus told the church that had soiled their garment, to:

- Wake up (v. 2)
- Strengthen (v. 2)
- Complete your works (v. 2)
- Remember (v. 3)
- Keep (v. 3), and
- Repent (v. 3)

On the other hand, Jesus instructed those who had not soiled their garment, to:

- Continue to conquer (do not fall asleep, remember, and keep what you have).

At this point, it should be made clear, on the day of judgement, none will escape God's wrath unless he/she is found worthy, in, and through Jesus Christ alone! Anyone found lacking will be unable to hide or excuse their behaviour and failure. The opening verse to the letter highlights that fact with the reference to the seven spirits of God (v. 1). The seven spirits refer to the Holy Spirit (Rev. 5:6), and His righteous judgement (see Isa. 11:2-5). Which, again, is to say, no one will escape His all-seeing eyes. The seven Spirits are the seven eyes of God and the seven eyes of Christ (Rev. 1:4c; 4:5b; 5:6; Zech. 3:9; 4:10).

In sum: The consequence of spiritual failure is that Jesus will come like a thief in the night, and those failing will not know what hour He will come against them. They will be 'left behind' to endure the great tribulation, their names will be blotted out of the book of Life, and consequently, their names will not be confessed before the Father. Yet Jesus, in His mercy, confronts the failing church and tells them to wake up, strengthen and complete their works, remember what they received and heard, keep that, and repent. Furthermore, continue in that until He returns.

"He who has an ear let him hear what the Spirit says to the churches."

Philadelphia

The church of Philadelphia is the sixth church addressed with the seven and only two of the seven that received no rebuke. The name Philadelphia means 'brotherly love.' Brotherly love is mentioned seven times in the N.T. (Rom. 12:10, 1 Thess. 4:9, Heb. 13:1, 1 Pet. 1:7 (x2), and Rev. 3:7). Love is an essential ingredient for every believer, for without it, you will not inherit eternal life. Such was the warning to the church of Ephesus (2:4). Although the church of Ephesus was rebuked for losing their first love, towards God, this lack of love is evident in the way we treat each other (1 Jn. 4:20).

Due to the love the church of Philadelphia had towards God, they kept His word (3:8, 10), and they did not deny His name (3:8). For this, God loved them (3:9) and would keep them from the great tribulation (3:10). Keeping God's word refers to not compromising, as the church of Pergamum had done, and staying free of corruption, unlike the church of Thyatira. Likewise, it relates to completing the works of God by bearing the fruit of repentance, whereas the church of Sardis failed by soiling their garments. In addition to keeping God's word, the faithful had not denied God's name, referring to not bowing down to anything false, such as the Jews in the synagogue of Satan. Furthermore, these Jews, no doubt, sought to force others to do the same. However, God would make these false scribes bow down to the faithful few in due time (3:9). Until then, the remnant had but one charge: Hold fast!

Holding fast is directly rooted in covenant language, referring to doing your part. While God alone established our covenant through Jesus Christ, we still have a role to play to remain in that covenant. This truth applies to both the O.T. and the N.T. Today, many dismiss the O.T. covenant conditions by claiming 'grace.' They state, because we are under the age of grace, the requirement of the O.T. does not apply. However, God's grace was given to all believers under every dispensation.

Moreover, grace is always followed by judgement. The judgement following this dispensation is the great tribulation, mirroring the Flood of Genesis 7 and the plagues of Egypt in Exodus 7-12. Judgement always follows grace, seen again where Israel was taken into captivity by the Assyrians (2 Kings 17), and when Judah was taken into captivity by the Babylonians (2 Kings 24-25). Judgement following grace was yet again seen where the Jews rejected Jesus, resulting in Jerusalem being sacked by the Romans in 70 A.D., fulfilling prophesy (Matt. 24:2). On each account, grace was given and rejected, and was subsequently followed by judgement. This will be repeated once more for Israel, the lukewarm church, and the world, shortly with the opening of the seals (Rev. 6). Within the letters to the seven churches, there are three references to the mentioned coming judgement, following this age of grace (2:22, 3:3, 3:10). Only those keeping God's word will escape the hour of trial coming on the whole world (Rev. 3:10).

Again, those escaping the great tribulation are those, and those alone, who are holding fast. The same command given to Israel (Deut. 20:10, 11:22, 13:4, Josh. 22:5, 23:8) applies equally to us. The writer of the book of Hebrews makes that clear, linking the commands of God, given through Moses and Joshua, to us today (Heb. 3-4, 10:19-31). Paul also provides support in 1 Corinthians 15:1-2 by stating, "IF we hold fast to the gospel he preached, we are being saved." The conditional IF is seen many times throughout all the passages mentioned above, both within the O.T. and N.T. alike. At this point, it is essential to note the difference between the gospel Paul preached and other versions that were getting around (2 Cor. 11:4, Gal. 1:8). Such was the situation within all of the addressed seven churches. Those receiving the rebuke had departed from what they first received and heard (Rev. 3:3), which is the gospel. Thus, they soiled their garments and were, therefore, in danger of judgement (Rev. 3:2-3). In addition to Paul's warning to the church of Corinth, he provides another to the saints at Philippi, encouraging the believers to hold fast to the word of life, or else their profession of faith is in vain (Phil. 2:16). The same warning was given to the church of Philadelphia (Rev. 3:11-12). They were to keep the word about patient endurance, they were to hold fast to their crown, and to remain by conquering the temptations of this world. Then, and only then, they would receive their reward.

In sum, the promise to the church is: IF they endure tribulation now (Rev. 1:9), they will not have to endure the great tribulation to come (3:10). Enduring now refers to dying with Christ, living for Christ, and not denying His name (cf. 2 Tim. 2:10-13). Enduring the great tribulation refers to the worst event humanity has ever seen or will see again (Matt. 24:21). So horrific will that time be, Jesus warned, "If the (tribulation) days had not cut short no human would be saved (Matt. 24:22), yet still, "Only those who endure until the end (in those days) will be saved" (Matt. 24:13).

Those who do endure this side of the tribulation will escape the things to come. They will be pillars in the temple, they will remain in the temple of God, they will receive new names, and they will abide in the new city of God, which is Jerusalem, that comes down from heaven (Rev. 3:12). The promise of being made pillars suggests that the weak believer who endures now will be made secure and given a permanent position in the temple of God in the millennium. While the church of Philadelphia was naturally weak (2:8), God would turn things around. On the other hand, those who had a reputation for being naturally strong, alive and rich, unless repentance came first, God would also flip things around for them too, resulting in judgement and damnation.

The theme of judgement is seen within the opening verse of each of the letters, capturing something of the introduction of Jesus from chapter one (vv. 12-16). Again, so frightening was the image of Jesus, John fell as a man dead. This same image of Jesus coming to judge the nations, and the church, is carried through each letter. For the church of Philadelphia, it is seen in verse one, referencing the keys of David. Chapter one, verse eighteen, pick up on the same referring to Jesus having power over life and death. Another link is seen in chapter one, verse eight, with chapter three, verse one, stating Jesus is God Almighty, which why He, and only He, has power over life and death. This applies to both natural life and death and spiritual life and death. Where the church of Philadelphia was naturally weak, Jesus is spiritually strong in and through them, enabling the faithful church to do what they could not do in their strength (3:7-8). Again, this refers to keeping God's word (3:8, 10), not denying His name (3:8), enduring (3:10), and conquering (3:12). Paul picks up on the same idea in his second letter to Corinth (2 Cor. 12:9-11). Paul's weakness stemmed from religious persecution in the same way the two faithful churches, Smyrna (2:9) and Philadelphia (3:9) experienced. Nevertheless, Paul received God's grace to stand (2 Cor. 12:8) and was made strong through the power of Christ (2 Cor. 12:9-10).

In conclusion: The church of Philadelphia was loved by Jesus despite being weak and unappealing by the world's standards. They were loved due to their commitment to Him and His word, while being under pressure and persecuted in poverty. On the condition that they remained faithful, they would avoid the coming great tribulation, and they would receive their eternal reward. The same is true today for any refusing to bow down to this world, who refuse to water down God's word, and who refuse to deny His name. For those, and those alone, Jesus gives these words: "I am coming soon" (3:11), "hold fast to what you have, and you will receive your reward" (3:11-12).

He that has an ear let him hear what the Spirit is saying to the churches.

Laodicea

The church of Laodicea is the last of the seven addressed within the book of Revelation and is prophetically fulfilled by the 19th - 21st -century church. That is to say, WE ARE the prophetic lukewarm church of Laodicea, being the last church before Jesus returns.

The evidence this last generation will prophetically fulfil the end times prophecy (Matt. 12:30, cf. Hos. 12:8, Zech. 11:8-12) is seen within the prophetic timeline within the church age. The order as outlined below is noted and agreed to by various serious scholars of eschatology: Ephesus, the Apostolic Church (AD 30–100); Smyrna, Roman Persecution (AD 100–313); Pergamum, Age of Constantine (AD 313–600); Thyatira, Dark Ages (AD 600–1517); Sardis, Reformation (AD 1517–1648); Philadelphia, Missionary Movement (AD 1649–1900); Laodicea, Apostasy (AD 1900–present-day).

In addition to the prophetic timeline, the condition of the Laodicean church is more prevalent today than at any other time previous. The state and the problems are due to the pursuit of prosperity, promoted today through the so-called prosperity 'gospel.' And, while the church of Laodicea was indeed materialistically rich (3:17), she was spiritually poor (3:18). This Laodicean condition is the complete opposite of the church of Smyrna. Smyrna was one of only two churches doing well, receiving no rebuke from Jesus. So severe was the state of the church of Laodicea, Jesus gave her no commendation, which meant, they were entirely unsaved, having nothing at all going well.

In fact, so dangerous was this church Jesus did not even ask to enter into it when standing at the door knocking, but instead said He would 'come into the one opening up to Him' (3:20). That same one needed to come out of that system (cf. Rev. 18:4), which is intuitional, organised religion. Opening the door to Jesus refers to opening up your heart to Him, receiving Him, obeying Him, following, and fellowshipping with Him. Against popular belief, Jesus knocking at the door of the church does not refer to evangelism but rather revival. Jesus is seeking to revive His spiritually lost church.

At this point, it is worth mentioning that the name Laodicea means 'people ruling,' which was precisely the problem and is the reason why Jesus is standing on the outside of the church knocking, while the members within are offering lip service by proclaiming His name (cf. Isa. 29:13, Matt. 15:8). Instead of recognising Jesus as the Head of the church, the church has replaced Him in pursuit of prosperity. And, the pursuit of wealth has led to their apostasies; such as the case with Judas (Matt. 26:15) and Demas (2 Tim. 4:10). In doing so, the church is fulfilling prophesy in a negative way (Matt. 24:12, 2 Thess. 2:3, 1 Tim. 4:1-3, 2 Tim. 4:3-4), which will result in Jesus saying… "I never knew you" (Matt. 7:21-23) unless first resolved through repentance (3:19).

Despite the problems mentioned earlier, and although the church of Laodicea is putrid in the mouth of Christ (3:16), Jesus loved/loves it (3:19). For this reason, He rebukes her, seeking to save the lukewarm church (3:20). The fact that Jesus is seeking to save this otherwise damned congregation is evident it is unsaved in its current condition. To be saved, this church must first repent and 'buy from Christ' (3:18, cf. Isa. 55:1-3) instead of buying from the world. Buying from Christ implies eating and drinking Him, that is, feasting on Jesus by partaking of His once and for all sacrifice on the cross, where He and we become one - Him in us, and us in Him.

The command to feed on the flesh of Jesus and to drink His blood (John 6:56) was the very thing that caused seventy-two disciples to depart (John 6:66). These were the same disciples who had previously been successfully ministering in Jesus' name, even casting out demons (Luke 10:17). The seventy-two, however, could not and would not fully commit to Jesus by going the whole way, as required. Therefore, instead of having their names written in heaven (Luke 10:20) they would be disqualified, and thus qualify for the judgement as prophesied in Matthew 7:21-23, as will be the case for many (most) from this generation.

Mentioned-above, Jesus is always seeking to save the lost (Luke 19:10). The very mission is seen throughout the book of Revelation, yet no more than through the letters of the seven churches. An example is seen with the invitation to 'come', found several times throughout the book. Although extended to different parties, in different periods of time, the intention is the same. The purpose of the word 'come' is invitational, drawn from the book of Isaiah 55:1-3, which is what Jesus is citing in the letter to the church of Laodicea (3:18).

On each account, not just to the church of Laodicea, the invitation is extended to seeking sinners, inviting them all to 'come,' that is, forsake religion and come to Jesus. Those responding to the invitation to come into a 'here and now' relationship with Him (3:18, 18:4), will be permanently positioned in the 'there and then' Messianic kingdom (2:26, 3:12, 21, 4:1, 11:14, 22:17). Those who come will be now and then 'rich in Jesus' (3:18) in the same way the church of Smyrna was (2:9).

Application: As mentioned above, the problem for the church of Laodicea is the same problem for us today, packaged by the prosperity gospel and promoted by a number of multimillionaire and even billionaire televangelists, who insist that God made them rich (cf. Hos. 12:8). If indeed that was the case, then God made these greedy peddlers (2 Cor. 2:17) wealthy by emptying the pockets of millions of their deceived followers, all trying to get rich by 'sowing' (giving to get) into their 'ministries.' In fact, there is actual biblical support for such a notice, for Paul said God would send the perishing a strong delusion because they did not love the truth in order to be saved (2 Thess. 2:10-11). The strong delusion refers to the antichrist. However, Satan right now has his false apostles, prophets, and teachers in place, and even behind pulpits masquerading as ministers of light (2 Cor. 11:13-15). The purpose is to condition the soon-to-be-left behind lukewarm church in preparation to receive the antichrist to come during the great tribulation.

He who has an ear, let him hear what the Spirit is saying to the churches.

Conclusion of the Seven Churches

When contemplating the seven letters to the churches (Rev. 2-3), alongside the list's issues, with a warning, repent or your salvation will be lost, it would be foolish to think the letters do not apply to us, also. The only exception to the five was with Smyrna and Philadelphia, who were both only commended, yet still charged to 'hold fast.' Failing to do so would cost them their crown. No crown, no salvation. While some say you cannot lose your salvation, a literal and honest interpretation of the seven letters to the churches in the book of Revelation, among other places, will quickly debunk that argument. The threat Jesus issued each church cannot be understood any other way than stated and summarised below:

Ephesus - they will lose their lampstand/testimony, they won't have access to Paradise, and they will not be able to eat from the tree of life unless they repent.

Smyrna - they will receive the crown of life IF they remain faithful.

Pergamum - Jesus will war against them with the sword of His mouth. They will not receive the hidden manner to eat (Christ, the bread of heaven), they will not receive the white stone (innocence), and they will not receive a new name unless they repent

Thyatira - they will be thrown into a sickbed and thrown into the great tribulation, where Jesus will strike her children dead (in the great tribulation), and they will be given in accordance with what they deserve if they do not repent.

Sardis - Jesus will come like a thief in the night - in an hour, they will not know. They will not be clothed in white garments (salvation), and they WILL have their names blotted out of the book of life. Their names will not be confessed before the Father unless they repent.

Philadelphia - they will be removed from the hour of trial coming on the whole earth (great tribulation), they will keep their crown, and be a pillar in the temple of God. They will never lose that position, and the name of God will be written on them IF they hold fast to what they have.

Laodicea - they will be vomited out, and they will not be granted access to sit with Jesus on His throne if they do not repent.

Based on the above, if you think Jesus will overlook your sin, you are worshipping the wrong God! The specific sins listed include: lovelessness, failing to endure, tolerating false teaching/teachers, sexual sin, tolerating false prophets, idolatry, learning the 'deep things of Satan' (learning and operating in the occult under the banner of Christianity, which includes Freemasonry), being spiritually dead, and being spiritually naked (full of religion yet empty of Christ).

The seven letters are written to the 'churches', which is extended to you and me. Every condition of every church is the reality and the experience today. The warning to them is a warning to us. And, in the same way, the churches received an opportunity to get right with God then, we do too, through the reading, hearing, and keeping of the word (Rev. 1:3).

CHAPTER FOUR

The Rapture

Rev. 4:1a

Revelation chapter 4, verse 1 sees a change in scenery from previous chapters and serves as an interlude from the following (6-19). The passage starts with "I looked up, and behold, a door standing open in heaven!" Exodus 19:20 should be compared where the Lord came down on Mount Sinai, and the Lord called Moses on the top of the Mountain, and Moses went up. In the following verses, God sent Moses back down to warn the Israelites, if they do not obey, they will perish. In fact, for this disobedience, they will perish by the hand of God who will 'break out against them.'

The importance of the Exodus account is this; in the same way, the Lord met Moses in the 'air', Jesus will likewise meet the church in the air (1 Thess. 4:17). However, instead of the church returning to warn the inhabitants of the earth, it will be the two witnesses (Rev. 11), one of which is most likely Moses. After three and a half years of ministry during the tribulation, the two witnesses will be put to death. They will lie dead in the street for three and a half days before rising from the dead, and then they will ascend into heaven. At that time, the exact words John heard "Come up here" (Rev. 4:1) will be heard by the two witnesses and understood by all as they ascend into heaven (Rev. 11:12). Everyone will see this event in the same way the world will watch the church ascend shortly. Like the event in Revelation 11, those left behind will also hear the trumpet blast, summoning the church into the air. This event is referred to as the rapture, which means caught up or snatched away.

While many today believe the doctrine of the rapture is one of the NT, even a theory of the 20th Century, they are mistaken. The OT alluded to the event in Zephaniah 2:3 and Isaiah 26:2, 20. Jesus picks up on it again in Luke 21:38 after providing a summary of end times signs. Jesus concludes by saying, those watching, waiting, awake, praying, and persevering (vv. 23-36), they (alone) will 'escape' the wrath to come. The same promise was given to the church of Philadelphia (Rev. 3:10), on the condition that they 'hold fast' and remain in a conquering state (vv. 11-12). On the other hand, those who do not, they will be cast into the great tribulation (Rev. 2:22-23). For clarity, in these passages, Jesus is talking to the CHURCH. Jesus makes the threat; I (Jesus) will cast you (members of the church) into the great tribulation if you do not repent (Rev, 2:21-22). For those who do repent and remain, they (only they) can expect to escape the things to come.

In agreement with Jesus, Paul continues with the same theme of escaping the wrath to come in Romans 5:9. And continues again in Romans 11:25b, but none more so than 1 Thessalonians 1:10, continuing in chapter 4:16-17, and onwards to chapter 5. Chapter 5, verses 1-11 spells out quite clearly; "God has not destined faithful believers to wrath (v. 9). The day will not catch us out (v. 2, 4), for we are not in darkness (v. 4) UNLESS we otherwise fall asleep" (v. 6-7). The promise of deliverance from the things to come was also picked up earlier in 1 Corinthians 15:50-52. Paul uses the same terminology of a sounding 'trumpet' (1 Cor. 1:52, cf. 1 Thess. 4:17, Rev. 4:1) to indicate, the church is removed.

Even though there are many warnings in scripture about this future event, few will be ready when it happens. That fact was clearly illustrated in the book of Revelation, where only two of the seven churches addressed were counted faithful. Further support of that claim is found in Luke, chapter 13, verses 22-30. Verses 23-24 confirm few will make it, only a remnant; therefore, we should strive (cf. Heb. 4:11) to make sure we are one of those. Those who don't strive, will be shut out, confirmed by Jesus' words "When the Master of the house has risen and shut the door' (v. 25), then those not ready will be shutout." This passage should be considered alongside Noah's account:

At the appointed time, Noah was told by God to GO into the Ark (Gen. 7:1, 16), where he would ESCAPE the things to come (v. 7); once in, God SHUT the door (v. 16). When the flood (tribulation) came, Noah and his family were lifted above and safely removed. Just like in Luke's account (v. 25), those locked out of the Ark, pleading to be let in, perished.

For Noah's generation, once the door was shut, the opportunity to heed the warnings and get right with God was lost. So likewise, will it be in this generation. Only those looking and living for the appearing of Jesus will Go Up and ESCAPE the Great Tribulation. Jesus reiterates this truth with the parable of the ten virgins (Matt. 25:1-13).

Further, support again to the argument of a pre-tribulation rapture is found in Paul's letter of 2 Thessalonians 2, stating the church will be gathered together to Him (Jesus) at the appointed time (v. 1). The appointed time that the church is gathered together takes place just before the Antichrist is revealed (vv. 3, 6-7). Right now, the Holy Spirit is restraining the Antichrist through the church. Once the church is removed (taken out of the way), the Antichrist is then released. The church is removed when the Holy Spirit lifts her up and presents her to Jesus in the air. Only then can the Antichrist be appointed his time of rule, which lasts for seven years (Dan 9:24-27). The seven-year period will make up the time of the tribulation (Dan. 7:25, 12:7, 11, Rev. 11:2, 3, 12:6, 13:4). Again, the church is not on the earth at this time, made evident in her absence from Revelation chapter 4:1. The church is not mentioned again as being on the earth until she returns with Jesus (Rev. 21-22). Until such time, the church is with Jesus, as foretold in John 14:1-3. There, Jesus promised the disciples that He would go and prepare a place for His followers. Jesus was referring to preparing a place in heaven; however, Christians are not destined to live in heaven, but on earth, as seen in Revelation 21-22. Therefore, believers will spend just seven years in heaven, escaping the tribulation on earth, before returning with Jesus. When Jesus sets up His millennial kingdom on earth, the new Jerusalem will come down, residing just above the earth (Rev. 21:2). The place Jesus has prepared for believers in preparation for our time in heaven with Him (Jn. 14:1-3) now descends upon the earth, from where we shall remain, ruling and reigning with Christ for 1000-years.

In a verse, the rapture of the church is the believers' blessed hope, waiting for the appearing of our Savior, Jesus Christ (Titus 2:13). When you are looking for Jesus, you live for Jesus; therefore, you are spiritually awake, ready, and patiently waiting for His return. However, when 'enjoying your best life now,' caught up by the cares of this world (Lu. 21:34), then the day of Jesus' return will come upon you like a trap, like a thief in the night (Matt. 24:43, 1 Thess. 5:2). You will not escape; therefore you will be left behind to endure what must take place 'after this' (Rev. 4:1b).

After This (4:1b)

After This… Everyone's Perspective will Change

Once the rapture takes place, regardless of whether you are caught up to be with Jesus or left behind to endure the tribulation, one thing is for sure, your perspective will change forever. Regardless of what position you hold now, it will change. You will either be fully enlightened, partially enlightened, or completely darkened. Whichever way it will be, EVERYONE will know that God is REAL (Rev. 6:12-17).

Following the rapture of the church (Rev. 4:1a), John was told he would be shown what 'must take place after this' (4:1b). The words 'after this' refer to what takes place after the removal of the church at the end of the church age (2-3). Those escaping the things to come (Rev. 3:10) are the faithful (Rev. 2:10), holding fast until the end (Rev. 3:11). Those failing to repent and wake up this side of the tribulation will, instead, wake up in the tribulation (Rev. 2:22), left behind to endure the seven-year event (Dan. 9:24-27).

When in heaven, John was told by Jesus to write down 'what must take place.' The word 'must' means 'necessary, inevitable, or unavoidable.' What must take place needs to for the purpose of saving the lost from their sin. The tribulation is purposed to reveal God and proclaim the gospel (Rev. 14:6) in an unprecedented way serving as one last attempt to redeem humankind through repentance before they perish eternally (cf. 2 Pet. 3:9-10).

Like John, Daniel also picks up on the same phrase of 'after this' (Dan. 2:29, 45, 7:6, 7, 24). On each occasion, Daniel was referring to the same events recorded by John, starting with Revelation 4:1. John goes further to write in detail what occurs during the tribulation (7:1, 7, 15:5, 18:1, 19:1).

Daniel 'saw' the things to come, progressing from one event to the next, as did John, revealed in Revelation 4:1 with the words 'I looked.' The words 'I looked' are recorded twelve times (4:1, 5:11, 6:2, 5, 8, 12, 7:9, 8:13, 9:7, 14:1, 14, 15:5). Furthermore, there are thirty-five references to the words 'I saw' from Revelation 5:1 to 22:8. The events that followed 'after this' (the rapture) that John saw are as follows:

- Jesus seated on the throne in heaven (chapter 4)
- The Lamb of God who breaks the seven seals, worshipped by the saints (chapter 5)
- The seven seals opened, releasing the four horsemen (chapter 6)
- 144,000 Jews sealed and set to evangelise the earth (chapter 7a)
- The slaughtered saints standing before the throne (chapter 7b)
- An interlude between the seven seals and the seven trumpets (chapter 8)
- The demon plagues of locusts and 200,000,000 horses (chapter 9)
- The seventh trumpet (chapter 10)
- The first beast (chapter 13a)
- The second beast (chapter 13b)
- 144,000 Jews proclaiming the gospel, alongside angels (chapter 14)
- The seven plagues (chapter 15)
- The seven bowls of God's wrath (chapter 16)
- The great prostitute and the beast (chapter 17)
- Babylon falling (chapter 18)
- The conclusion of the marriage supper of the Lamb (chapter 19a)
- Jesus returning to the earth (chapter 19b)
- The battle of Armageddon (chapter 19c)
- The defeat of Satan (chapter 20a)
- The great white throne judgement (chapter 20b)

- The new heaven and new earth (chapter 21a)
- The new Jerusalem (chapter 21b)
- God as the temple (chapter 22a)
- Recap over everything seen (chapter 22b)

John looked and saw everything that followed 'after this,' triggered by the removal of the church via the rapture. He saw the events taking place on the earth from heaven. While in heaven, John saw what was about to happen and then watched as it actually happened. He also saw the response to the events of both those in heaven and those on the earth. 'After this,' and all of the judgements, John then saw Jesus returning to the earth with the saints, where His kingdom would be set up and established for 1000-years. John also saw the judgement of the false prophet, the beast, and Satan, followed by the judgement of the nations at the end of the 1000-year reign. Finally, John saw the new heaven and earth being refurbished. Everything John saw covered the entire tribulation period, and the 1000-year Messianic reign, concluding with everything fully restored and made new. Essentially, John saw the fulfilment of prophetic literature/bible prophecy and every prosperity promise stemming from Israel to the church.

The book of Revelation, as John saw, following the rapture, flows from heavenly perspective to an earthly perspective as seen in the following chapters:

- 4 – heaven
- 5 – heaven
- 6 – heaven/earth
- 7 – earth/heaven
- 8 – heaven/earth
- 9 – earth

- 10 – heaven
- 11 – earth/heaven
- 12 – heaven/earth
- 13 – earth
- 14 – earth
- 15 – heaven
- 16 – heaven/earth
- 17 – earth
- 18 – earth
- 19 – heaven/earth
- 20 – heaven
- 21 – earth
- 22 – earth

Throughout the seven years, John saw the saints worshipping God in heaven while at the same time, he saw the rebellious of the earth cursed Him. John also saw multitudes of earth dwellers coming to faith through repentance in Jesus during the tribulation. Involved in this great revival were the 144,000 sealed Jews, the two witnesses, and angels, concluding with Jesus. Revelation 4:10-11, 5:12-14, 7:11, 11:16, and 19:4 reveal the saints worshipping God in heaven, while five more verses show calling for the now converted saints on the earth worshipping God (11:1, 14:7, 11, 15:4, 20:4). Eight more verses acknowledge the rebellious worshipping the Antichrist on the earth (9:20, 13:4, 8, 12, 15, 14:11, 16:2, 19:20). Although the book concludes by saying, worship God, alone (22:9), most will not. Throughout the seven years, the book of Revelation reveals three different perspectives, 1). heavenly, 2). earthbound, yet heavenly minded (Col. 3:1-4), and 3) worldly.

In sum, on this side of the tribulation, we have an earthly perspective; but after the rapture takes place, we will have a heavenly view from there on out. Paul said it this way: "For now we see through a glass, darkly; but then face to face: now I know in part; but then shall I know even as also I am known" (1 Cor. 13:12). Others, left behind, who come to faith through repentance, will have a heavenly perspective, albeit in the tribulation. And then, there are those darkened by unbelief who will reject God and worship Satan. Although the rebellious will not be able to deny God in this time, they will be able to 'choose' to reject Him by choosing to deny and refusing to accept His authority. In fact, they will even go as far as to hide in the caves and have rocks fall on them than repent of their sins (Rev. 6:12-17, cf. 9:20-21, 16:9, 11). And, as seen throughout this book, God will grant them their desire.

Come Up Here

John saw the vision of the heavenly throne after he heard the Revelation of the messages to the churches.

Following the rapture call 'Come up here,' yet before what John saw 'must take place after this,' John's attention was firmly fixed on the throne of God, concluding the church age. Today, there are several people 'saying' that they have also been to heaven and talk about what they 'believe' they saw, but John actually did see heaven, and this is what he saw and heard:

John first heard the announcement of Jesus (trumpet), as in chapter one (1:10, 4:1), and then saw something of the imagery of Jesus, also as in chapter one. This time, however, the experience of Jesus is quite different from that of chapter one. In chapter one, John fell as a man dead in sheer terror of what He saw. This time he was in awe. Chapter one is a revelation of impending judgement, while chapter four follows the rapture and is then met with the reward. When John was caught up to heaven, it was symbolic of the rapture to come, which will involve the true church of God. When John saw Jesus from the earth (chapter 1), it was symbolic of the coming judgement which will be poured out on all earth dwellers, left behind, following the rapture. Now, in heaven and standing before God on that day, John had no reason to fear because he was, then, like Jesus (1 John 3:2). At that raptured point, perfect love casts out all fear. That is the fear of judgement (1 John 4:18).

Despite the many false testimonies of those claiming they have been to heaven, John was not alone in what he saw. What John saw, Ezekiel also saw, albeit some 400 years before John (Ezekiel 1:26-28, 28:13). Similarly, when Ezekiel saw what John saw, he responded the same way; he fell on his face in fear and awe (1:28, cf. Rev. 1:17). Isaiah likewise had a heavenly experience and responded in the same way (Isa. 6:2-3). The only other reference to someone going to heaven is with Paul, as recorded in 2 Corinthians 12:2—4. Paul's response was that "He heard things that cannot be told, which man may not utter" (v. 4). John wrote something similar in Revelation, chapter 10, verse 4, where he was told not to write down what he saw at that point.

There is one more exception found in the Bible, which is with Stephen, while being stoned, he too got a glimpse of heaven just before he died, recorded in Acts 7. In verses 54-56, Stephen saw an open heaven where Jesus was standing in preparation to receive him. As with Stephen, each testimony of a heavenly experience narrows in on one thing, Jesus! Jesus is the centre of a heavenly vision/testimony, which is the quickest way to debunk false claims of those stating they have had heavenly experiences when void of seeing Jesus. Think of it this way. If you are invited to a king's palace, what would be the most important and most treasured aspect of that visit? It would be seeing and experiencing the king, right! The same is true with any heavenly experience. Remembering, the revelation and the blessing of the prophecy (the book of Revelation) is Jesus (1:1, 3). And it was this blessing that John received by having an experience of heaven – John saw God (Jesus) face to face.

John also saw many spectacular things taking place in heaven, such as lightning and thunder around the throne of God. Lightning and thunder around the throne are seen seven times in the book 4:5, 6:1, 8:5, 11:19, 14:2, 16:18, 19:6 and should be compared to the Exodus account found in Exodus 19:20. Remember, God does not change (Mal. 3:6). Other imagery includes the reference to the sea of glass (4:6-8), seen again in 15:2, 21:18, and 21. Similarly, Ezekiel saw the same 1:5-10, 22, 10:14, as did Isaiah 6:2-3. The sea of glass speaks of purity and perfect reflection. Only purity abides in heaven, nothing corrupt, and nothing tainted is found there, including the spotless saints (21:27).

Relating to purity, John saw the everlasting activity of those who had inherited eternal life. The action is worship, pure worship. John saw the saints worshipping Jesus as God. The worshippers John saw were those (alone) who had inherited crowns (4:10). These are those who had remained faithful (2:10), and held fast (3:11). As for the rest, at this point, they were left behind and cast or vomited into the great tribulation (2:22, 3:16). Another observation is that only those (those alone) wearing white garments were seen in heaven (4:4). These were the ones who kept their garments white (3:5), who were refined by fire, thereby having white garments (3:18). And, these were those who had woken up (3:3, cf. Luke 21:34-36) and have remained awake (16:15). As for the rest, the ones who had soiled their garments (3:4), who did not repent, because they did not wake up, they missed the rapture due to Jesus coming like a thief in the night (Matt. 24:43, 1 Thess. 5:2, Rev. 3:3), and were left behind to experience the wrath to come (Rev. 6-19).

In sum, a heavenly experience is centred on Jesus, which each of the three dominant biblical testimonies were bearing similar witness (Ezekiel, Isaiah, and John). Furthermore, worship is what takes place in heaven, confirmed by verse 4. That being the case, if you don't like worshipping God, you won't like heaven, and neither will you be going there, as heaven is reserved for those who worship God alone. Chapter 5:8-14 provides something more of what that pure and heavenly worship will look like, again, being reserved alone for those holding onto their crowns and keeping their garments white. Throughout the book of Revelation, worship is, in fact, an ongoing central theme and activity, as seen in the below chart.

Moreover, the book of Revelation is all about worship, either worshipping Jesus, or the antichrist, God, or Satan. Chapters 13 and 14 illustrate that best where on the one hand there is a demand to receive the Mark of the Beast (13:16), while on the other hand, an angel is flying directly overhead proclaiming the everlasting gospel saying, with a loud voice, to fear God and worship Him (14:7). Revelation 14:7 brings us back to 4:11, where God alone is worthy of worship (cf. 19:10, 22:8-9). False worship, or idolatry, was the problem addressed with 5/7 of the churches in chapters 2-3. Due to idolatry they were in danger of being left behind, either cast or vomited into the great tribulation, receiving one more chance to get it right.

14 Doxologies in the Book of Revelation

References	The One(s) Giving the Praise	The One(s) Receiving the Praise
4:8	4 living creatures	God the Father
4:11	24 elders	God the Father
5:9–10	24 elders and 4 living creatures	The Lamb (Christ)
5:12	Many angels	The Lamb
5:13	Every creature	God the Father and the Lamb
7:10	Tribulation martyrs	God the Father and the Lamb
7:12	Angels, 24 elders, and 4 living creatures	God the Father
11:16–18	24 elders	God the Father
15:3–4	Tribulation saints	God the Father and the Lamb
16:5–6	Angel	God the Father
16:7	"The altar"	God the Father
19:1–3	A great multitude	God the Father
19:4	24 elders and 4 living creatures	God the Father
19:6–8	A great multitude	God the Father

Source: Walvoord, J. F. (1985). <u>Revelation</u>. In J. F. Walvoord & R. B. Zuck (Eds.), *The Bible Knowledge Commentary: An Exposition of the Scriptures* (Vol. 2, p. 943). Wheaton, IL: Victor Books.

In conclusion: Throughout the book of Revelation, worship revolves around four things:

- Jesus is God (1:8, 11:7, 15:3, 16:7, 14, 19:6, 15, 21:22)
- Jesus is the Creator (4:11, 5:12-13, 10:6, 14:7, cf. Col 1:16-17)
- Jesus is the Redeemer (5:9, 12, 7:9, 10, 14, 17, 12:11, 13:8, 14:1, 4, 19:7, 9, 21:9)
- Jesus is the returning King (5:10, 13, 6:16, 19, cf. 1:6, 20:16, Isa 61:6)

So, the next time you hear a testimony about someone getting a glimpse of heaven, test that testimony against scripture, against the recorded experiences of what such an experience was like for those who went there or got a glimpse of it. Notice, none of the examples given in scripture talked about a mansion and or an individual appointment or a promotion or gaining a higher office. Instead, every example, without exception, points to fear, awe, and worshipping Jesus.

CHAPTER FIVE

(5a)
The Scroll

Chapter 4 of the book serves as an introduction to chapters 4 and 5, which go together. The central point is the scroll and seven seals, narrowing in on the Lamb (Jesus). The critical question of the text provides confirmation: Who is worthy to break the seal and open the scroll? (vv. 2-5). Only one, the Lamb, Jesus Christ! The scroll is the title deed of the earth similar to a title deed of a property, where only the owner of that property has the power to process the deed and break its seal to open. Furthermore, the owner has the authority to execute certain judgements such as evicting bad tenants and making various changes, whether to tear down, rebuild, and or renovate.

Interestingly, the Greek word for scroll is biblion, from where we get the word Bible. Again, only the Lion (Jesus), the root of David (v. 5, 22:16), can open it. The reference to Jesus as the Lion is found one time in the book of Revelation (v. 5), while references to Jesus as the Lamb are found twenty-seven times. The significants of this are that, the Lamb is symbolic of salvation, pointing to Jesus' reason from coming the first time (Jn. 1:29,

36). The Lion is symbolic of judgement and rulership, which looks to Jesus' second coming (cf. Dan. 7:9, 13-14, 2 Thess. 1:5-10, Rev. 19). When Jesus returns for His church, He does not return to the earth but instead meets the church in the air (1 Cor. 15:51-52), ushering the church into heaven. What John experienced following the words, 'Come up here' (4:1), signifies the rapture (cf. 11:12). When in heaven, the church will be among the OT saints, witnessing the twenty-four elders and the living creatures (angels) surrounding Jesus, loudly proclaiming 'Who is worthy?' (v. 2). The Lamb is worthy (v. 5). Worthy is the Lamb (v. 12).

Throughout the book of Revelation, there are twenty references of Jesus, people, and angels making proclamations with a loud voice. The references for Jesus are 11:12, 16:1, & 17. The references for angles are 5:2, 7:2, 10, 8:13, 10:13, 11:15, 14:7, 9, 15, 18. Tribulation martyrs will also cry out with a loud voice (6:10), likewise will the 144,000 sealed evangelists (14:2). Lastly, there will be a collection of the above making proclamations throughout the tribulation period, with a loud voice (5:12, 12:10, 19:1), concluding with 21:3. Every reference gives glory to God/Jesus and points to His redemptive work, which further supports the point and purpose of the tribulation being to save. Jesus is always seeking to save the lost (Lu. 19:10), and the tribulation period makes no exception for that mission statement.

One more important reference is found in chapter one, which applies to us: "Blessed is the one who reads ALOUD the words of this prophecy" (v. 3). The promise of blessing is directly followed by a proclamation of Jesus' love for us, His redemptive work, and His promise to return (vv. 5-8). There is no other book in the Bible offering such a blessing to the one who reads aloud. The blessing is Jesus, the revelation of Him (1:1), and the testimony of Him (1:2, 19:10).

Throughout the tribulation period, repeatedly seen in the book of Revelation, worship is the central theme, as seen in 4:8, 11, 5:8-10, 12-14. Chapters 13 and 14 are pivotal in the prophecy where Satan and God are competing for worship. Satan, through the Antichrist, is deceiving and even forcing humanity to worship him (13:15-18), while angels are flying overhead saying with a loud voice, "Fear God and worship Him" (14:7). Worship God alone, or else suffer the consequences (14:9-11). However, the first occurrence of worship seen in the book is, following John praising God (1:5-8) where he then falls at the feet of Jesus (1:17), seen again in chapter 5, verse 8 where the elders also fall at the feet of Jesus, and then again with the four living creatures in verse 14. This is repeated in 7:11, 11:16, and 19:4. There are two more occasions where John falls down and worships an angel in heaven, and both times is rebuked by the angel, saying, "Worship Jesus ALONE" (19:10, and 22:8-9).

Adding to the references above, there are twenty-four worship songs recorded in the book of Revelation:

1. In Revelation 1.5b-6, John praises the God who saved us and made us a kingdom of priests.
2. In Revelation 4.8, the four living creatures praise God's holiness.
3. In Revelation 4.11, the 24 elders sing that God is worthy because he is the Creator.
4. In Revelation, 5.9-10, the elders and the living creatures say that the Lamb is worthy because he is the Redeemer.
5. In Revelation 5.12, the angels, elders, and living creatures exclaim that the Lamb is worthy.
6. In Revelation 5.13b, every creature praises God and the Lamb.
7. In Revelation 5.14, every creature says Amen.

8. In Revelation 7.10, a great multitude sings that salvation belongs to God and the Lamb.
9. In Revelation 7.12, the angels ascribe praise, glory, etc. to God.
10. In Revelation 11.15, heavenly voices say that the kingdom has passed to God and his Messiah.
11. In Revelation 11.17-18, the 24 elders thank God for reigning and for beginning to judge.
12. In Revelation 12.10-12, a heavenly voice calls the heavens to rejoice and the earth to lament, because the dragon has been thrown from heaven to earth.
13. In Revelation 14.3, the 144,000 receive a new song that only they know.
14. In Revelation 15.3-4, the ones who conquer sing about the works of God.
15. In Revelation 16.5-6 an angel sings that God is just for judging the persecutors of the saints.
16. In Revelation 16.7b, the martyrs exclaim that God is just.
17. In Revelation 18.2-3, an angel sings that Babylon has fallen.
18. In Revelation 18.4-7, a voice calls out for people to flee Babylon.
19. In Revelation 18.20, someone (the author?) calls the saints and apostles to rejoice over Babylon.
20. In Revelation 18.21-24, a powerful angel sings that Babylon has fallen.
21. In Revelation 19.1b-3, the great multitude praises God for condemning Babylon.
22. In Revelation 19.4, the elders and living creatures sing Amen, Alleluia.
23. In Revelation 19.5, a voice from the throne calls God's servants to praise him.

24. In Revelation 19.6b-8, the great multitude praises because God reigns, and the wedding supper of the Lamb has arrived.

There are also three other references of the rebellious singing over their loss:

1. In Revelation 18.10, the kings of the earth sing a lament for Babylon.
2. In Revelation 18.16-17a, the merchants sing a lament for Babylon.
3. In Revelation 18.19, the sailors and sea travellers sing a lament for Babylon.

Sources: Mark S. Wilson, Charts on the Book of Revelation. (Grand Rapids: Kregel, 2007), pp. 74-75, augmented by the author's personal study.

The book of Revelation is about Jesus, who alone is worthy of our worship. The following event from chapter six is designed to bring lost humanity to their senses to worship God, starting with repentance (6:12-17, 9:20-21, 16:8-11).

Again, as in the conclusion of chapter four, only a few have seen heaven this side of going there. However, through chapters 4-5, every believer can get a glimpse of it. And, through the verses referenced here, we can also learn what happens there, and everywhere else for that matter (5:13-14). In sum, Jesus alone is worthy to open the scroll because He alone is worthy to be praised/worshipped. In short, Jesus IS God.

CHAPTER FIVE

Part Two

"And you have made them a kingdom and priests to our God,
and they SHALL reign on the earth"
(Rev. 5:10).

To understand the verse above (Rev. 5:10), Revelation 1:6 must first be taken into consideration: "And hath made us kings and priests unto God and his Father."

Recently someone asked me if I believed Revelation 1:6 was true, which was a strange kind of way of asking whether I thought we are called to rule and reign 'as kings and priests' here and now on the earth. While I absolutely believe what Jesus said in Revelation 1:6 is 100% true and reliable, as with every other verse in the Bible, I do NOT accept we are called to rule and reign on earth here and now in the way the inquirer intended. And, this is why…

Firstly, that interpretation of scripture is simply ridiculous. It fails to take into consideration the immediate context, or more comprehensive text and the original source from where the quote is first found, which is Exodus 19:6, and again later in Isaiah 61:6. Furthermore, the passage is also found in the book of Revelation, chapters 5:10, and 20:6. When considering these supporting verses, the reader gains an understanding of what Jesus is referring to and when it will come into full effect.

Secondly, starting with the verse itself, the better translation is 'a kingdom of priests' (ESV), and we are that because we have been reconciled to God through Christ Jesus, the King of kings (v. 5). That being the case, our priesthood and rulership fall directly under Jesus' rulership. And, that statement alone should do most of the work for us in establishing 'when' we rule on the earth. That would be when Jesus returns (Dan. 7:13, Zech. 12:10, Matt. 24:30, 2 Thess. 1:7b-9, Rev. 19:11-21), with us (2 Thess. 1:10), just before the millennial dispensation. From that point onwards, Jesus sets up His rule and reign on the earth (Zech. 14:6-11, 16-21), and the saints will share in that under His Kingship. To clarify, see Revelation 11:15b, "The kingdom of the world has become the kingdom of our Lord and of His Christ, and He shall reign forever and forever." Clearly, the fulfilment of this verse is set for a future date.

Thirdly, from the wider text, we learn from chapters 5:10 and 20:6, the saint's rule with Jesus after this dispensation (church age and tribulation period) is complete. At the close of this age (tribulation), the so-called kings of this world are being slaughtered, which was the case since Jesus was crucified. It is happening today, and it will increase leading up to and during the Tribulation (Matt. 24:8-9, 21). During that time, the coming earthly king, the Antichrist (Dan 7:24, Matt. 24:15, Rev. 17:10-13), will target both Jews (Rev. 12:15) and Christians (Rev. 20:4), killing them on an unprecedented scale.

So, after taking into consideration those mentioned above, the delusion that we are ruling and reigning here and now as kings on the earth is short-sighted and overlooks the fact that Satan is the current god of this world (2 Cor. 4:4), and its ruler (Jn. 14:30, 1 Jn 5:19). That is why he was able to offer Jesus all of the kingdoms of the world when tempted in the wilderness (Matt. 4:8).

Furthermore, when comparing the account recorded in the book of Exodus and the book of Revelation, if we are to rule and reign here and now, the question needs to be asked and answered: Whenever did Israel rule and reign on the earth following their deliverance? They didn't! And they won't until Jesus returns. And, only those calling on Jesus, confessing (Matt. 23:39) and committed to His Lordship (Rev. 14:4-5), and enduring until the end (Matt. 24:13), will do so during the millennium.

As mentioned earlier, another verse besides Exodus 19:6, in need of consideration, is Isaiah 61:6. Here, the passage is broken up into two prophetic parts: 1). The arrival of Jesus (vv. 1-2a), confirmed by Luke (4:18-19), and 2). The return of Jesus (2b). On Jesus' return, He will set up His kingdom on the earth, which is described in verses 2c-11. Within those verses, verse 6 falls and remains to be fulfilled, taking place during the millennium.

As for what Revelation 1:6 implies in the here and now: We need to consider the original source and quote (Exodus 19:6) again. In that event, Israel had been delivered, set free, or freed from slavery at the hand of Egypt. They were set free to become a covenant people of God. When comparing that event with Revelation 1:5-6, we see a repeat of the same: We are set free from slavery/sin, redeemed to God (Rom. 6) by being brought into the covenant. For us, this was achieved through Jesus Christ's finished work on the cross; therefore, our ruling and reigning here and now is over sin (Rom. 5:17). As freed people, we are currently commissioned to bring others into the same (Matt. 28:18-20) by preaching repentance and offering the forgiveness of sin in Jesus' name (John 20:23).

In sum: Revelation 1:6 should be understood in two parts, 1). We are being delivered from sin through Jesus Christ, 2). As such, we are a kingdom of priests under the Kingship of Jesus. As for now, we are called to be ministers of the new covenant, reconciling the lost to God by preaching repentance and the forgiveness of sin. And, in the future, we will be caught up to meet Jesus in the air, then seven years later, we will return with Him to rule and reign on the earth under His Kingship.

The danger of subscribing to 'made kings and priests' now, theology is that it places your focus on the 'here and now' instead of the 'there and then.' For which, I would argue the reason Jesus has John write two chapters (4-5) on our coming heavenly experience, following the church age-for those that conquer the world; those who remain faithful and overcome, is so we fix our eyes on the promised inheritance. In doing so, we turn away from worldly pursuits. There is an old saying, 'look where you are going, or you will go where you are looking.' If we are looking at the world, we shall have the world and all its troubles. Said another way, 'we shall have the world and share in its end'. But, if we fix and focus our eyes on Jesus, we shall have Jesus. When setting our focus on Jesus, the things of the world grow strangely dim. For such a person, worldly materialism, such that the prosperity gospel 'promises' (kingdom now theology), holds no attraction.

CHAPTER SIX

The Seals

Chapter 6 of the book of Revelation introduces the white horse (v. 2), who is the Antichrist, but not before referring to Jesus. Making reference first to Jesus is an important point and continuous theme throughout the prophecy. The importance of this is that the prophecy is the Revelation of Jesus (1:1), for He is the prophecy of the book (19:10b). Too many readers of the prophecy forget this critical point when becoming too focused on the Antichrist, the false prophet, the Mark (666), and Satan. Even the events unfolding throughout the seven-year tribulation period all point back to Jesus, as we have seen and will see in the following chapters. To illustrate further, the opening verse of chapter 6 points back to chapter 5 regarding the scroll and seals. Only Jesus is worthy to open the scroll (5:5), and Jesus alone is worthy of worship (5:9-10, 12-13).

Second, to observing Jesus, there is the angel with a voice like thunder, saying, "Come!" Here, there is clear evidence that God is in complete control of the events unfolding. The word 'Come' indicates 'what follows after this.' Again, the words 'after this' are found numerous times throughout the book, pointing to the unfolding events in progression during the seven-year ordeal. Note also the words 'a voice like thunder.' Having a voice like thunder illustrates authority and command, like a sergeant major perhaps. When a sergeant major thunders a command, the rattled troops stand to attention and quickly act upon his order. It further supports the absolute sovereignty of God, which makes the unholy trio (Satan, the Antichrist, and the false prophet) look pathetic by comparison.

The word 'Come' is repeated with the opening of each of the first four seals (vv. 1, 3, 5, 7), again indicating moving forward progressively. Each new announcement comes with another event unfolding. The progressive nature of the book is illustrated powerfully in chapter 9, verse 12, with the words, 'The first woe has passed; behold, two woes are still to come.' Again, in chapter 11, verse fourteen, 'The second woe has passed; behold, the third woe is soon to come.' There are thirty-eight references in the book of Revelation using the word 'come' to indicate progression with time and events, and all point towards the return of Jesus. When Jesus returns, He quickly and effortlessly deals with the unholy trio (19:20, 20:2-3), progressing then to the establishment of the millennial dispensation (20:4b). Before the millennial reign of Jesus Christ commences, God effortlessly deals with the unholy trio illustrating how insignificant they are by comparison to Him.

Now that the stage is set, the reader is positioned correctly to understand who controls what, including the release and limitation of the white horse, the Antichrist. The white horse is the first of four apocalyptic riders and was initially referred to by the prophet Zachariah (1:8-11, 6:1-7). These riders will inflict havoc throughout the entire Tribulation period under the leadership of the first, the Antichrist. The Antichrist is a counterfeit Christ having a bow, which is seemingly without arrows. Although the description of this white horse is void of arrows, they are not missing. The arrows are deception, accompanied by the activity/traits of the following horsemen, which is war, famine, and pestilence (6:8).

The Antichrist is, in fact, Satan's weapon of mass deception (WMD). He is Satan's son of perdition (2 Thess. 2:3), yet it is God who sends him (2 Thess. 2:11). God sends the Antichrist due to people refusing to love the truth and be saved (2 Thess. 2:10); therefore He gives them what their hearts desire. These are the same that cannot endure sound doctrine; instead, seek teachers who tickle their ears telling them what they want to hear (2 Tim. 4:3). Their inability to endure sound doctrine leads them to be devoted to demonic doctrines (1 Tim 4:1), conditioning these so-called believers for the strong delusion to come, the Antichrist. The Antichrist, or mystery of lawlessness, is already operating today (2 Thess. 2:7) and does so through many pulpits failing to proclaim Christ's second coming. In doing so, that preacher is a deceiver/distractor, operating through/in the spirit of Antichrist (2 Jn. 1:7).

Instead of pointing to Jesus' return, the spirit of Antichrist deceives and distracts from the pulpit by preaching what hearers want to hear, such as promises of prosperity (your best life now). The Antichrist will continue to deceive and distract lovers of pleasure through the tribulation period, delivering billions who refused to love the truth, into a Christless eternity. As mentioned earlier, the spirit of Antichrist is very much alive and well in the church today (1 Jn. 2:18-23, 4:3, 2 Jn. 1:18), preparing, conditioning and delivering the deceived into the tribulation, to accept 'the' Antichrist to come.

When the Antichrist does come onto the scene, he will appear to be a man with 'little' power (Dan. 7:8b), which is a part of the illusion. At this point, it is worth noting; the Antichrist is a literal man and not a system (Dan. 9:26, 11:21, 36, 2 Thess. 2:3, Rev. 13:18, 19:20). This man, the Antichrist, will be revealed only after the church is taken out of the way

(2 Thess. 2:4), by way of the rapture. The tribulation is then triggered around the same time by signing the seven-year peace treaty, presented by the Antichrist (Isa. 28:15, 18, Dan. 9:27, 11:21b). In sum, the rapture and the signing of the peace treaty happen around the same time, and both will serve to reveal and unveil the Antichrist. On this side of the tribulation, any attempt to identify the Antichrist is mere speculation.

When the Antichrist does appear on the scene, he, as a little horn (power), will be in the company of ten nations from the revived Roman Empire (Dan. 2, Rev. 13, 17). The peace treaty signed at the commencement of the tribulation will be broken forty-two months in (Dan. 9:27b, Isa. 28:18), which is the halfway point (cf. Rev. 12:13). At that point, the 'little' horn will attempt to rule the world (Dan. 8:9-23, Rev. 13:7, 17:12-13), deceiving billions with lying signs and wonders (2 Thess. 2:9, Rev. 13:13, 16:16, 19:20). One of the signs and wonders will be his resurrection after receiving a mortal wound to the head, again, at the forty-two-month mark (Rev. 13:3, 12-13). He will be resurrected by his father (Satan) to do his will (Dan. 11:36). At this point, he will demand to be worshipped (Rev. 13:14-15), claiming to be God (2 Thess. 2:4) from the third Temple (Rev. 11:1-2). This act will fulfil the prophecy of the 'abomination of desolation' (Dan. 11:31, 12:11, Matt. 24:15-17, Mk. 13:14).

To ensure alliance and worship, the Antichrist will make his Mark (666) mandatory, which will be connected to the then introduced new world order and economic system (Rev. 13:16-18, 14:11, 16:2, 20:4). The Mark (666) is being prototyped today through a soft strategy of microchipping incorporating blockchain technology, previously promoted through convenience, and now through health and security under the umbrella of 'vaccinations.' However, today's introduction merely serves to condition and prepare the naïve. You cannot take 'the' actual Mark (666) of the Beast until you first have 'a' Beast. In other words, to take his Mark, you have to first recognise and acknowledge him; thereby he has to be made known and announce that he is God. Nonetheless, the stage is set, and soon, very, very soon, the white rider will come galloping onto the scene, which is the world stage of the new world order, established at the commencement of the Tribulation. Albeit, it is already in place with a plan soon to be established.

The Red, Black and Pale Horse (Sword Famine & Pestilence)

Like with the introduction of the white horse, it is God who sends or releases the red, black, and pale horses (Rev. 6:3-8). The trio has been patrolling the earth for thousands of years, waiting, while growing impatient, for their time of release (Zech. 1:8, 6:2, 7). Upon their release, they will bring great distress through Tribulation, where billions dwelling on the earth will perish. Many perishing will be those who have since come to faith in Jesus during the Tribulation period (Rev. 6:8, 7:14, 13:15, 17:6, 18:24, 20:4b). Together with unbelievers, the believers will be slain by a combination of the sword, famine, and pestilence. The sword represents the red horse; the black horse represents famine, and the pale horse, pestilence.

The Tribulation is not the first time God has used this combination of the sword, famine, and pestilence to deal with the rebellious. There are over thirty verses found in scripture, which can be divided into three separate events. The first is 1 Chronicles 21. The next is 2 Chronicles 20, and the last is Jeremiah and Ezekiel's accounts, which refer to the same issues and timeframe. This section will deal with the first account found in 1 Chronicles, and the next section will deal with that of Jeremiah and Ezekiel.

As previously revealed, the sword, famine, and pestilence are sent by God to deal with the rebellious, bringing correction, resulting in repentance. And, that is precisely what we will see with every account recorded in scripture. There is no exception to this. With the report filed in 1 Chronicles, chapter 21, God gives David, as a result of sin, a choice of either judgement by famine for three years, the sword for three months, or pestilence for three days. This sin David committed was putting his trust in himself, or his military, rather than God, despite Joab advising him not to. David's instructions were abhorrent to Joab (v. 6). Nevertheless, David, incited by Satan (v. 1), overrode Joab, instructing him to take a census of his army, which displeased God (v. 7). Later, David realised the error of his ways - that he had dealt foolishly and repented, pleading with the Lord for forgiveness and mercy. But there was a price to pay for his disobedience; and that payment required blood by the hand of God. However, David got to choose the means.

David had to choose between famine, the sword, or pestilence from God. He was having to make the choice caused in great distress, knowing full well of the severity and that there was no avoiding it. No amount of repenting and pleading would turn back the hand of God; payment was required and in full. David's only hope was to 'fall into the hands of God, believing His mercy is very great' (v. 13). In doing so, David said to the Lord, "You choose!" And, He did. God sent pestilence, and 70,000 Israelites died. No doubt that number was made up of the mighty warriors David was so proud of in the first place. But it wasn't going to end there, for God sent an angel to destroy Jerusalem. The angel was standing by the threshing floor and between heaven and earth with a drawn sword stretched out (vv. 15-16). Before striking the nation, God stopped the angel, saying, "It is enough" (v. 15). David also saw the angel of death and fell on his face, repenting of his evil (vv. 16-17). David realised that he had sinned greatly (vv. 8, 17).

David repented (vv. 8, 17), and God relented from the calamity (v. 15), but not before 70,000 Israelites died with a single brushstroke of God's hand. Just imagine how much worse it would have been if the sword-bearing angel had not been stopped! The account recorded in 1 Chronicles gives us a glimpse into how it will be in the Tribulation for those left behind, only it will be far, far worse than what David experienced. For there will be no stopping the sword-drawn angel, nor the angel of famine to follow the angel of pestilence joins. And, they will continue to strike earth dwellers for seven years. Here, the reader should be reminded of the word Jesus, that there has never been a time like the Great Tribulation to come, and there never will be again after it (Matt. 24:14). The Tribulation will be the most incredible time of testing (Rev. 3:10) and sifting (Rev. 14:14-20) ever known in the entire history of humanity.

The idea of testing and sifting is picked up in 1 Chronicles 21, where David saw the sword-bearing angel by the threshing floor (v. 15). On the threshing floor, David built an altar to the Lord and made a sacrifice for his sin (v. 18). Before doing so, David paid 'full price' for the land from Ornan, that the plague may be averted (v. 22). David paid 600 shekels of gold for the property and made a peace offering to God (vv. 25-26). The Lord answered David with fire from heaven, burning up the offering on the altar (v. 26), and then commanded the angel to put his sword away (v. 27). From then on, David was afraid of the sword of the Lord (v. 30). Through this account, David was indeed both tested and sifted.

When reading the account of David, it is crucial to pay careful attention to the mentioned threshing floor. The threshing floor is, in fact, the exact location the temple of Solomon was later built on (2 Sam. 6:6). There is also an interesting parallel with the story of Ruth (3:6-9). In the same way, David found redemption on the threshing floor, so did Ruth, by submitting herself to Boaz, her redeemer. Redemption for both David and Ruth came at the threshing floor, but also through and by threshing (testing). Both suffered, as both were sifted before they found/gained redemption.

The process of threshing separates one from the other, as the threshing floor does for wheat and chaff. Interestingly, the word 'tribulation' in Latin is 'tribulum,' which is where we get the name 'trib'. A trib is the wooden board used to separate wheat and chaff. The connection is clear; Tribulation is purposed to separate one from the other. Jesus said that in this world, we will have tribulation for this purpose (Jn. 16:33), testing and separating. This is also the reason that Jesus came (Matt. 3:12), and unless we have separated to Him this side of the Tribulation, there will be a far more severe sifting in the great Tribulation to come (Matt. 13:24-30, 36-43, Rev. 6-19).

Like the sifting process that puts pressure on the wheat to separate it from the chaff, God's sifting does the same to His people for the same reason. During the threshing process, the grain is crushed, and the chaff is then thrown up into the air with the winnowing fork (cf. Jer. 15:7, Matt. 3:12) and blown away. An example of a church being sifted and crushed is with Smyrna (Rev. 2:8-11). Smyrna was tested (crushed) through persecution yet remained faithful to God. Smyrna means 'myrrh', which when crushed, releases a pleasing, pleasant fragrance. In the process of being crushed, Smyrna remained faithful to God and was thereby separated from those who say 'they are of God' but are not (Rev. 2:9). Another example of a believer being sifted is found in Luke 22:31-32, where Satan demanded to have Peter, that he might sift him like wheat. Peter was indeed sifted, and he did fall but was restored again as Jesus said he would be (vv. 32-34).

During the Tribulation to come, there will be a most severe sifting for seven years (Dan. 9:27), separating one from the other. During that time, God's angels with sharp sickles will reap the earth for the end-time harvest (Rev. 14:16-18, cf. Matt. 13:37-42), only the reaping here is for the purpose of everlasting damnation (Rev. 14:19-20).

In sum, the purpose of the Tribulation is to separate one from the other. Tribulation sifts and separates by producing godly fear as it did in David (1 Chron. 21:30, 22:1). God's sifting will continue both this side of the Great Tribulation to come and in it until Jesus returns. In the hour of trial to come, set to try those who dwell on the earth (Rev. 3:10), God will use the same method that He did with David, only in much greater measure. In fact, in just the first few months of the Tribulation, billions will perish

(Rev. 6:8). By the time Jesus does return, there will only be a remnant remaining (Matt. 24:22), which gives the reader just a glimpse of what that time will resemble. The point and purposes of the sign are that perhaps we might avoid it by allowing God to sift us here and now rather than there and then. Remember always, however, that redemption is the Redeemer's plan and intention – for, Jesus came to seek and save the lost (Lu. 19:10), that God would have none perish, but all come to repentance (2 Pet. 3:9).

In the following section, we will be considering the writings of Jeremiah and Ezekiel, dealing with the same threat of the sword, famine, and pestilence.

Sword Famine and Pestilence – Jeremiah (Revelation 6:1-8) 'A Time of Trouble'

As seen in the previous section, the combination of the sword, famine, and pestilence played a major role in the judgements of Israel. This continues when dealing with the southern kingdom, Judah. Addressing Judah in their apostasies were prophets Jeremiah and Ezekiel, who threatened God's people with God's judgement. The threat of judgement came about as a result of forsaking (2:13; 5:7, 19; 9:13; 16:11, 17:13; 19:3b; 22:9), replacing and forgetting God (13:25, 18:15). Judah had forsaken God and had replaced Him with self-centred pride. This was why David got himself into trouble (1 Chron. 21), costing the lives of 70,000 Israelites (v. 14). The problem of pride will be the same reason this twenty-first-century generation will likewise find itself in trouble, vomited out into the Tribulation to come (Rev. 3:10b, 16). Pride, by way of believing we (the church) have everything and no need for anything, that is, nothing missing, nothing lacking, and nothing broken (Rev. 3:17a). However, after waking up in the tribulation, the left behind lukewarm church will soon realise there was plenty broken, namely God's commands, resulting in broken fellowship and estranged relationships. Overall, wretched, pitiable, poor, blind, and naked (Rev. 3:17b)!

Shortly following the realisation that they (the lukewarm church) have been left behind, the next revelation will follow the opening of the scroll and the breaking of the seals (Rev. 5), which releases the four apocalyptic horsemen (Rev. 6). This revelation will result in the fifth seal, mass martyrdom (Rev. 6:9-11). Martyrdom will come about by deadly, demonic lying signs and wonders (white horse), the sword (red horse), famine (black horse), and pestilence (pale horse). With the release of the horsemen comes the opening events of the seven-year ordeal, which will escalate and increase in intensity, and severity as time draws to a close (Rev. 6-19). The first half of 'the hour of trial' (Rev. 3:10) is said to be the 'Tribulation', while the second half is known to be the 'Great Tribulation.' To understand what these periods might look like, a study of the Old Testament is required; following 1 Chronicles, 21, the next stop is Jeremiah, chapter 14.

Jeremiah 14 is headed, 'sword, famine, and pestilence' for a good reason. Due to the sins (vv. 7, 9, 10) of Judah, the said combination is what God is sending upon His people (v. 12). Specifically, God is sending plagues due to His people backsliding, wandering, and not restraining their sin. The plagues of God will result in the people of God enduring 'a time of trouble' (v. 8, 19). After twenty-three years (25:2-3) of failing to heed the warnings of the prophet, the people of God are now beginning to realise the weight and error of their ways and seek God's forgiveness (vv. 7-9), pleading with the Lord not to forsake them (v. 9). But it is a case of too little, too late, for God will not forgive or accept them (vv. 10, 12) but will instead only remember their sins (v. 10). Furthermore, God instructs Jeremiah not to even pray for them (v. 11); instead He will not hear that prayer, but will consume them by the sword, by famine and by pestilence (v. 12, 15-16).

Like today, the problem for Judah is deeply rooted in the deception of lying prophets (v. 14, 15), who contradicted the word of God. They did so by proclaiming, "You (Judah) shall not see the sword, nor shall you have famine." Instead of warning, the worthless shepherds assured the congregation and sinful nation that God will give them peace (v. 13, 15). Filling the deceived with vain hope (23:16, cf. Matt. 7:22-23), saying, "It shall be well with us" and "No disaster shall come upon you" (23:17). This empty talk is not dissimilar to that of our own modern-day prosperity preachers, who promise something and deliver nothing (see 8:10b-12, 22:13-17, 21).

Because of these failed preachers, God's people were deceived, delivered, and destined unto destruction (v. 16). Instead of receiving godly instruction, they inherited lies (16:19b, cf. 2 Thess. 2:9-12). And, in the time of trouble (v. 8), due to following preachers without knowledge (v. 18), promising peace, when there was no peace (6:14), they will find none, nor healing, but only terror (v. 19). Terror, not peace, was the proclamation of God. No amount of praying, pleading, and repenting would cause God to relent from what He was about to do (15:2-4, 6b-9). Judah was now destined for disaster where nothing and no one can save them (v. 5).

Due to ongoing sin, the central theme of the book of Jeremiah is judgement, pointing to a 'time of trouble' (2:27, 28, 8:15, 11:12, 14:8, 19, 30:7, cf. Ezek. 7:7, Dan. 9:25, 12:1, Rev. 3:10), for the purpose of salvation. Through the Tribulation, God will tear down so that He can build up again (1:10, 31:28). Still, and as always, the purpose of the threat is to bring about change through true and lasting repentance (17:8-11, 18:20-23). A lesson, that's sadly missed, for most do not learn and turn (17:12), ending in Tribulation (21:5-7). Tribulation always follows a time of grace. Following a period of grace, in affliction, Judah will have a choice, once more, to either submit to God in hardship, or perish by the sword, famine, and pestilence (22:7, 9 24:10, 27:8, 13, 29:17, 18, 29:18, 32:36, 34:17, 38:2, 42:22, 44:13). The purpose, once again, is to save their eternal souls.

In sum, through the Tribulation, Judah will be sifted and separated (see Lamentations). Judah's Tribulation was pronounced by Jeremiah for twenty-three years yet fell on deaf ears. Speaking on behalf of God, Jeremiah (15:7) proclaimed that during the trial, "I (God) have (will) winnowed them with a winnowing folk." The winnowing fork takes us back to the topic of the threshing floor, as discussed in the previous section with David (1 Chron. 21), now repeated for Judah. The threshing floor is directly connected to the theme of the sword, famine, and pestilence, and also redemption, which continues through to chapter 16. In chapter 16, Jeremiah instructs Judah (and the reader), in the tribulation, no amount of pleading with God will save your flesh due to forsaking Him and following after and worshiping false gods and refusing to listen to God (16:11-12).

So, what now for us? Like Judah, the lukewarm liberal congregation, failed by false, worthless preachers, who were preaching peace, peace, when there was no peace will be vomited out into the time of trouble (30:7, Dan. 12:1, Matt. 24:21, Rev. 3:10). Then, while in the tribulation, the left behind will be winnowed. Those (then) who fear and worship God, alone (Rev. 14:7), are eternally saved, but slain (Rev. 13:15, 20:4). Those bowing down to false worship are temporally spared, but eternally damned (Rev. 14:9-11).

Conclusion: The book of Jeremiah is one of prophesied judgement against the people of God for forsaking, replacing, and forgetting Him. For all of Judah's sins, they can be summed up in a single verse: "Cursed is the man who trusts in mankind, who makes the flesh his strength and turns his heart from the LORD" (17:5). Virtually the entire book threatens judgement for this sole reason. As mentioned earlier, King David was once on the wrong side of the Lord's sword for the same reason (1 Chron. 21). Likewise, will we be too unless lasting repentance comes first, and fast? (Rev. 3:14-22). To remedy this, God's requirement is simple and summed up in another single verse: "Blessed is the man who trusts in the LORD, whose confidence is Him" (17:7). All Judah had to do was 'turn.' That's it! Turn from self (and man) to trust in God alone. That was the only requirement, and in doing so, everything else would have fallen into line. David did just that and saved Israel from further calamity (1 Chron. 21:15-17, 25-30). The same is required of us (Rev. 3:18-21) or else be vomited out and into the time of trouble coming on the whole earth (Jer. 30:7, Rev. 3:10b).

Sword Famine and Pestilence – Ezekiel (cf. Rev. 6:1-8).

The very thing that separates us from God (i.e., wealth), God is about to remove (Ezek. 7:11, 19), and while at it, putting an end to pride (v. 25). That was the message to Judah. Now think forward 700 years to John's letter, the book of Revelation, and for our time, explicitly addressing the church of Laodicea (Rev. 3:14-22). Laodicea, the final church before Jesus returns, was warned unless they repent, they would be vomited out (into the Tribulation). Laodicea, meaning 'People ruling' was full of wealth, yet empty of God. While the Laodicean church was a literal church in 95 A.D., the letter falls within a prophetic timeline, referring to us today, 1,900 years later. We are prophetically that church, having everything worldly, yet lack Jesus, and subsequently are wretched, pitiful, poor, blind and naked, spiritually speaking. Due to the condition of this church, Jesus warned her to, 'seek Me now, or else meet Me in Tribulation.' For this reason, the religious and lukewarm are given such insight into the Tribulation events following the rapture of the Bride, so they might flee the wrath to come (Matt. 3:7).

The Tribulation will commence with the release of the four apocalyptic horsemen (Rev. 6:1-8). Following the white horse (the Antichrist/deceiver) are the red horse (war), black horse (famine), and the pale horse (pestilence). As written earlier in the previous sections, this combination is first seen in 1 Chronicles, 21; there are also references in 2 Chronicles 20, followed by Jeremiah with eighteen more references. Finally, Ezekiel uses the same language, specifically from chapters five through to chapter seven. The purpose of examining O.T. passages is to allow scripture to interpret scripture. What the events looked like in the O.T. is what they will look like in the N.T., only next time dwarfing anything of the past (Matt. 24:21).

So, what did Tribulation look like for Judah? That day was described as an inescapable disaster (7:5, 26) and doom (vv. 7, 10), where God was judging (vv. 3, 8) and punishing His people (vv. 3, 4, 8, 9). God announced, "Your end has come" (vv. 2, 6), and "Your doom has come" (vv. 7, 10), paralysing the people with terror (v. 27). The reason for the judgement was: "That you will know I am the Lord" (vv. 4, 9, 27). The same rationale will be exact for the coming Tribulation (Rev. 9:21; 16:11); God will remove every obstacle preventing us from acknowledging and worshipping Him alone (Rev. 19). Therefore, when reading the O.T. prophets, we see history is repeating itself, as it always has done. Echoing the announcement to Judah, the same is applied to us: "The day is near" (v. 7), and "The end has come" (vv. 2, 6); repeated for the same point and purpose that we would 'know (experience) God' (Jn. 17:3).

The quote, "That you will know I am the Lord," is repeated twenty-seven times in the book of Ezekiel, and on each occasion, it speaks of Tribulation. God will reveal Himself to His own rebellious people through a time of trouble, and that time of trouble will entail the sword, famine, and pestilence (5:12, 17, 6:11, 12, 7:15). Chapter 14 picks up on the same, throughout verses 13-19. There, Ezekiel predicts what the coming judgments will look like: (a) cut off the food supply and send famine (v. 13), (b) send wild beasts through that country (v. 15), (c) bring a sword (v. 17), and (d) send a plague (v. 19). Chapter five, however, introduces the said combination with the introduction of the sharp sword (v. 1).

The word Ezekiel used for 'sword' is 'hereb,' mentioned eighty-three times in the book of Ezekiel, which refers to the weapon carried by Israel's enemies. With 'this' sword, Ezekiel cut off a third of his hair (vv. 1-4) symbolising a third of God's people will die of the pestilence and be consumed by famine, and a third by the sword (v. 12). Which is to say, if you survived the famine, you would meet with the sword. Amos said something similar when describing the tribulation awaiting Israel (5:18-20). In short, none who are destined to die will escape the things to come. The parallel to Revelation 6, verse 8, is striking, and for a good reason!

In the same way, the last church before Jesus returns was/is wretched, Judah; at this point, it was also worse than any other nation before it (vv. 6-7). Their condition caused God to deal with her in a manner He has never done before (vv. 8-9). God's judgement on these sinful people will exceed anything seen before, which, again, parallels the Tribulation period (Dan. 12:1, Matt. 24:21). Moreover, the prophesied judgement to come cannot be removed or 'prayed away' (8:18, 14:12-23), for 'it has been spoken, and it will/must come to pass.' In the same way, birth pains cannot be prayed away (i.e., COVID-19 – Lu. 21:11).

The word that God has spoken must come to pass (vv. 13, 15, 17), for the purpose: "That they shall know that I (God) am the Lord" (vv. 13, 6:8, 10, 13, 14, 7:4 9, 27). For this reason, God's wrath will be poured out in full until fully satisfied. The same threat is given eleven times in the book of Revelation, and for the same reason. God will use any means and method to reveal Himself. Interestingly, in addition to the sword, famine, and pestilence, Ezekiel includes wild beasts (5:17, 14:15, 21, 29:5, 34:5, 8), which is seen again in Revelation, 6:8. Once more, it is worth pointing out that God, not Satan, sends the plagues (5:8, 6:3). And, the same will be true in the coming Tribulation where it is Jesus who pours out the judgement on every earth dweller (Rev. 14:10, 16:1), in full fury, and until completed (15:1, 16:19, 19:15), to bring people to their senses and turn them away from their sin. Following the Tribulation, repentance and restoration, God reverses the curse (34:35).

Ezekiel, chapter 6, narrows in on the specifics of sin, being idolatry, which is, again, precisely the same reason Jesus addressed the lukewarm church of Laodicea. Highlighted in both Ezekiel and the letter to the last church (Rev. 3:14-22), before Jesus returns, is the contrast and conflict of true worship against false worship. The same is also the central theme of the entire book of Revelation (13-14), and indeed the Bible starting with Adam and Eve.

To summarise -, in the same way, God was about to remove everything false in Israel (6:3-6), He will do again through the Tribulation (Rev. 18). Ezekiel, chapter 20 provides more information, about the specifics of Judah's sin, where he had rebelled against God by turning to idols (v. 8), by not walking in His statutes (vv. 13, 16, 18, 24, 25), by rejecting His rules (v. 16, 18, 24, 25), and for child sacrifice (vv. 26, 31). Child sacrifice is carried out today through abortion, with some churches approving it and even blessing clinics that conduct the procedure. Child sacrifice was the final straw that brought tribulation to Judah. No amount of pleading and praying would avert God's judgement (8:18).

In Tribulation, God will not hear their inquiry (prayer) but instead will pour out His wrath against them (20:33). In doing so, He will deal with them face-to-face (v. 35) for their betrayal, purging the rebels from among them (v. 38). God said, "As I entered into judgment with your fathers, I will enter into judgment with you" (v. 36). Amid judgement, some will, however, find mercy (5:3-5, 6:8-10, 12:16) through belated repentance, returning to God in recognition, that 'He is the Lord;' but, not before experiencing something of His wrath. Alas, God's judgement has come (6:11, 30:2, Jer. 30:7, Rev. 6:17, 18:10, 16, 19).

Chapter 7 describes 'The Day of the Wrath of the Lord,' stating it has come; the end is upon you (vv. 3, 5, 6, 7, 24). Again, God, not Satan, strikes His people (vv. 3, 4, 8, 9, 24). And, when He does, in that day, what was once so valuable to them previously, is now worthless (vv. 11-12, 19). The same will be repeated with the church of Laodicea, who replaced Jesus with wealth and false promises of position, peace, and prosperity.

Like Jeremiah, the false prophets proclaimed peace in a time of judgement (Jer. 6:14, 8:11, 9:8), and found none; the same was true with Ezekiel (13:10, 16). In a time when they should have been condemning the wicked, turning them away from sin that they might live, they instead encouraged them (13:22b). The problem for Ezekiel, then, is just as prevalent today. Actually, the church is rife with it. Failing shepherds promising peace when there is no peace (7:25), but instead disaster, and doom (7:5, 7, 10, 26), looming by way of the sword, famine, and pestilence, and wild beasts (5:17, 7:15, cf. Rev. 6:1-8).

To recap, the problem was, instead of addressing sin and building solid walls for protection (against sin), the false prophets were 'whitewashing' God's word (13:10). In other words, they were covering up cracks (sin) in the wall with flimsy paste, instead of pointing to the coming danger. Like today, these preachers distract God's people with a false proclamation of peace and security (1 Thess. 5:3). And, if the above mentioned wasn't bad enough, Judah's prophets went even further by leading women into witchcraft (13:17-23), prophesying (falsely) for payment (13:19).

The same activity is seen and increasing today through lying signs and wonders operating in the church, as predicted by Paul (2 Thess. 2:8-9). And, because churchgoers refused to love the truth, that would have saved them (2 Thess. 2:10), soon, God will instead cast them into the Tribulation. In the Tribulation, their blind eyes will be opened where God will expose the lies and the false prophets, just as He did in Judah's day (13:20-21). Micah, chapter three addressed the same, where the false prophets promised, peace (v. 5) and that no disaster will come on them (v. 11). In a time of looming judgement, the false prophets minister for payment (v. 11) but would be denounced and disgraced when judgement came (v. 7). The fulfilment of Micah's prophesy is reserved for the latter days (4:1), where the sins of the religious will be declared against them by those empowered by the Holy Spirit (v. 8, cf. Rev. 11).

Conclusion: In Judah's tribulation, there was no defence against God's wrath (vv. 15-16), which will be repeated for those left behind (Rev. 6:9, 17). When judgement finally came for Judah, their hands and knees went limp with fear (vv. 17-19, cf. Rev. 6:14-17). The purpose of the tribulation is to bring about repentance (v. 18) through a mixture of grief and terror (v. 27). Remembering always, through affliction, God is seeking to save the lost (18:23, 30-32; 33:11, cf. Ps. 83 (vv. 16, 18), 2 Pet. 3:9). God confirms, "I have no pleasure in the death of the wicked, but that the wicked turn from his way and live (33:11, 14b). When ANYONE turns to God through repentance and remains (33:19) in that repentant state, the promise is, they shall live (18:21-22; 33:16). The promise is also accurate in reverse: Even if you start off well and then turn back, your end state will determine your final outcome, which is death (18:24; 33:18, cf. 2 Pet. 2:21).

Although the above mentioned is a timely warning for us, as much as it was for Judah, it is not one you will often here preached in most churches today. Albeit, the consequences of failing to issue a warning are severe. Within chapters 3 and 33, God warns, if you fail to inform, then you will be held responsible (3:18, 20, 33:6, 8-9).

The book of Revelation, starting with the confronting image of Jesus in chapter 1, then the warnings to the seven churches (2-3), followed by the threat of judgment for those left behind, serves the purpose of turning hearers away from sin. Hence the warning, He who has an ear, let him hear what the Spirit is saying to the CHURCHES before it is too late!

Martyrdom
The Fifth Seal

"When he opened the fifth seal, I saw under the altar the souls of those who had been slain for the word of God and for the witness they had borne" (Rev. 6:9).

Following the release of the four apocalyptic horsemen, billions upon the earth will perish (6:8). Within the first year or two of the Tribulation alone, it is predicted upwards of two billion people will die by the sword, famine, and pestilence (Rev. 6:8). With those statistics, it is not surprising Jesus said, unless those (Tribulation) days were shortened, no one would survive (Matt. 24:22). In the Tribulation those perishing will start with the saints (6:9), with continual and increasing persecution throughout the seven-year plight (Matt. 24:9, 7:13-14, 12:17, 13:15, 14:12, 17:6, 18:24, 19;2), right up until the end (20:4).

During the Tribulation, many will break away from the loveless, compromising, corrupt, dead, and lukewarm churches (Rev. 2-3). They will come to faith, finally finding salvation through Christ alone, and grace, and faith. churchgoers who failed to respond to the gospel this side of the event will wake up in the Tribulation, having one last chance to get right with God. Instead of counting the cost and accepting Jesus this side of the trial, they followed a different gospel; they received a different spirit and accepted another Jesus (2 Cor. 11:4). In doing so, they were deceived by 'super-apostles' (2 Cor. 11:5) (celebrity preachers), preaching prosperity, 'Your Best Life Now', instead of Christ crucified (1 Cor. 1:23, 2:2, 15). Christ crucified, requiring we be likewise (Matt. 16:24-27, Gal. 2:20, 5:24, 6:14).

When Jesus was asked, "What will be the sign of your coming and the end of the age" (Matt. 24:3), He responded by listing several, yet of the many, He repeated only one several times - 'deception' (vv. 4-5, 11, 15, 23-26). Deception is the most significant sign of the end times, preparing and conditioning people for the greatest deceiver to come, the Antichrist (2 Thess. 2). The Antichrist spirit is already at work (1 Jn. 4:2-3), causing entire churches and whole denominations to fall away from the gospel (v. 7, 2 Thess. 2:3). Churchgoers thinking, they are Alive when they are Dead (Rev. 3:1b-2) and Rich when they are Poor (Rev. 3:17). Instead of enduring sound biblical doctrine, many have itching ears seeking teachers telling them what they want to hear (2 Tim. 4:3). Instead of having ears to hear what the Spirit is saying to the churches (2:7, 11, 17, 29, 3:6, 13, 22), the left behind have departed the faith, giving heed to deceiving spirits and doctrines of demons (1 Tim. 4:1). In other words, they were deceived by compromised and corrupt doctrine (Rev. 2-3), promising 'Your Best Life Now.' Adding to the mix is Gnosticism (secret knowledge), going ahead of the teachings of Christ (2 Jn. 9), going beyond what is written (1 Cor 4:6). Gnosticism is readily seen in the New Apostolic Movement (NAR), which has evolved from the Word of Faith movement.

AFTER being deceived into the Tribulation through another gospel (2 Cor. 11:4), only THEN, embracing THE gospel, millions will be ushered and welcomed into heaven, martyred for their commitment to Jesus and their testimony of Him (Rev. 6:9). Revelation 6:10-11 provides support: "They cried out with a loud voice, 'O Sovereign Lord, holy and true, how long before you will judge and avenge our blood on those who dwell on the earth?'" Then they were each given a white robe and told to rest a little longer until the number of their fellow servants and their brothers should be complete, who were to be killed as they themselves had been."

Chapter 7 also provides confirmation: "Then one of the elders addressed me, saying, 'Who are these, clothed in white robes, and from where have they come?' I said to him, 'Sir, you know.' And he said to me, 'These are the ones coming out of the great Tribulation. They have washed their robes and made them white in the blood of the Lamb'" (7:13-15).

Chapter 7 introduces the 144,000 Jewish evangelists, seen again in chapter 14. These faithful witnesses preach the gospel to a great multitude that no one could number, from every nation, all tribes and people and languages (7:9). Those coming to faith through their ministry are persecuted unto death (7:14). Joining the 144,000 Jewish evangelists are the two witnesses in chapter 11. They will be preaching repentance (11:3), pointing to Jesus while operating in powerful signs and wonders likened to Moses and Elijah (11:5-6). Alongside the 144,000 Jewish evangelists and the two witnesses are angels preaching the eternal gospel (14:6, 8, 9). Joining the collective in the proclamation of the gospel are the saints who are being slain for the word of God and for the witness they had borne (Rev. 6:9).

In sum: The same 'saints' who refused to wake up, repent and get right with Jesus this side of the Tribulation will find themselves waking up in the Tribulation. Having missed the opportunity to escape the things to come (Lu. 21:34-36, Rev. 3:10), they will now have to endure the Day of Wrath. Waking up in the tribulation, the 'left behind' trade the empty promise for their 'Best Life Now' for the cross, counting the cost to follow Jesus. And, they follow Him wherever He goes (by taking the narrow and difficult road) through unwavering belief and obedience (14:4, 12). In doing so, where they once had compromised, they now refuse to do so by resisting and rejecting false worship of the beast and refuse to take his mark (Rev. 13:15, 20:4).

For this reason and their treason, they are hunted down and beheaded (Rev. 20:4). Many others will be slain by the sword, through famine, pestilence and wild beasts (Rev. 6:8). Adding to the mix are earthquakes (Rev. 6:12 11:13, 16:18), hail, and fire, mixed with blood, of which a third of the earth is destroyed (8:7). Meteorites also, where a third of the sea becomes blood (8-9); and, nuclear warfare, poisoning a third of freshwater (8:10-11). Others will be sun struck, blinded in darkness, where a third of the earth's natural light is removed (8:12-13). And then, there is the release of the fallen angels from the pit, unleashing hordes of demons and (Nephilim) spirits wreaking unprecedented havoc on the earth.

In conclusion: In the Tribulation, there will be a combination of persecution, both natural, and supernatural affliction, and both natural and supernatural catastrophes. When considering the mix, it is no wonder Amos said of the Day of the Lord: "Woe to you who long for the day of the Lord! Why do you long for the day of the Lord? That day will be darkness, not light. It will be as though a man fled from a lion only to meet a bear, as though he entered his house and rested his hand on the wall only to have a snake bite him. Will not the day of the Lord be darkness, not light—pitch-dark, without a ray of brightness?" (5:18-20). In other words, there will be no escaping the terrors to come after waking up, left behind in the Tribulation! However, the terror is purposed to produce godly fear, missing this side of the event. Godly fear will produce repentance, resulting in salvation and evangelistic motivation: "I saw under the altar the souls of those <u>who had been slain for the word of God</u> and <u>for the witness they had borne</u>" (Rev. 6:9).

To avoid the tribulation, you must 'endure unto the end now' (Matt. 10:22, Lu. 21:19, Rev. 1:9, 3:10), or else you will have to 'endure in the tribulation, until the end' then (Matt. 24:13, Rev. 2:13, 12:17, 13:10, 14:12). And, providing you do endure, you will only THEN reap the reward of eternal life (Rev. 22:7, 14). That is, 'Your Best Life THEN', not and never NOW (see Jn. 16:33, Rev. 1:9).

The Sixth Seal

Revelation 6:12-17 introduces the sixth seal, following the martyred saints (fifth seal), resulting from the release of the four horsemen (first, second and third seals). Following the sixth seal will be the sealing of the 144,000 Jewish evangelists, confirmed by the words 'After this' (7:1). There are seven references for the words 'After this' in the book of Revelation (1:19, 4:1, 7:1, 9, 15:5, 18:1, 19:1). There are over one hundred groupings of sevens in the book, being heptadic (sevenfold) in structure. Each time the words 'After this' are used, there is a change of scenery shifting from an earthly focus to a heavenly one, or visa-versa. Whichever way, the shift always points to the purpose of the tribulation, which is salvation.

Accompanying signs of the sixth seal are a combination of natural catastrophes and signs in the sky. The most significant symbol in the sky is Jesus where the sky is rolled back, announcing His wrath (vv. 14, 16). The sixth is the most dramatic judgement of the seals so far, and this is just the first round of three in the seven-year tribulation period, followed by the trumpet and bowl judgements.

With the opening of the sixth seal, so powerful are the events in the heavens; every mountain and island are removed from the earth. According to this statement, only large landmasses remain. Not only are the mountains and islands shaken, but the population also. Even those who were 'great' on the earth (6:15) are shaken and terrorised by the great events (6:12), and the great day of their wrath (6:17). So frightened are they that they hide themselves in the caves and among the rocks (6:16).

Here, their response reminds me of Saddam Hussein and Osama bin Laden, both once great men, yet they were found hiding away like scared little mice. Soon, Saddam and Osama's experience will be a global reality for every 'great' man. Not just the great, rich, and powerful men, but everyone left behind will be subject to the same, utterly terrified by the things to come (6:15). All walks of life, whether rich or poor, free or slave, will respond in the same way to the unfolding events, calling on the rocks to hide them from the wrath of the Lamb (6:16). So frightened, they would rather be crushed by rocks falling on them than face the wrath of the Lamb (6:17).

Based on the above, the Tribulation will be unlike anything the world has ever seen before or will see again, just as Jesus predicted (Matt. 24:21), and Daniel (12:1). The event of Revelation 6:12 is repeated in 16:18-21. On that occasion, instead of hiding in the caves and among the rocks, the earth dwellers cursed God for the plagues because the plagues were so severe (16:21). Their cursing is a repeat of 16:9 and 11. Instead of repentance (16:9, 11, cf. 9:20-21), they hardened their heart all the more, entirely given over to sin (Rom. 1:28-32), serving the purpose of the Tribulation. The Tribulation will sift and separate one from the other, where some come to repentance, finding salvation, most will go in the opposite direction. In the tribulation, unlike now, there will be no grace extended for lukewarm Christianity; you will either be sold out to Jesus or sold out to the Antichrist. Either way, there will be no atheists or agnostics.

Furthermore, Revelation, chapter 6 puts every false teacher to rest, who says, "God is (only) a God of love and will not judge us." The same empty rhetoric heard today is a repeat of Jeremiah's day, saying, "God will not judge; instead, He will pour out His blessings; peace, peace, and prosperity." But God did arbitrate Judah, and He is about to judge this generation for the same reason, to separate one from the other for salvation.

When Jesus returns for His Bride, only those working (Lu. 19:13), waiting, and watching will escape the things to come (Lu. 21:34-36). Only those who have kept His word and who endured will be removed from the hour of trial (Rev. 3:10). As for the rest who had itching ears, running after teachers they wanted to hear (2 Tim. 4:3), they will be introduced to THE Jesus of the Bible (Rev. 1:12-17, 6:16-17). The biblical Jesus is another Jesus other from the one they heard and received (2 Cor. 11:4), which is why they were left behind. For others, while they may have started on the right foot, they drifted away, they backslid and fell into apostasy.

The Bible has a lot to say about drifting from the faith; the book of Hebrews is the most prominent on the subject. The writer of Hebrews compares Israel and the church, stating that, just like Israel, you too can lose your promised inheritance. Paul made the same argument in Romans 11. And Jesus, through John, says the same in the letters to the seven churches (Rev. 2-3); hence the warning, repent, or else! The 'or else' is a threat of judgement to the churches, referencing the Tribulation.

Isaiah gives similar warnings to the people of God that parallel Revelation 6:12-17, found in chapter 2:17-22: "And the haughtiness of man shall be humbled, and the lofty pride of men shall be brought low, and the LORD alone will be exalted in that day. And the idols shall utterly pass away. <u>And people shall enter the caves of the rocks and the holes of the ground, from before the terror of the LORD, and from the splendour of his majesty, when he rises to terrify the earth in that day</u> mankind will cast away their idols of silver and their idols of gold, which they made for themselves to worship, to the moles and to the bats, to <u>enter the caverns of the rocks and the clefts of the cliffs, from before the terror of the LORD, and from the splendour of his majesty, when he rises to terrify the earth</u>. Stop regarding man in whose nostrils is breath, for of what account is he?"

Because humanity has put their trust in false teachers, false worship, and themselves, the Lord will soon terrorise the earth when opening the seals of chapter 6, commencing with the white horse, who represents the Antichrist. The Antichrist's weapon of mass destruction is deception, which is already operating in the church today, hence the great falling away (2 Thess. 2:3).

The apostate church is not one falling away from religion but from Jesus. Again, instead of enduring sound doctrine, the deceived chase after teachers tickling their ears telling them what they want to hear (2 Tim. 4:3). In response, it is God who opens the seals and sends the deceiver (Antichrist), even handing the deceived (churchgoers) over to him for their destruction (2 Thess. 2:9-12), which will be a repeat of 1 Kings 22:19-28:

And Micaiah said, "Therefore hear the word of the LORD: I saw the LORD sitting on his throne, and all the host of heaven standing beside him on his right hand and on his left; and the LORD said, 'Who will entice Ahab, that he may go up and fall at Ramoth-Gilead?' And one said one thing, and another said another. Then a spirit came forward and stood before the LORD, saying, 'I will entice him.' And the LORD said to him, 'By what means?' And he said, 'I will go out, and will be a lying spirit in the mouth of all his prophets.' And he said, 'You are to entice him, and you shall succeed; go out and do so.' Now therefore behold, the LORD has put a lying spirit in the mouth of all these your prophets; the LORD has declared disaster for you." Then Zedekiah, the son of Chenaanah came near and struck Micaiah on the cheek and said, "How did the Spirit of the LORD go from me to speak to you?" And Micaiah said, "Behold, you shall see on that day when you go into an inner chamber to hide yourself." And the king of Israel said, "Seize Micaiah, and take him back to Amon the governor of the city and to Joash, the king's son, and say, "Thus says the king," 'Put this fellow in prison and feed him meagre rations of bread and water, until I come in peace.'" And Micaiah said, "If you return in peace, the LORD has not spoken by me." And he said, "Hear all you peoples!"

The same will be true for those preaching peace, peace, and prosperity today, or else the Lord has not spoken: "Hear all you people" (1 kgs:22:28). "He that has an ear hear what the Spirit says to the churches" (Rev. 2:7, 11, 17, 29, 3:6, 13, 22).

Matthew 24 and Revelation 6

"The one who endures until the end shall be saved"
(Matt. 24:13)

"Here calls for the endurance of the saints"
(Rev. 13:10, 14:12, cf. 1:9, 2:10, 3:10, 12:17)

Revelation, chapter six, was foretold by Jesus when asked, What will be the sign of your coming and the close of the age? (Matt. 24:3). The chart below lists the top ten signs of the end times. The number one sign of the end times is deception through false teachers, teachings, and lying signs and wonders. So deceptive will they be, even the elect would be led astray, if possible (24:24). During the Tribulation, for the elect's sake, the days are cut short (24:22), and the elect will be gathered up at the end of the seven-year period (24:31). The 'left behind' elect wake up in the Tribulation, failing to do so this side of the event.

Birth Pains	Event	Verse	Where	Prediction
1	False Teachers	24:5, 11, 23-26	Hyper Faith/ Grace, NAR, Ecumenical	Every book of the NT, bar Philemon
2	War (Technology)	24:67 (Dan. 12:4)	Middle East, Turkey, Russia North Korea	Isa. 17:1, Jer. 49:24-27, (Rev. 9:12-19)
3	Famine/ Sickness	24:7a	Developing Nations	Lu. 21:11 Rev. 6:5-8
4	Earthquakes	24:7b	Global	Rev. 6:12 11:13, 16:18

	5	Delivered Up	24:9	Global	Lu. 12:12-18 Rev. 6:9
	6	Falling Away	24:10	Apostasy	2 Thess. 2:3 Rev. 2-3
	7	Lawlessness	24:12	Faithless/ Loveless	Matt. 7:21-23
Peace Treaty		Antichrist Revealed	Isa. 28:14-16,18	Israel	Isa. 28:15, 18 Dan. 9:27
Tribulation		Last Call	24:9-28	7-Years	Rev. 6-19
	8	Third Temple	24:15-23	Jerusalem	Dan 9:27, 11:31, 12:11
Three Woes		Supernatural	24:21	Global	Rev. 9:1-11. 13-16, 12:7-8
	9	Signs Wonders	24:24	2-Witnesses Third Temple	Zech. 4 Rev. 11:1-13
Jesus Returns		Judgement	24:36, 42, 44, 50	Armageddon	Dan. 12. Rev. 19:11-21
	10	Sun, Moon, Star	24:29-30	Signs in the Sky	Joel 2:30, Acts 2:17, Rev 16:14

Having failed to heed the warnings, such as recorded in each of the letters written to the seven churches (Rev. 2-3), the loveless, compromising, corrupt, dead, sleeping, and lukewarm churchgoers now have to endure the Tribulation, until the end (of their lives) to be saved. Foretelling this event, Matthew chapter 24 is an exact fit and in the precise order of Revelation chapter 6. The chart above shows the sequence of events from birth pangs to the signing of the peace treaty, which will trigger the Tribulation. The Tribulation will not happen before the church is removed; therefore, the signing of the peace treaty and the rapture will coincide.

The tribulation is then split into two parts, the first and second half, each three and a half years long, or 42 months, being 1260 days each. The third woe will commence the second half of the Tribulation, known as the Great Tribulation. This is referenced in Matthew 24:21, Revelation 2:22, and 7:14. On the third woe, Satan is cast to the earth, and the Antichrist announces himself to be 'God' from the rebuilt third Temple. At that point, all hell breaks loose, literally. Revelation, chapter 6, is an introduction to the events unfolding throughout the seven-year period.

Matt 24	Matt 24	Matt 24	Matt 24	Matt 24	Matt 24	Matt 24
Deception vv. 5, 11, 24	War vv. 6-7, 22	Famine vv. 7b-8	Pestilences v. 7	Martyrdom v. 9	Earthquake vv. 7	Cosmic events vv. 29
Seal 1	Seal 2	Seal 3	Seal 4	Seal 5	Seal 6	Seal 7
White Horse 6:2	Red Horse 6:3-4	Black Horse 6:5-6	Pale Horse 6:7-8	Martyrdom 6:9	Earthquake 6:12	Cosmic events 8:5 (cf. 6:12)

When Jesus was describing the Tribulation, He was not just referring to the first period but the entire seven-year period. Revelation chapter 6 serves both. It is the first of three sets of judgements, and it also covers the whole seven-year period. The evidence for the latter is in the words, "Immediately after the tribulation of those days…" (Matt. 24:29). Matthew 24:29 lines up with Revelation 6:12, and 8:5, the seventh seal. The seals are followed by the trumpet judgements, concluding with the bowl judgements, before Christ returns to the earth. In sum, the same story is told three times, only intensified. Further evidence for the above mentioned is seen in Matthew

24, where Jesus provides a detailed account, and outline for the entire book of Revelation. The following chart illustrates how:

Section	Matthew 24	Revelation	Events
Introduction	Verses 1-3	Chapters 1-5	Opening scene
Part 1	Verses 4-14	Chapters 6-8a	Seals
Part 2	Verses 15-28	Chapters 8b-14	Trumpets
Part 3	Verses 29	Chapters 16-17	Bowls
Conclusion	Verses 30:52	Chapters 18-22	Be ready / Come

In conclusion, when His disciples asked Jesus, "Tell us, <u>when</u> will these things be, and <u>what</u> will be the sign of your coming, and the end of the age?" (Matt. 24:3), Jesus answered both questions. Jesus answered 'what will be the signs…?' with what we have covered above, and also 'when will these things be?' within verses 32-35. Verses 32-35 refer to Israel becoming a nation again, which happened in 1948. Jesus said the generation that saw that event would be alive to see His return (v. 34). Israel is now 72-years old; therefore, the youngest living person who saw the nation of Israel reborn is 72-years old today. The scripture says we can expect between 70-80 years of life (Ps. 90:10), on average. Although we do not know the 'day and hour' (24:36, 42, 50), we do know the times by the signs, and the seasons, discussed above. Of the signs, no other sign is greater than the rebirth of Israel. Of which, *IF a man can expect a maximum of 80-years, and the youngest of those witnessing the rebirth of Israel is 72-years old today, then by taking into consideration seven years of tribulation, the rapture could happen as soon as 2020/21, leaving seven Tribulation years before Jesus returns. To escape the trial, you must endure now (Matt. 10:22, Rev. 1:9, 2:10, 3:10), failing to do so, you must endure then (Matt. 24:13, Rev. 12:17, 13:10, 14:12).

CHAPTER SEVEN

The 144,000 Sealed Jewish Evangelists

> *This gospel of the kingdom will be proclaimed throughout the whole world as a testimony to all nations, and then the end will come*
> *(Matt. 24:14, cf. Rev. 7:9-10)*

Following the sixth seal, 'after that,' the angels of God standing at the four corners of the earth hold back the four winds of the earth for the purpose of sealing and salvation. The four winds refer to God's judgments being poured out, such as the four horsemen (6:1-8). In the previous chapter, verse 17, the question was raised, "Who can stand the great day of God's wrath?" Chapter 7, verses 3-8, provides the answer: 1). Believing Israel, and 2). Everyone/anyone else who comes to faith in Jesus through the testimony of the Jews (vv. 9-10), albeit at the cost of their natural lives (vv. 14-15). The second group is the same as described in the previous chapter, verses 9-11. While those coming to faith in Jesus through the testimony of the 144,000 Jewish evangelists are slain, the 144,000 are sealed and protected (v. 3). God instructs the angels who have been given the power to harm the earth and people of the planet not to proceed until the sons of Israel have been marked with God's divine seal of protection (v. 3-4).

During the Tribulation, God will separate 144,000 Israelites from the plagues that He pours out on Earth. The separation will be a repeat where God distinguished between Israel and the Egyptians when He poured out His plagues on Egypt, as seen from the fourth plague of ten (Ex. 8:22). The shift came only after Pharaoh's magicians acknowledged the third plague was 'the finger of God' (Ex. 8:19). Chapter 9 makes a further distinction between Egypt and Israel, adding livestock (9:4, 7), that all would know 'there is none like God' (9:14). Those that feared God were protected (9:20, 26, 10:23, 11:6b, 12:12-13, 23). Even non-Israelites found relief temporally through short-lasting repentance (9:27-28, 33-34), repeated a few times over (10:16-20). The last of which was Pharaoh himself, who told Moses to leave, but before he did, to first 'bless him' (12:32b).

Here lies the problem with many confessing Christians today. They acknowledge God temporally (when it suits them) and want to be protected from His wrath through false repentance, and they even want His blessing, but they do not want… Him! The church of Laodicea is a classic example of this where they wanted all the blessings and benefits of being a believer but were not interested in counting the cost to follow Jesus. Remember, the church of Laodicea means people ruling. Like today, instead of serving God, they would have God serve them, commanding and demanding of God, declaring and decreeing, naming and claiming, blabbing, and grabbing.

Not only do the liberal believers use God as an ATM card to get what they want, when they want it, but many also remain in sin. Deceived by hyper-grace demonic doctrines, they justify their sin by saying, "I am a child of God, and He knows my heart." God does know our hearts, which is precisely the problem, and that fact alone should bring godly fear to us all. Jesus said, "I am the one who searches the mind and heart, and I will give to each of you as your works deserve" (Rev. 2:23, cf. Jer. 17:10, 1 Pet. 1:7). The judgement will be in accordance with the gospel that Paul preached (Rom. 2:15-16), not the watered-down version proclaimed today (2 Cor. 11:4). Simply said: there will be no excuses, no faking, and no escaping what is due on the day of judgement.

To avoid judgement, those who genuinely repent must also endure until the end (Matt. 10:22). Those who do not repent or do not remain in a repentance state will find themselves in the Tribulation, where they will then have another opportunity to come to genuine and lasting repentance, enduring until the end to be saved (Matt. 24:13). The same call for endurance is echoed throughout John's revelation, repeated seven times. Five times refer to the here and now (Rev. 1:9, 2:2, 19, 3:10), and twice more referring to those left behind, having to endure the Tribulation period (13:10, 14:12).

Adding to the mentioned prophecies of Jesus is another, "And this gospel of the kingdom will be proclaimed throughout the whole world as a testimony to all nations, and then the end will come" (Matt. 24:14). While many have said the rapture would not occur until the whole world has first heard the gospel, the verse contextually applies to those cast into the Tribulation, then and there, proclaiming Christ until He returns. The 144,000 are God's chosen people who will primarily fulfil this prophecy, where every nation will hear and respond through them, either for or against the gospel (Rev. 7:9). Moreover, the 144,000 are ISRAELITES (vv. 4-8), not and never the church or anyone else. Nowhere in the Bible does a reference to Israel ever mean the church. The church has not and will never replace Israel as replacement theology suggests.

During the tribulation, Israel will wake up after their eyes have been opened (Rom. 11:25b-27, Matt. 23:39), following the signing of the peace treaty and the removal of the church. The awakened Jews will then make up a powerful evangelistic force bringing in the final Pentecostal wave and revival before Jesus returns. Countless millions will respond and holdfast to 'the' gospel being proclaimed (14:6-7), having failed to do so this side (3:10). Again, the great multitude being saved in the Tribulation is first mentioned in chapter 5, verses 9-10. These 'will' reign with Christ on His return, not and never before, indicated by the words: "And THEN they shall reign on the earth" (v. 10b). The saints reigning with Jesus takes place AFTER a time of persecution (1:9), which will increase during the Tribulation. Again, those being saved in the Tribulation are mentioned in chapter 6, as the slain. The 'lucky' ones will die early in the Tribulation, which is the fifth seal (v. 9-12, cf. Lam. 4:9). When the number of saved Tribulation saints is complete, THEN Jesus will return (v. 12).

The reference to the number being completed is also mentioned in Romans 11, verse 25. There, it refers to the Gentiles being saved and removed this side of the Tribulation. Once all the Gentiles (church) have come in (been rescued and removed), it is Israel's turn. First, the church is removed, and then Israel's eyes are opened, albeit in the Tribulation. Again, Revelation 7, verse 14 clarifies that those saved through the testimony of the Jews are the same who are slain. They are killed for resisting and rejecting the Antichrist system in the Great Tribulation. While in the Tribulation, they suffer terribly, but through death, they are delivered, comforted, and consoled (vv. 15-17) before the throne of God day and night. While the left behind who come to Christ suffer temporally in the Tribulation, those rejecting Jesus will suffer day and night for all eternity following the final judgement (Rev. 14:11, 20:10).

Until Jesus returns to the earth, the slain saints rest in heaven before the throne, shepherded by Jesus (v. 17). Having been deceived by false shepherds leading up to the Tribulation, the deceived go 'through' the Tribulation. While there, they realise the error and foolishness of their ways (cf. Lam. 3:42). Now before the throne, they worship and serve the True Shepard, Jesus (v. 15). Instead of declaring and decreeing through kingdom now theology, that teaches: Jesus will do unto me/thee, by twisting scripture: "Thou shalt also decree a thing, and it shall be established unto thee" (Job 22:28); they now only seek and desire that, "His will be done" in the kingdom to come (Matt. 6:10, Rev. 5:10).

Three times more, the Tribulation saints are mentioned following chapter 7. Chapter 13, verse 15, chapter 14, verses 1-5, and chapter 20, verse 4 mention them as those who have been slain for refusing to compromise and or bow down to the Antichrist. Martyrdom will be an ongoing and increasing theme throughout the seven years. The shift from self-seeking and self-serving to seeking and serving Jesus alone is seen through the letters to the seven churches where five of seven churches were in serious trouble and in danger of Tribulation. Only two were doing well but were also encouraged to remain faithful and to holdfast, or else…

In sum, chapter seven serves to prove the point and purpose of the Tribulation. God is ALWAYS seeking to save the lost and will use any means to do so. The threat of Tribulation is intended to wake God's people up this side; it is also purposed to wake up the left behind that side of it. While it is not God's will for any to go into, and through the Tribulation, He will allow it to save some who would otherwise spend eternity separated from Him. No matter which way it goes, God's arm is not too short to save; however, man must return to Him to benefit from His saving work. "Surely the arm of the LORD is not too short to save, nor His ear too dull to hear. But your iniquities have built barriers between you and your God, and your sins have hidden His face from you so that He does not hear" (Isa. 59:1-2). While God has made a way where there was no way (Isa. 59:16), we must respond by 'turning from transgression' (Isa. 59:20), or else our sin will eternally separate us from Him (Isa. 59:2).

CHAPTER EIGHT

The Seventh Seal
The Sound of Silence is Sobering

Chapter 8 introduces the seventh seal, which is the most severe of the judgements to date, indicated by silence in heaven for about half an hour (v. 2a). Within the seventh seal is the seven trumpets (v. 2b), and the same is true of the seventh trumpet regarding the seven bowls (15:7). Said another way, the seventh judgement contains the next seven to come, only intensified. Each set of experiences progresses in time and increases in severity. As indicated by the half-hour of silence, time is recorded in heaven (v. 2). In other words, time, as in heaven, is paralleled on the earth. Minute by minute, while the population of the planet is suffering from the plagues of the Lamb, the rescued redeemed are in heaven resting at the foot and throne of the Lamb (6:15-17). Here, the reader should be reminded, "Note then the kindness and the severity of God: severity towards those who have fallen, but kindness to you *PROVIDED you continue in His kindness" (Rom. 11:22).

When reading about the Tribulation events, the reader should always be reminded of the purpose of the prophecy, which is linked to the condition of the recipient of the letters. The seven churches are the first recipients of the book of Revelation (2-3); and, all were given the same opportunity to repent and or holdfast. Those who did were guaranteed to be removed and rescued from the Tribulation (3:10); those who did not would be thrown into it (2:22). Remember, the letters to the seven churches are just as much addressed to believers today as they were sent to the churches then; the same conditions, threats, and promises are equally shared.

'Believers' failing to heed the warning, left behind to endure the Tribulation will be the collective churchgoers who missed Jesus. They have a reputation of being Alive, yet were Dead (3:1), and or seemingly had everything, yet actually had nothing (3:17). They are those who corrupted (2:14) and who compromised (2:20) God's word. They are also the same who Jesus warned that He would come as a thief (3:3, 16:15), leaving them behind unless they first wake up (3:2, 3, cf. 16:15).

Paul warned the church of Corinth of the same, saying, "Wake up from your drunken stupor, as is right, and do not go on sinning, for some have no knowledge of God. I say this to your shame" (1 Cor. 15:34). Paul starts chapter 15 with an introduction to 'the gospel that he preached' (v. 1) and that, according to 'his gospel,' we are being saved *IF we hold fast to the word 'he preached' (v. 2). The gospel Paul preached is vastly different from today's empty rhetoric (2 Cor. 11:4). The gospel that Paul preached is summed up in 1 Corinthians 15, starting with Jesus, who died for our sins and delivered us from sin through His resurrection. Paul goes onto say because Christ was resurrected, so will we be. This is our hope and what we live for (cf. Titus 2:13). In the meantime, there are conditions. 1). We must die daily to the flesh (v. 30); therefore stop sinning. Those who do and hold fast to 'this gospel' can expect to be rescued and removed when Jesus returns for His Bride (vv. 51-52). Those who do not can expect to be left behind (v. 50). Adding to the first condition, there is another 2). To reinforce the 'covenant conditions,' Paul closes the chapter with the words, "Be steadfast, immovable, always abounding in the work of the Lord, knowing that in the Lord your labour is not in vain" (v. 58). Points 1 and 2 are therefore the fundamental differences to what is preached today, lacking repentance, holiness, and endurance. How Paul starts this chapter is how he finishes: We MUST obey and remain; those who do not have believed in vain (v. 2).

Sadly, like Israel and Judah, instead of being delivered from the wrath to come, most churchgoers have been deceived by a false gospel (1 Cor. 15:33) and will not wake up before they find themselves in the Tribulation. Although many confess Jesus as Lord, they do not know Him, evident by failing to obey Him (Lu. 6:46, 1 Cor. 15:34). The Tribulation is purposed to remedy that, introducing them to the 'real' Jesus of the Bible, opposed to the one they have so readily received (Gal. 1:6), often peddled by prosperity preachers. In the Tribulation, there will be no place for modern-day prosperity preachers, hyper-grace, or kingdom now seven mountain dominionists; instead, they will be hiding away in their underground bunkers. Following the Tribulation, in the millennium, those who once falsely prophesised this side will be ashamed and will even lie to cover up their former deception (Zech. 13:4-6). But, before then, the Tribulation will serve to either wake up the deceived or delude them further for damnation (2 Thess. 2:11), starting with the seven seals.

Although the tribulation begins with the seals, the seals, trumpets, and bowls are one in the same thing, where the story is simply retold three times over, yet intensified. Walvoord (1985) records C.A. Blanchard saying it this way, "The series of three sevens are really included in one series of seven, that is, the seven trumpets are included under the seventh seal, and the seven bowls are included under the seventh trumpet so that we have in fact a single series in three movements" (Light on the Last Days, p. 58).

The seventh seal accordingly is important because it actually includes all the events from 8:1 through 19:10.

Within each of the judgements, there is a shift of focus from sinners to saints with correlating activities. For example, the conclusion of the seals and introduction of the trumpets sees the seventh angels standing before God, who is given seven trumpets (v. 2). This event is immediately followed by another angel who came and stood at the altar with a golden censer (v. 3a). The censer was given much incense, with the saints' prayers before the throne (v. 3b). Here, there is a direct link to a previous verse mentioning bowls full of incense, which are the prayers of the saints (5:8). In chapter 8, the reference states that the prayers are of 'all' the saints before the throne, not just those previously fallen asleep, joined by those raptured.

Traditionally, bowls of incense were poured out over hot coals at the tabernacle and temple altar. Smoke would then go up, symbolic of prayer rising to heaven and ascending to God. In chapter 8, we see the reverse. The saints are before God, and their prayers fill the censor with fire, and from the altar in heaven, the fire is thrown down on the earth. This is the seventh seal. Again, so severe is the seventh seal, there is silence in heaven in preparation; and, the silence will be sobering! The reason is the silence is connected to the prayers of the persecuted saints, which are often made in silence. In chapter 6, the slain saints before the throne ask for revenge (v. 10). They are continually collected in chapter 7 out of the great tribulation (v. 14), and then they are avenged, in part, in chapter 8, verse 5.

As a result of the seventh seal, the silence in heaven is broken with peals of thunder, rumblings, flashes of lightning, and an earthquake (v. 5). The same collective was seen in Revelation 4:5 and will be again in 11:19 and 16:18. The first occurrence is before the throne in heaven, and the last is after the bowl of judgements just before Jesus returns. Revelation 11:19 refers to the event taking place in heaven, adding 'heavy hail.' This event follows the seventh trumpet (11:15). Like the seventh seal, the seventh trumpet follows an evangelistic proclamation of the gospel through the two witnesses (11:1-12). The two witnesses are OT prophets, Elijah is one (Mal. 4:5-6), and the other is likely to be either Moses or Enoch. Moses is more likely than Enoch due to his and Elijah's appearance at the transfiguration (Matt. 17:2). Either way, the message coming through the two prophets will be one of repentance (11:3), like that of John the Baptist (Matt. 3:3), who would have fulfilled the Elijah prophecy if he and his message had been received (Matt. 11:11-15, 17:10-13). Because Elijah (John) and Jesus were both rejected by most, Elijah and Jesus will meet their rejectors, who mainly were religious, in the tribulation.

The religious, in context, are the churchgoers addressed in chapters 2 and 3 of the revelation. They are the same that either had a reputation of being alive or had everything and no need for anything, and they are those that rejected and persecuted the faithful followers of Jesus (2:9, 3:9). As for those who continue to reject Jesus in the tribulation, they will now be dealt with, starting with and flowing from the prayers of the saints, resulting in the fire being poured out upon them (8:5). The judgement will mirror James and John's (sons of thunder, Mk. 3:17), request (Lu. 9:54), only this time, for repentance (16:8-9). When James and John asked Jesus whether or not they should call down fire from heaven, the request was denied, and they were rebuked due to not being the time for judgement. However, in the Tribulation, the request through prayer is granted. Fire will be poured down from heaven upon the people of the earth. Hence the warning to five of the seven churches, repent, or else!

The First Trumpet

The seventh seal contains the seven trumpets given to seven angels. Following the first angel who blows the first trumpet, the first set of seven judgements commence with: "Hail and fire, mixed with blood, and these were thrown upon the earth." The result: "A third of the earth was burned up, and a third of the trees were burned up, and all green grass was burned up." Like most symbols, signs, and segments within the book of Revelation, the first trumpet is no exception to the rule. Most of what is seen in the book is found in the OT. In particular, is the divine stoning by hail and fire! A similar sign took place through Moses, which is another reason Moses is likely to be one of the two witnesses (Rev. 11). Exodus 9:23-26 records the paralleled event:

"Then Moses stretched out his staff toward heaven, and the LORD sent thunder and hail, and fire ran down to the earth. And the LORD rained hail upon the land of Egypt. There was hail and fire flashing continually and in the midst of the hail, very heavy hail, such as had never been in all the land of Egypt since it became a nation. The hail struck down everything in the field in all the land of Egypt, both man and beast. And the hail struck down every plant of the field and broke every tree of the field. Only in the land of Goshen, where the people of Israel were, was there no hail."

Before stoning the Egyptians with hail and fire, God distinguished between the pagan nation, Egypt (the world), and the people of God, (Israel). The distinction and separation are seen in Exodus 8:22-23, which was in itself a sign (8:23). After separating the Israelites from the rest, through the seventh plague, God purposed to make Himself known, supported by the statement: "There is none like God in all the earth" (Ex. 9:14). Through the plagues, God even used the rebels to proclaim His name (9:16), bringing godly fear resulting in salvation (9:20). Despite the overwhelming evidence, some refused to fear God and consequently perished (9:21), paralleling Revelation 9:20-21, 16:8, and 21. However, those who feared God were delivered (9:26), just as promised (9:20). As seen in both passages (Exodus and Revelation), the purpose of the plagues is to save. While many did and will perish through the plagues, the intention is to turn them around and protect them from the final judgment to come (Rev. 20:11-15).

The difference between the Exodus account and what is to come through the Tribulation is the trumpet judgment will affect a third of the earth (Rev. 8:7), where the hail and fire will be mixed with blood. No doubt, the referenced blood responds to the judgment of the martyrs (Rev. 2:13, 6:9, 7:14, 13:15, 16:6, 17:6). Chapter 16, verse 6, couldn't be more precise: "For they have shed the blood of saints and prophets and you have given them blood to drink. It is what they deserve!"

The added fire to hail should also serve as a reminder of the judgement on Sodom and Gomorrah (Gen. 19:23-29). And, as prophesied by Jesus and Jude (Lk. 17:28, Jude 7), it will be repeated in the Tribulation. Note Jude's reference is aimed at those who pervert grace (v. 4) and pursue greed (v. 11). The mention of perverted grace and greed is best illustrated today with prosperity preachers, who have 'crept in unnoticed' (Jude 4). Unnoticed by most, but not all!

Again, the first trumpet judgement will affect a third of the planet, but not just the first trumpet, the following six trumpets will do likewise (8:8, 9, 10, 11, 12, 9:15, 18). In the previous chapter (7:3), the angel with the seal of God forbids the four angels given the power to harm the earth and sea to proceed until he had first sealed the servants of God (7:4). The servants of God are the 144,000 Jewish evangelists (7:4-8). Now that the servants of God are sealed, the plagues of God can continue. So severe will the following judgements be that possibly a third of humanity will be killed upon each, as indicated by the sixth (9:15, 18). So severe are the trumpet judgments; they make up two of the three tribulation woes (9:12, 11:14). The three woes are announced by an angel flying overhead, saying, "Woe, woe, woe to those who dwell on the earth" (9:13). The third woe will be fulfilled in chapter twelve when Satan is cast to the earth (11:14, 12:12-13), which marks the halfway point of the tribulation (12:6, 14, 13:5) following the ministry of the two witnesses (11:3).

When the particular plague of reference took place in Egypt, nothing before that time had matched it (Ex. 9:18). When the same plague occurs in the great tribulation, it will be unlike anything in the history of the world, nor will it be repeated (Matt. 24:21). When considering a third of the earth's population will perish on the sixth trumpet alone, following a fourth of the population being killed by the four horsemen, the collective is broken down to 1,250,000,000 killed by the four seals, leaving 3,750,000,000. A further 1,250,000,000 perish on the sixth trumpet. The combined sum is 2,500,000,000 (2.5bn); half of the remaining population if we allow for some 2,000,000,000 being raptured before the tribulation commences. And, at this point in the tribulation, two of the three woes have been fulfilled. The two woes include the demonic locusts (9:1-12), and a great earthquake (11:13). When considering the great earthquake, the numbers perishing will be much higher than 2.5bn, not to mention, when adding the fifth, sixth, and seventh seals, combined with the first five trumpet judgements, and then the seventh to come. With these statistics, the odds of survival are pretty grim; therefore, there is no little wonder the question was asked: "Who can stand the day of the wrath of the Lamb?" (Rev. 6:16-17). The answer is, none unless sealed by the Lamb (Rev. 7:3-4).

In sum, following the seals and the first six trumpets, less than half of the remaining population will be left to endure the worst part, being the great tribulation, containing the third woe (11:14). Here, it is essential to note that the judgements are a literal and pending event, not symbolic, as some suggest. Poof alone is provided by the historical account of the Exodus event. Through those plagues' vast numbers of the Egyptian population perished in the same way humanity will die in the Tribulation period. Therefore, the Revelation text leaves no grounds or support for any other interpretation, whether allegoric or already historically fulfilled. Further support for a literal translation is found with Jesus and Jude's reference to Sodom, warning; the plague will be repeated in the Tribulation. The tribulation will be triggered by the removal of the church, coinciding with the signing of the Middle East Peace Treaty, which will reveal the Antichrist.

To avoid the judgement to come, we must separate ourselves from Egypt and Sodom (the world); and hear what the Spirit says to the churches (Rev. 2:7, 11, 17, 29, 3:6, 13, 22). The message to the churches, then and now, was never, 'God wants you to be wealthy, healthy, and happy,' but rather to repent and remain. Instead of prosperity, Jesus promised His disciples trouble: "In the world, you will have Tribulation" (Jn. 16:33). However, our Tribulation on this side (Rev. 1:9) does not compare to 'the Tribulation,' never mind 'the Great Tribulation,' to come. For those who remain faithful (2:10), and hold fast to the end (3:10), like Israel did when God poured out His judgements on Egypt, and Lot when God poured out His judgement on Sodom, they (alone) will be set apart from those perishing, which includes corrupt, compromising, and lukewarm churchgoers.

The Second Trumpet

Revelation 8:7-8 introduces the second trumpet, and like the first, it is not the first time we have seen a particular judgement, in part at least.

Again, like the first, the second is found in the book of Exodus (7:20-21).

"Moses and Aaron did as the LORD commanded. In the sight of Pharaoh and the sight of his servants, he lifted up the staff and struck the water in the Nile, and all the water in the Nile turned into blood. And the fish in the Nile died, and the Nile stank so that the Egyptians could not drink water from the Nile. There was blood throughout all the land of Egypt."

And, again the judgement aims to save, indicated by verse 17

"Thus, says the LORD, 'By this, you shall know that I am the LORD: behold, with the staff that is in my hand I will strike the water that is in the Nile, and it shall turn into blood.'"

Through each plague, God targeted false Egyptian gods demonstrating that He alone is God, which was even acknowledged by Pharaoh's magicians, in part (8:19).

Possible Egyptian gods and goddesses of Egypt Attacked by the Plagues:

1. Nile turned to blood
   Exodus 7:14–25
   Hapi (also called Apis), the bull god, god of the Nile; Isis, goddess of the Nile; Khnum, ram god guardian of the Nile; and others

2. Frogs
   8:1–15
   Heqet, goddess of birth, with a frog head

3. Gnats
   8:16–19
   Set, god of the desert

4. Flies
   8:20–32
   Re, a sun god; or the god Uatchit, possibly represented by the fly

5. Death of livestock
   9:1–7
   Hathor, goddess with the cow head; Apis, the bull god, symbol of fertility

6. Boils
   9:8–12
   Sekhmet, goddess with power over disease; Sunu, the pestilence god, Isis, goddess of healing

7. Hail
   9:13–35
   Nut, the sky goddess; Osiris, god of crops and fertility; Set, god of storms

8. Locusts
   10:1–20
   Nut, the sky goddess; Osiris, god of crops and fertility

9. Darkness
10:21–29
Re, the sun god; Horus, a sun god; Nut, a sky goddess; Hathor, a sky goddess

10. Death of the firstborn
11:1–12:30
Min, god of reproduction; Heqet, goddess who attended women at childbirth; Isis, goddess who protected children; Pharaoh's firstborn son, a god

Source: Hannah, J. D. (1985). Exodus. In J. F. Walvoord & R. B. Zuck (Eds.), *The Bible Knowledge Commentary: An Exposition of the Scriptures* (Vol. 1, pp. 119–120). Wheaton, IL: Victor Books.

To produce saving repentance, God must first deal with false worship, which is idolatry. What God did to the idolatrous Egyptians He also did to the Israelites shortly afterward (Ex. 32). Another example, apart from the Exodus account, is seen in Ezekiel 14. The context of Ezekiel 14 is addressing stumbling religious men (v. 3), who stumble due to having a multitude of idols in their hearts (v. 4). As a result, they have cut themselves off from God (v. 5). Through the prophet Ezekiel, the stumbling prophets are told to repent by turning away from their idols (v. 6), by separating themselves from idolatry. Unless they do, in the same manner, God dealt with the Egyptians and Israel, He will deal with them (Judah), making a 'sign' of them that others may know that He is the Lord (v. 8). The same applies to the church (Acts 5:5, 11, Rev. 2:23) for the same reason: They may know and fear God.

The phrase "That they/you shall know that I am the Lord" is found fifty-two times in the book of Ezekiel alone when dealing with Judah. Isaiah narrows in on something of the same: 43:10-13, 44:6b, 8b and 45:5-6, 14c, 15, 18, 21b, 22, 46:9, 47:8, 10b, when dealing with Israel.

The shared deception then and today is that 'due to (hyper)grace, we can do whatever we like and that it will be alright.' But it will not be the case. In fact, when God does execute His judgement, even if Noah, Daniel, and Job (Ezek. 14:14) stood together and interceded, none will be delivered (v. 16, 20) outside those repenting.

Referring to the judgements of Noah, Daniel, and Job, God, threatened, "How much more/worse (will your judgement be) when I send upon Jerusalem my four disastrous acts of judgement, sword, famine, wild beasts, and pestilence to cut off from it man and beast!' (v. 21, cf. Rev. 6:8). The judgement God warned Judah of through Ezekiel for twenty-three years, was executed through the Babylonians (586 B.C.). And, as horrific as that was, the coming tribulation threatened through the prophets, and the book of Revelation will dwarf anything previous (Matt. 24:21), and for the same reason, idolatry. For this reason, God will strike 'His' people who replaced Him with idols. In the 21st century, idols often refer to self and materialism.

Contrary to post-modern popular belief, God strikes those who confess to being His own to show He is God and 'they are not.' God will do whatever is necessary to remove false worship from His people. God threatens and executes judgement in this way throughout the OT and the NT. Nearly all of the NT parables taught by Jesus have the same theme, albeit the book of Revelation is chief. The letter to the church of Laodicea (Laodicea meaning: People ruling) perhaps provides the strongest warning yet, where 'confessing Christians' act like 'they are gods,' today even confessing to being 'little gods.' The same prosperity-driven liberal and lukewarm believers state that they have everything and no need for anything, including Jesus!

They have no room for Jesus due to their pride-filled hearts being so full of idols, worldly idols of self, and materialism. However, the Tribulation will serve to break them free of such things by removing deception and distractions from their lives. In the Tribulation, they will be stripped so bare that the only thing left will be Jesus - if they still want Him. In short, the tribulation will serve to reveal that Jesus is Lord and that they are not!

As addressed in the book of Revelation, the warning to the churches is, 'How much worse will our Tribulation be for forsaking Christ through idolatry!' The writer of Hebrews joins in on the conversation, saying, "It will be so much worse due to having been given so much more" (Heb. 6:6, 10:29), confirmed again by Peter (2 Pet. 2:21). The coming trial is so severe that five of the seven churches were warned to repent in the book of Revelation. They were warned that unless they repent, they would suffer the worst of judgements in the history of humankind.

The five letters each deal with false worship, yet none more so than the last, representing the last church before Jesus returns, which is us on the prophetic timeline. Unless we, the lukewarm church, renounce the idolatrous, 'name it and claim it,' false prosperity gospel, we will be vomited into the Tribulation, where God will make a show of every false god and idol of the heart. Again, the pronounced judgement will demonstrate that He is God, and we are not, no matter how much we confess it, name and claim, blab and grab, demand and command, declare, and decree.

In sum, through the Tribulation, God will deal with false worship severely due to its deceptive nature, conditioning liberal churchgoers for the ultimate deceiver, the Antichrist, who will be central to the Tribulation judgements (Rev. 13-14). Evidence of such is seen in Revelation 16, where the angels pour out on the earth the seven bowls of God's wrath (16:1). The first of which is directed at the Antichrist and his followers: "So the first angel went and poured out his bowl on the earth, and harmful and painful sores came upon the people who bore the mark of the beast and worshipped its image" (vv. 2, 10). Following the first bowl is the second, which parallels the second trumpet, and similar again is the third. Verses 5 to 7 confirm the judgements are from God (cf. Isa. 45:7b), they are just, and they are well deserved.

Not only is the judgement of turning water into blood seen through the trumpet and bowl judgements, but they are also seen through the two witnesses. Revelation 11:6 confirms the same phenomena of water being turned into blood will occur through the two witnesses preaching repentance (11:3b). Again, Moses is the only person in the OT to have been used by God to turn water into blood; therefore, that sign, among others, supports that he will be one of the two witnesses in the Tribulation.

Water being turned into blood (Ex. 7:14-21) should also be compared with Jesus turning water into wine (Jn. 2:1-11). The story illustrates two things, 1). Christianity (new wine) is superior to Judaism (old wine); 2). God saves the best for last. When Jesus turned water into wine, it was symbolic of life. The sign points to Jesus as the Word in the flesh, the Mighty Creator alone, the Author of life. As with all signs, they are designed to save, even in Tribulation. In a sense, the Tribulation will be 'the best saved until last,' for it will both slay and save. The next time you hear a liberal preacher say, "The best is still yet to come," think on this with the above mentioned in mind,

The best of God will be accompanied by the worst of God (Rom. 11:22). When God saved us through the shed blood of His Son, He saved us, not from hell, but from HIMSELF: "Since, therefore, we have now been justified by His (Jesus') blood, much more shall we be saved by Him (Jesus) from the wrath of God (Rom. 5:9)." While the kindness of God is meant to lead us to repentance, because of hardheartedness, we store up wrath for ourselves (Rom. 2:4-5), which will be administered throughout the Tribulation (the best is yet to come).

On the sound of the second trumpet, as a result of a great mountain burning with fire, thrown into the sea, one-third of the sea will become blood, a third of everything living in the sea will die, and a third of the ships will sink. Undoubtedly, they will sink due to the tsunami effect caused by the great mountain thrown into the sea, which will most likely kill millions of land dwellers. And yet, the Tribulation is just warming up. For the best is still yet to come!

In conclusion, God sent plagues to separate Egypt (the world) from His people through the Exodus account and then used plagues to separate the true from the false worshippers of God throughout the OT. Those plagues came primarily through the Assyrians (to Israel) and Babylon (to Judah). Soon, God will do the same again to the compromising, corrupt, and lukewarm churchgoers through the Tribulation, hence the warnings provided through the letters to the churches (Rev. 2-3).

Remember, God had 3000 Israelites put to death for making a golden calf (Ex. 32) and warned, "Whoever has sinned against Me will be blotted out of the book of life" (v. 33), with a paralleled warning given to the church (Rev. 3:3). However, God would have none perish, but all come to repentance (2 Pet. 3:9); therefore, He has provided a way of escape (Lu. 21:34-36). He will not pour out His wrath before taking true worshippers out of the way (Rev. 3:10). As for the rest, those who stumble around, the lukewarm idolaters, they will be left behind and sifted through the Tribulation, exchanging 'their best life now,' for God's 'best, yet still to come.' God's best will come with an introduction to Jesus, the 'real' Jesus, in an unprecedented way (Rev. 6:12-17, 19:11-16).

The Third Trumpet

Immediately following the second trumpet, affecting one-third of the sea, is the third trumpet of the Tribulation, seen in Revelation 8:10-11, where a great star fell from heaven, blazing like a torch. The reference to 'great' is seen 57 times in the book of Revelation, referring mainly to the severity of judgment. For example, there will be great Tribulation (x2), as a result of the great sword, a great earthquake (x2), the great day of wrath (x2), great mountain, a great star, great furnace, great fear, great power, great signs (x2), the great red dragon, great authority, and great Babylon. The last three references refer to great deception. Two more references are given to the great and small, meaning everyone without exception will be affected by the great Tribulation; the great and powerful included. Not only every person and every living creature but also creation will be affected, including the land, sea and sky, and everything within. In other words, nothing will escape the great terror to be unleashed upon the earth. The whole earth is even now under judgement, confirmed by what Paul said in Romans 8:18-25, where creation groans in childbirth until now. With the great Tribulation ahead of us, today's groaning is nothing by comparison.

Today we see some significant groaning through birth pains, which will not stop until Jesus returns on the scene. In fact, the birth pains will intensify in severity with multiple contractions blended into one final burst. Jesus warned about this in Matthew 28, verse 8, recorded again in Mark 13, verse 8. As the birth pangs increase in intensity, men's hearts will fail them for fear (Lu. 21:26). The same is picked up by the prophet Jeremiah in chapter 48, verse 41, and chapter 49, verse 22.

Jeremiah 48, verse 41, references birth pains associated with the hearts of warriors failing for fear. The prophecy is reserved for the last days, confirmed by verse 47. The judgement pronounced is on Moab because they trusted in their works and treasure (v. 7), as did the church of Laodicea (Rev. 3:14-22). Jeremiah, chapter 49, verse 22 also refers to birth pains, and again, the heart of warriors will race due to the intensity. The prophecy in chapter 49 refers to the judgement pronounced on Edom due to the pride in their hearts (v. 16). Again, just like the church of Laodicea.

Through the prophet Jeremiah, God warned 'His people' not to be deceived by their own 'wisdom, might, and riches,' but instead to boast on their understanding and knowledge of Him (Jer. 9:23-24). The prophet's warning to the people of God is that they have forsaken God and disobeyed His voice by not walking in His commands (vv. 12-13). Instead of following God, they stubbornly followed their hearts by going after false gods (v. 14). As a result, God will give them bitter food and poisonous water (wormwood) to drink (v. 15). Verse 15 should be considered alongside Revelation 8:11, where the waters became wormwood, and many people died from the water because it had been made bitter. The same will be repeated in the third bowl in chapter 16, verse 4.

Jeremiah, chapter 9 concludes with a collective warning to Egypt, Judah, Edom, Ammon, Moab, and all who dwell in the desert, including Israel, that God will judge them (vv. 25-26). The pronounced judgement addresses the same collection in the closing chapters of Jeremiah, which is still yet to be fulfilled. Chapter 10 of Jeremiah narrows in on the same, warning not to be deceived by other nations (v. 2) who are stupid (vv. 8, 14). God then draws closer to home, where through the prophet, God says, "And so are the shepherds stupid who do not inquire of the Me" (v. 21). In other words, Judah's religious leaders are deemed by God to be stupid for trusting in themselves over God. Again, just – like – the – church – of – Laodicea.

Chapter 23 picks up on the same again, this time calling the stupid shepherds lying prophets. The lying prophets are likened to our current day prosperity preachers (22:14, 17a, 21), who were discussed earlier in chapter 8, verses 10b-11—instead of prosperity, there is a warning, terror awaits and it is even knocking at the door (v. 15). God said that because of their deception (23:13), by preaching peace instead of repentance (v. 14c), their way will be like slippery paths in the darkness (12). God will bring disaster upon them in the year of their punishment (v. 12), which will include bitter food and poisoned water (wormwood) to drink (v. 15).

Through the prophet Jeremiah, God warns His people not to listen to the lying prophets (prosperity preachers) who filled them, and even deceive the ungodly, with vain hope (23:16): "It shall be well with you, no disaster shall come upon you" (v. 17). These are people who have not stood in the council of the Lord; they have not paid attention to His word and listened to His voice (v. 18). They speak in God's name, yet they have not been sent by God, evidenced by not speaking His word and turning sinners from their evil ways (vv. 21-22). Instead of bringing a fiery word (v. 30), they preached fluff. These stupid shepherds and lying prophets are nothing but dreamers who prophesy lies and deceit in God's name, who say, "I had a dream." They make God's people forget Him through their fantasies and fairytales. For this reason, God said, they shall suffer everlasting judgement that will never be forgotten (v. 40, cf. 21:11-14).

When reading any of the major and minor prophets, the message is clear; God is against prophets/preachers who lead His people astray with lies and recklessness (Jer. 23:32). These are the ones who proclaim peace when there is no peace, and in doing so, they fail to warn of the danger ahead. They comfort sinners instead of turning them to repentance. They are the burden of God who perverts the word of the Lord (v. 36) and will be eternally cast off (vv. 33, 39-40). The message coming through the prophet

Jeremiah, aimed at the stupid shepherds, has been partly fulfilled (see Laminations) and is still yet to be fulfilled. The book of Revelation will see in the fulfilment, linking the third trumpet with the threats seen in Jeremiah 9:15 and 23:15. For Judah, the threat was fulfilled as predicted, in part, and will be again, fully and fulfilled in the Tribulation. The Tribulation event will be aimed at the same; only this time will include lukewarm churchgoers. But, none more so than the stupid shepherds who bring a fluffy word, proclaiming peace, peace, when there is no peace, who comforted people in their sins instead of warning them to repent and remain.

The comparison and application of the warning to Judah are found with the seven churches in the opening chapter of the book of Revelation. Here, Jesus, through John, similarly addressed drifting pastors and churchgoers as Jeremiah did Judah, and for the same reason, idolatry. In the same way, Judah was judged and will be again, so will the compromising, corrupt, and lukewarm church be. Those having a reputation of being alive but are dead, and those having everything, yet nothing of Jesus, are in the same sinking boat as the failing prophets and people addressed through Jeremiah.

Today, in fulfilment of scripture, we are surrounded by these false prophets who have crept into the church. They are the people who God has not sent, preaching empty words that tickle the ear in a time when judgment is looming. These weak, deceptive individuals will lead multiple millions into the tribulation, where, while in the Tribulation, they themselves will be subject to the great wrath of God in order to restore. The purpose of the Tribulation is to produce fear, resulting in genuine repentance, that some might be saved. The judgement is to 'test' the whole world (Rev. 3:10), drawing them to Jesus where they drink from Him (Rev. 22:17), in an exchange of bitter for sweet (cf. Ex. 15:23-25), death for life.

In sum, the third trumpet is just a small part of what God has in store when His great wrath is poured out on the whole earth. On this occasion, one-third of the rivers and springs will become poisonous, following one-third of the sea turned to blood. The judgement of the third trumpet turns the water into wormwood (bitter or poisonous). Many will die as a result (Rev. 8:11). The word 'wormwood' has been translated into Chernobyl by some, linking it with nuclear warfare. The idea is that due to nuclear warfare, the waters will become toxic and undrinkable. That understanding is possible, but a more favourable interpretation lies with the 'great star' that fell from heaven like a blazing torch, which from the Greek, is either interpreted 'angel,' or a 'literal star.' The latter could refer to a breakaway from an exploding star, such as a meteorite.

There is now a threatening meteorite circling the earth called wormwood with a predicted collision set for 2029/30. Either way, whatever it is that causes freshwater to become poisonous, the event will be cataphoric, killing millions of people on top of those who have already perished due to trusting themselves and or listening to the deceit of stupid shepherds.

God is the same God today as He was yesterday. He does not change (Heb. 13:8)! We must never forget who the book of Revelation was given to (the church), and for what reason (repent and remain). When we read Jeremiah's book and compare it to today, we quickly learn that nothing has changed from Judah's apostasy to our own, and neither has God changed. What God did to Judah; He is about to do again. The way God dealt with His people in the OT is the same way He will deal with His people at the close of the NT, only with much greater severity, due to being given much more (Lu. 12:28).

To think God will not judge this generation for doing the same as those in the OT is short-sighted at best. Remember the warning Jesus shared with His disciples: "Truly I tell you; it will be more bearable for Sodom and Gomorrah on the Day of Judgment than for that town" (Matt. 10:15). The warning is repeated for the city of Capernaum: "And you, Capernaum, will you be lifted up to heaven? No, you will be brought down to Hades! For if the miracles that were performed in you had been performed in Sodom, it would have remained to this day. But I tell you that it will be more bearable for Sodom on the Day of Judgment than for you" (Matt. 11:23-24).

The Fourth Trumpet

Within the first few years of the Tribulation, one-third of the earth was struck, then one-third of the waters then one-third of the heavens, resulting in darkness over one-third of the earth (Rev. 8:12). Like every other judgement in the book of Revelation, Jesus prewarned of this coming darkness, recorded by Matthew (24:29), Mark (13:24-25), and Luke (21:25).

Luke puts it this way:

> "And there will be signs in the sun and moon and stars, and on the earth distress of nations in perplexity because of the roaring of the sea and the waves, people fainting with fear and with foreboding of what is coming on the world. For the powers of the heavens will be shaken. And then they will see the Son of Man coming in a cloud with power and great glory. Now when these things begin to take place, straighten up and raise your heads, because your redemption is drawing near" (21:25-28).

Luke addressed this event again in the book of Acts, quoting Joel 2:28-32:

> "The sun shall be turned to darkness and the moon to blood before the day of the Lord comes, the great and magnificent day" (2:20).

When reading Acts, chapter two, the focus is on the outpouring of the Holy Spirit (vv. 17-21). But, take note, the fulfilment of the prophecy is reserved for the tribulation, which leads to salvation, which is the entire point and purpose of the hour of trial coming upon the whole earth (Rev.

3:10): "And it shall come to pass that everyone who calls upon the name of the Lord shall be saved" (v. 21). Those calling upon the name of the Lord, in context, are the left behind, they failed to heed the warning this side of the Tribulation (Rev. 7:9). John picks up something similar in chapter six of the book of Revelation with the fifth seal, where millions lose their earthly lives in exchange for a heavenly existence (Rev. 6:9-11). 'Their best life THEN will mean their worst life NOW!'

Following the mass murder of the Tribulation saints is the sixth seal (vv. 12-17), which is similar to the fourth trumpet, as is the fourth bowl (16:8). The only difference between the fourth trumpet and the fourth bowl judgement is that with the latter, the sun was allowed to scorch the people with fire, which resulted in them cursing God. The reference to the people cursing God indicates they knew that it was God inflicting them, but instead of repenting, they further rebelled.

Again, the whole point and purposes of the Tribulation are picked up in the people's response. By this time, no one on the planet will be able to deny God but only accept or reject Him. In short, the Tribulation plagues will bring everyone to the knowledge and awareness of Him, in the same way, the plagues of Egypt did. God will use the same plague of darkness He inflicted the Egyptians with to achieve the same outcome in the coming time of trouble.

Exodus, chapter ten, mentions the ninth plague, where darkness fell over Egypt, causing a portion of the land to be darkened. Like with the trumpet judgements, only a part of the land, sea, freshwaters, and heaven will be struck. In Egypt, throughout the plagues, God divided from one to the other as a sign (Ex. 8:23), that everyone would know - He is the Lord God (7:17, 8:10, 9:14). God will do the same in the tribulation, by removing His people from the earth before pouring out His judgements (Lu. 21:34-36, Rev. 3:10). He will also distinguish between His people and the rest during the Tribulation (Rev. 7). However, God would have not have any go through the hour of trial, which is why He called the churches to repent, this side, that they may be taken out of the way. God's 'true' children are not destined for His wrath (1 Thess. 5:9). God's wrath (Rom. 2:5) and fury (Rom. 2:9) are reserved and even being stored up for the self-seeking (Rom. 2:9). It is the self-seeking who place their trust and confidence in themselves and their false gods.

Remember, with each plague that God struck Egypt, He was targeting their false gods, demonstrating that they had no power to save. With the plague of darkness, God struck the Egyptian sun god, which was considered to be the greatest of gods, outside of Pharaoh himself. Pharaoh would be struck in the subsequent plague where his first-born son, the heir to the throne, died (12:29-30).

Through these events, the message from God is precise: "I am God, alone!" Even the great Pharaoh recognised this by saying, "I have sinned against the Lord your God, therefore forgive my sin" (10:16b-17). Later, he asked Moses to 'bless him' before the Israelites departed Egypt (12:32). While it took a little longer for Pharaoh to respond to God than his magicians (8:18-19), he got there in the end, albeit short-lasting. The same will be true in the Tribulation; everyone will acknowledge God. To reiterate, there will be no atheists, and neither will there be any agnostics by that time. Yet still, like Pharaoh, most will not come to a place of genuine and lasting repentance (Rev. 9:20-21, 16:8-11).

Another point of interest with the ninth plague over Egypt is that darkness could be 'felt' (10:21). Clearly, the darkness was not due to an eclipse, evident by Goshen (8:22), where Israel lived, and they still had light (10:23). Therefore, the darkness could be considered the cause of something supernatural, that the 'felt' darkness was as much spiritual as it was physical.

Before reading on, take a moment to think of a time wherein the pitch-blackness of night, you 'felt' a demonic presence. Remember how the atmosphere changed and how frightening that was! Now, times that experience by one thousand, then you will have some inkling of what the prophesied event might feel like. People will be scared out of their wits. Exodus 10:21 gives the same sense and makes a direct link to Revelation 16:10, where: "The fifth angel poured out his bowl on the throne of the beast, and its kingdom was plunged into darkness. People gnawed their tongues in anguish. In other words, the darkness was felt in such a way that it caused fear and pain.

Another example of this is found in Isaiah 8:22, where God judged His people for inquiring of mediums and necromancers (8:19), resulting in distress, darkness, gloom, and anguish. Instead of seeking God, God's people chased after 'words and wonders' from clairvoyants. God warned them not to do this many times, but they failed to heed the warning and even called the pronounced judgement, a conspiracy (vv. 12-13), just – like – today! While walking in the ways of the world (8:11b), they became like the world and lost their fear of God (8:13). As a result, they could no longer hear the truth and instead replaced it with a lie (vv. 14-15). In an ironic twist, because they preferred demons to God, God said that they would join them in Hell (8:22). After all, God does give us the desires of our heart, and He will reward us according to our heart's desire (Rev. 2:23).

Joining rebellious Israel, many 'believers' will likewise find their full reward in Hell (cf. Matt. 7:21-23), despite numerous warnings not to go that way, which include the warnings to the seven churches addressed in the book of Revelation (Rev. 2-3). Even today, we see denominations doing the same (Isa. 8:19) by consulting with clairvoyants, thereby practicing and promoting the occult within the church. Examples of this are seen with those who confess to being Christian, seeking information from the dead, also practicing angel (tarot) card readings, and conducting grave soaking sessions (necromancy), and fire tunnel walks. These demonic practices are a repeat of Israel's sins. Jezebel was also guilty of the same, referenced both in the OT and the NT. Jesus warned the CHURCH of Thyatira if they do not repent of tolerating that woman, they would be cast into the great tribulation, with her (Rev. 2:22). Again, Jesus warned the CHURCH to repent or else be thrown into the great Tribulation. The name Jezebel means Unhusbanded, which means, unruled, and unsubmitted to authority. The church of Laodicea has a similar meaning: People ruling (instead of God). The church of Laodicea was warned to repent or else be vomited out. This church was the last to be addressed in the book of Revelation, which is prophetically the last before Jesus returns. Therefore, the application of being vomited out would be vomited out into the Tribulation. The Greek implies, violently, which translates, violently vomited out.

Picking up again on Isaiah chapter eight, the prophet narrows in on the same, with another yet to be fully fulfilled prophecy (13:10). This time the judgement is on Babylon due to their arrogance and pompous pride (v. 11). While the literal judgement has been fulfilled (v. 22b), the spiritual application is still yet to be achieved and will be in the great Tribulation. Revelation chapter 18 provides insight into what that will look like.

Once more, like that of Egypt, God distinguishes between His people and the rest by calling them out of the end times religious system (Rev. 18:4). Following, God pours out His judgement on the end-times harlot church, or religious system, where her iniquities are heaped as high as heaven (v. 5). Her iniquities are glorifying in herself (v. 7a), boasting in her security (v. 7b), and prosperity (vv. 11-13). All of which will be lost in a single day (v. 8), in a single hour (vv. 10, 17, 19). Like the Egyptians (Ex. 7:11), and the Israelites (Isa. 8:19), and like the churches of Thyatira, Sardis, and Laodicea, the end-time church is being deceived by the same sorcery, worldly reputation and prosperity. Therefore, it will face judgement through tribulation, as Egypt did, and Israel, however, much more severely (Matt. 24:21).

To summarise, we have seen that the coming judgement of darkness is much more than just the absence of light; it is the absence of God! Essentially, God gives the rebellious what they want – darkness due to not loving or wanting the light (Jn. 3:19). God gives them a taste of what it might 'feel' like to be consumed by absolute darkness, that they might repent before it becomes their eternal reality, in Hell (Matt. 8:12, 22:13, 25:30). Note carefully that each reference (Matt. 8:12, 22:13, 25:30) is aimed at those who 'thought' they were saved, warning them that they are not, just like five of the seven churches (70%) addressed in the book of Revelation.

The Three Woes of the Tribulation
The Worst is Yet to Come

Following the fourth trumpet that cast darkness over one-third of the earth (8:12) came the announcement of the coming three woes (8:13). The fourth trumpet introduced a wave of demonic darkness, not merely physical, as discussed in the previous section. The following three trumpets are the three woes that will unleash demonic activity upon the earth, unlike anything anyone has ever seen before, or will again (Matt. 24:21), concluding with the return of Jesus. The unprecedented events are confirmed by the words of Jesus (Matt. 24:21), and the prophecy (Rev. 6-22), which is about to be fulfilled. While some say John's prophecy (the revelation) was fulfilled in 70 A.D., they overlook the fact that we have seen worst since then through WWI and WWII alone. We will again through WWIII, which is set to occur at the end of the Tribulation, known as the battle or campaign of Armageddon (Rev. 19). Furthermore, Jesus has not yet returned to the earth (Rev. 1:7, 19:11-21).

Further support for future fulfilment is found with the opening chapters of the book of Revelation that plainly state a fourth of the planet's population (not Israel), will be slain on the release of the apocalyptic horsemen (Rev. 6:8). Putting the prediction into perspective, suppose we consider some two billion are raptured (for argument sake), leaving five billion (rounding down) left behind to endure the tribulation. In that case, subtract one-fourth (1.25 billiion), leaving 3.75 billion, with another third (one billion) killed through the sixth trumpet judgement. Then add the many Tribulation saints who are slain (6:9, 7:9). Combined we can safely say less than half the population, left behind, will survive the first few years of the Tribulation. Again, LESS THAN HALF the people will remain, reducing to less than 2.5 billion, and the worst is still yet to come! The above mentioned alone should be enough to debunk and discredit preterist (past, history, and already fulfilled) theology.

To recap on what we have covered so far: The seals cover the entire tribulation period. The trumpets cover the first half (chap. 6-9), and the bowls cover the second half (chap. 15-16). Chapters 10-14, 17, and 18 are informative, not chronological. The three woes pick up on the key events leading into the last three and a half years, concluding the seven years of Tribulation with the intention to save. The three woes announcement serves as a warning call, much like an altar call SHOULD. Sadly, however, many altar calls today are likened to 'who wants ice-cream?' Moreover it should be, 'who wants to be saved from the wrath of God?'

During the Tribulation, the invitation for salvation primarily comes through the Jewish evangelists, seen in chapters seven and fourteen, and the two Jewish witnesses seen in chapter eleven. And, here is another problem for preterists who subscribe to replacement theology, stating God has done away with Israel and replaced her with the church. Question: When have we ever seen anything like the events of the said chapters take place? Never! Not even close! During the Tribulation, not only will the Jews proclaim salvation through Christ alone, but angels will also:

"Then I looked, and I heard an eagle crying with a loud voice as it flew directly overhead, "Woe, woe, woe to those who dwell on the earth, at the blasts of the other trumpets that the three angels are about to blow!" (8:13).

Compare the image of the eagle to Rev. 19:17-19:

"Then I saw an angel standing in the sun, and with a loud voice he called to all the birds that fly directly overhead, "Come, gather for the great supper of God, to eat the flesh of kings, the flesh of captains, the flesh of mighty men, the flesh of horses and their riders, and the flesh of all men, both free and slave, both small and great. And I saw the beast and the kings of the earth with their armies gathered to make war against him who was sitting on the horse and against his army."

And again, to the angel proclaiming the eternal gospel, issuing a threat that some may turn (Rev. 14:6-7):

"Then I saw another angel flying directly overhead, with an eternal gospel to proclaim to those who dwell on the earth, to every nation and tribe and language and people. And he said with a loud voice, "Fear God and give Him glory, because the hour of his judgement has come, and worship him who made heaven and earth, the sea and the springs of water."

Remember, during the Tribulation, like the plagues of Egypt, God will target false gods. The Tribulation plagues will target the land, sea, freshwater, and heavens in a direct assault on everything that humanity worships. For example, God will make a show of climate change proponents who forsake the Savior and, instead, seek to save the planet, even claiming Greta Thornburg is the New Climate Messiah.

Following the assault on the land, sea, freshwater, and heaven, the fifth plague and first woe introduce the demonic locusts. This time, the ground and vegetation are off-limits, replaced with people (9:4) Again, following the fourth trumpet judgement of darkness, spiritual darkness verses spiritual light is the central theme of the Tribulation. Upon opening the bottomless pit, the angel of God will release a demonic horde of locusts, led by Apollyon (9:11). Apollyon means 'the destroyer.' Apollo is the Greek god of death. The locust was an emblem of this god, who poisoned his victims. In the tribulation, the poison will be administered through the painful and poisonous scorpion-sting of the locust (9:5, 10). During that time, death will not be found by those inflicted, even though desperately sought (9:6).

Some five months after the first woe comes the second. We know that there are at least five months between the first and second woe due to in the first, none die (9:6), but in the second, one-third of the population will perish (9:18). We also know precisely when the first woe concludes, and the second commences by the announcement: "The first woe has passed; behold, two woes are still to come" (9:12). The second woe is the sixth trumpet that releases the four bound angels (9:14) who kill one-third of humanity (9:15) through the 200m mounted troops (9:16). The mounted troops are riding horses (9:17), but not just any horse! We will look at the army of 200m more closely when considering the sixth trumpet, but suffice to say, as the demonic locust, the army of 200m is not natural, but instead, supernatural. Worth noting, the supernatural armies of both the locust and mounted troops are under God's authority, released on God's say-so. God prepares them for 'the hour, the day, the month, and the year' (v. 15a). During that time, they are limited (by God) to kill one-third of humanity (vv. 15b, 18). Of course, the affliction's purpose is to save, drawing humankind to repentance, although not achieved (vv. 20, 21).

While some say the severity of the plagues is too much and unnecessary, the plagues are in proportion to the blasphemy of men and their rejection of God. Again, the Tribulation will parallel the plagues of Egypt. Similarly, God used the judgments (Ex. 7-12) to reveal Himself (Ex. 7:5, 17; 8:10, 22; 9:14, 29; 10:2), yet Pharaoh refused to repent (Ex. 7:13, 22, 23; 8:15; 9:35; 10:27; 11:10; 14:8) even after he had acknowledged God (Ex. 8:8, 28; 9:28; 10:17). Furthermore, his magicians gave testimony to the Living God (Ex. 8:19) yet did not seek repentance for themselves (Ex. 9:11). It resulted in the crippling of a great empire, so severe were the judgments that Egypt never recovered and remained that way even to this day. The literal plagues of Egypt targeted the nation's drinking water (Ex. 7:19) and food source (Ex. 9:3, 22; 10:5), thus their economy. Egypt's military was also wiped out (Ex. 14:27-28).

Following the second woe is the last (Rev. 11:14). The third woe is the seventh trumpet, which contains the seven bowls described in chapter

16, verses 1-21, pointing to Jesus Christ and His return. Chapter eleven, verses 15-18, announces that the kingdom of the world has come to the kingdom of our Lord (v. 15) and that He has begun His reign (v. 16). The same is picked up in chapter fifteen. At His appearance, Jesus will judge the nations (Rev. 19:11-21), which fulfils the third woe, as introduced through the sixth seal in chapter six (vv. 12-17). The prophet Jeremiah mentions something similar in chapter four, verse 13, which is likened to Revelation, chapter eight, verse 13, and linked to chapter nineteen, (vv. 11-21).

To gain a full understanding of the event that Jeremiah describes, read chapters four and five, and note the similarity to the coming tribulation. Pay careful attention to the closing verse addressing the false prophets who told Judah God will not judge them (5:12, 6:13). God responded by asking, "What will you do when the end comes?" (5:31). Joining Jeremiah, Joel predicts the same in chapter two of Joel's book, cited by Peter in Acts 2. Mentioned earlier, nothing close to the anticipated events have occurred before. In fact, so severe will the time of trouble be, Jesus said, "If those days had not been cut short, no one would survive" (Matt. 24:22). Once again, the statement completely debunks preterist teaching.

Although the third woe was announced through the seven trumpets, which contains the bowl judgements, and leads to the conclusion of the tribulation with Jesus' return, there is yet another woe in-between. The woe in-between the second and third woes describe Satan being cast down to the earth (Rev. 12:12). Satan is thrown to the earth at the halfway point of the Tribulation, which will be appropriately addressed after discussing the seventh trumpet.

Until then, it is important to note that Satan is freely operating from the heavenly realm today (Eph. 2:2, 6:12), seeking whom he may devour (1 Pet. 5:8). He is the ruler (Jn. 14:30) and god of this world, blinding unbelievers. And, he will continue to do so until he is first cast to the earth (Rev.

12:12), and then judged by Jesus forty-two months later (Rev. 20:1-3). When Jesus returns, then the devil will be cast into the pit for one thousand years. However, preterists state that Satan is already bound, but, if that were true, then I suggest, Satan's chain is way too long, and Jesus' ruling rod of iron (Rev. 2:27) is way too short!

The Fifth Trumpet
Such as has not been before and never will be again

As previously written, the fifth trumpet (Rev. 8:1-11) is the first woe (8:13) of the Tribulation, and it is the first wave of demonic activity following an escalation of spiritual darkness coming upon the earth (8:12). The previous section of this study argues that the locust plague unleashed on the planet is supernatural, not natural. During the Tribulation, not only will the left behind suffer natural catastrophes, including wars (Matt. 24), but supernatural plagues as well, starting with the demonic locusts, which are released on God's say-so.

Chapter nine of the book of Revelation introduces the demonic locusts, but before doing so, gives the careful reader cause for self-reflection with the opening verses. Verse 2, in particular, is not only a repeat of 8:12, but the fulfilment of Hebrews 12:26, which glances back at the event described in Exodus 19:18, and then takes a glimpse forward towards Revelation 8-9. The warning of Hebrews 12 is "Not to grow weary in your struggle against sin" (vv. 3, 4). The message encourages the believer to endure (v. 7), to strive for peace and holiness (v. 14), and to remain sexually pure (v. 16), for without which, no one will see the Lord (v. 14).

In sum, if you grow weary in your struggle against sin, you will not see Jesus when He returns for His Bride. The warning is similar to that given to five of seven of the churches addressed in Revelation, chapters 2-3. Those not having ears to hear what the Spirit is saying to the churches will be left behind to endure the Tribulation, which contains the plague of the demonic locusts. Sadly, in fulfilment of scripture, the majority will not hear the warning, and it is not the first time!

Throughout the OT, various tribulation plagues, including locusts, were sent by God to punish spiritually deaf religious and rebellious people, to produce repentance. An example of this is seen in Exodus 10:12, where through the eighth plague on Egypt, God sent an army of locusts that every plant might be destroyed (v. 12). The event was like nothing anyone had ever seen before, nor will again (v. 14). The purpose is confirmed in verses 16-17, to bring about repentance. Another example is found in the book of Joel. The prophet Joel predicts something similar, only this time concerning the 'Coming Day of the Lord.' Joel references the Day of the Lord seven times (1:15, 2:1, 11, 31, 3:1, 14, 18). The central theme of Joel's book is repentance (1:5, 8, 9, 11, 13, 2:12-17) following the acknowledgment of God (2:27, 3:17) in preparation for the Messiah's rule and reign (3:17-21).

Like with the Egyptian plague, what Joel describes has never been seen before is confirmed by chapter one, verse 2, "Has such a thing happened in your days, or in the days of your fathers?" (Joel 1:2). The answer is NO! Repeated in chapter two, verse 2, where the things to come, 'Has never been seen before, nor will it be again after them through the years of all generations." Going by these verses (1:2, 2:2), we know Joel's prophecy is quite different from what took place in Egypt. Remember, with the plague on Egypt - God said what He was about to do has not been seen before and would not be seen again (Exodus 10:14).

Like the Egyptian plague of locusts, Joel's prophecy is also purposed to bring about repentance (vv. 12-17). Once God's great locust army had done what God sent it to do, God will then restore (2:25, 3:1). But, not before Armageddon's battle takes place (3:9-16), which is the day Jesus returns. When Jesus returns, that day will be unlike any other; Joel states it will be, "a great day and very awesome; who can endure it?" (2:11). The same rhetorical question was raised in John's prophecy regarding the same event (Rev. 6:17). Jesus mentioned something similar when speaking about the last days, issuing a warning to, "Stay awake that we might escape it" (Lu. 21:36). Like Moses and Joel, Jesus also confirmed that what is to come, has never taken place before or will again (Matt. 24:21). Jesus was referring to the Tribulation, which includes the supernatural locusts of chapter nine (vv. 1-11).

With the first two judgements (Exodus and Joel), they speak of two different, yet natural events. And, the third is different again, and supernatural. The supporting argument for the Tribulation locusts being supernatural is based on their appearance, ability, purpose, leader, and origin. Their appearance is described in verses 7-10. When reading these verses (vv. 7-10), even allegorically, to conclude, the locusts are natural creatures would be to perform some serious exegetical gymnastics (twisting scripture).

Furthermore, their ability to sting people with a scorpion tail is nothing like anything we have seen from a natural locust—locusts attack crops, not people. But, with these creatures, they are told not to harm the vegetation, but only people (v. 4), and only those without the seal of God (v. 4, cf. 7:3). That last statement also rules out weapons of war, such as helicopters or drones engaging with chemical warfare. The fifth trumpet is the first that targets people, the four trumpets beforehand targeted the land, sea, freshwaters, and heavens.

The next supporting argument for the creatures being supernatural over natural is their purpose. The purpose of the locusts is to harm humanity, not kill. They are to torment people to the point that they would rather die than endure the pain (vv. 6, 10). God effectively gives humanity time to repent rather than allowing them to perish into a Christless eternity. The locust will torment humanity for five months, either with a single sting or a continuation of stings (vv. 5, 10).

Another reason supporting why the creatures are not natural is their leader. Their leader is Apollyon, whose name means 'destroyer.' The Greek god Apollo derives from the demon Apollyon who is said to be Satan's commander and chief, much like the angel Michael is for God.

Further support for the creatures being supernatural is drawn from their origin. Verses 1, 2, and 11 tell us the locusts come from the bottomless pit and appear only after a 'fallen angel' (probably Satan, cf. Rev. 12:12) opens it (vv. 1-2). The "Abyss" (abyssos) is the home of demons (cf. Luke 8:31; Rev. 9:11; 11:7; 17:8; 20:1, 3; in Rom. 10:7 it is translated 'deep'). Once opened, the creatures then come out of the smoke of a great furnace, which is so great, it darkens the sun and the air. First, the earth is darkened, like with the fourth trumpet, then the locusts appear. The appearance and the ability of these demonic creatures will be unlike anything the planet has seen before, making the worst of horror movies look tame by comparison. Once released, there will be nowhere to hide and no cure to be found for the painful and poisonous sting they deliverer. Not even through death will humanity be able to escape or find relief (v. 6).

In sum, through the three different examples (Exodus, Joel, and the book of Revelation), we have seen God using a plague of locusts to reveal Himself and bring about repentance. However, on each occasion, the locust army represented something different. First, they were a literal insert army of locusts. Second, they represented a literal army of men. Third, they are supernatural and demonic creatures released from the bottomless pit, inflicting pain and torment for five months. On each occasion, just before the locust army was released, God said through the prophet, "What was about to happen has never happened before, nor will it happen again." Although the judgement is confronting and severe, we must never lose sight of the reason, that through Tribulation, God is still desperately seeking to save the lost (Lu. 19:10).

Perhaps, Joel says it best with these words:

"Yet even now (in the tribulation)," declares the LORD, "return to me with all your heart, with fasting, with weeping, and with mourning; and rend your hearts and not your garments." Return to the LORD your God, for He is gracious and merciful, slow to anger, and abounding in steadfast love; and He relents over disaster" (2:12-13).

Verse 12b was first recorded by Moses (Ex. 34:6), following God's judgement on those who worshipped the golden calf (Ex. 23). Again, the saying was repeated by Jonah when God relented from destroying Nineveh after they repented (Jon. 4:2). Joel repeats these words aimed at those left behind in the Tribulation to come. The affirmation was true then, and it is just as accurate today, and it will still be valid for those left behind in the Tribulation.

"Yet even now, return to Me with all your heart, says the Lord."

The Sixth Trumpet

Possibly only five months after the fifth trumpet is blown, the sixth trumpet of the tribulation follows. No one has been allowed to die (9:6) during the fifth trumpet and first woe (8:13, 9:12). With the sixth trumpet and second woe (8:13, 11:14), one-third of the remaining population will perish (9:18). There is still a third woe remaining (8:13, 11:14), which is the seventh trumpet (11:15-19).

As argued in the previous section, each of the three woes is spiritual or, at least, has a spiritual component. The second woe and sixth trumpet are revealed to be spiritual with the release of the four angels who are bound at the great river Euphrates (9:14). The bound angels are demons; holy angels are not bound. Quite possibly, they are the same bound angels that crossed the line in Noah's day (Gen. 6, 2 Pet. 2:4, Jude 1:6). The apocryphal book of Enoch has plenty more to say about these angels. If they are indeed the same bound angels from Noah's day, they have been bound for five thousand years, and are soon to be released. When these four demons are released, they will be at a specific time, right down to the minute (v. 15a). Up until that time, they have been prepared for a particular purpose. God is the one who bound them, and prepared them, and He is the one who releases them, and indirectly commands them. When they are released, they are limited by God to kill one-third of the population, and no more. Remember, at the fourth seal opening, one-fourth of the population perished, amounting to 1.25 billion, if we consider some two billion are raptured before the Tribulation. On the release of the four bound angels, 3.75 billion, less the martyred, left behind, saints (6:9-11, 7:9-14, 13:15, 14:12-13, 20:4), remain. Due to not knowing the numbers equating to the martyred saints, working only with the known number of

3.75 billion, less another third (one billion), around 2.75 billion people remain on the planet after the sixth trumpet.

At this point in the tribulation, we are not even at that halfway point. The second half of the Tribulation is the Great Tribulation due to being saliently worse than the first half, or 42-months.

The bound angels, who are released in the latter part of the first half of the Tribulation, kill one-third of the population through 200 million mounted troops (vv. 15, 18). Again, one-third of the people will amount to around one billion people. To put that number into perspective, in World War I, 17 million people perished. In World War II, 73 million more lost their lives; it is predicted that World War III would result in 500 million lives lost through nuclear warfare alone. If you combined the loss of life through World War I, II, and III, the numbers amount to just over half of that perishing through the 200 million mounted troops. These troops will lead the Tribulation period into the final war, the great battle, or campaign of Armageddon, picked up again in chapter sixteen, with the sixth bowl judgement. The sixth bowl and the sixth trumpet are one in the same thing. The bound angels at the great river Euphrates, lead the 200 million mounted troops, under the command from the kings from the east, prepared (by God) to march across the great dried-up river Euphrates (16:12).

Deceived by Satan, the Beast, and the False Prophet (16:13), the kings from the east, alongside the kings of the whole world, gather together for the battle on the great day of God the Almighty (16:14), which is Armageddon (16:16). Chapter nineteen picks up on this battle from verses 11-21, as does Daniel, chapter eleven, verses 40-45. Revelation 19:18 reveals the unstoppable army is slain by Jesus at the plains of Megiddo where, "The flesh of horses and their riders are consumed by the birds gathering for the great supper of God" (v. 17).

When considered the above mentioned, it is no wonder both Daniel and Jesus said the coming Tribulation will be unlike anything we have seen before and will again (Dan. 12:1, Matt. 24:21). In fact, if Jesus did not come back early, there would be no person left alive (Matt. 24:22). Simply put, the tribulation will dwarf everything and everything else combined by comparison. Not only will the Tribulation dwarf every other natural or man-made event, but every previous supernatural event also, as discussed in the previous section.

Again, the supernatural element is seen with the 200 million mounted horses, who are under the king's command from the east and are led by four powerful demons. If these are the same bound fallen angels from Noah's day, then these were the ones responsible for corrupting human flesh by producing the Nephilim. The Nephilim are a corrupt blend, or hybrid, of humankind and angels whom God destroyed through the Flood (Gen. 7). Many believe the Nephilim spirit is in the demons that roam the earth today and will be unleashed during the tribulation. The argument makes sense and has biblical support where Jesus said, "The tribulation will be as the days of Noah" (Matt. 24:37-39). The reference refers to the corruption of God's creation, being God's creative design of humanity made in His likeness.

Today, we see something of the same through transhumanism, where humanity's very DNA is being altered with an incorporated combination of robotics and A.I. Furthermore, the coming Mark of the Beast (666) is also argued to have a DNA altering component, which is why anyone who receives that Mark cannot be saved after that (Rev. 14:9-11). Due to DNA alteration, even by 1%, the altered being is no longer human, as God designed; therefore, they are unredeemable. Salvation is reserved for humankind alone, which is why fallen angels cannot be saved. Again, Enoch has much to say on this matter.

If I am correct in the previous statement, then the 200 million mounted troops are no longer considered to be human, but rather transhuman. They are the super-soldiers of the future. Even now, we are seeing the first of these super-soldiers being rolled out with implants incorporating A.I and robotics. We have been watching it for decades thanks to Hollywood with the likes of Universal Soldier, released in 1992. Other similar movies include, but are not limited to, Terminator, Robocop, The Matrix, Elysium, Iron Man, X-Men, Spiderman, the Hulk, Avatar, Transcendent, and more recently Bloodshot.

Essentially, Hollywood has been conditioning us for decades in preparation for the things to come. They include these 'super-soldiers' described in chapter nine of the book of Revelation. And, John is not the only one who received a revelation of this futuristic army; the prophet Joel did likewise.

When considering Joel's prediction (Joel 1-2), with the acknowledgment, the prophecy will be fulfiled in the Tribulation. It would be reasonable to state that what Joel saw is the same as what John saw regarding the 200 million mounted troops. Although Joel's prophecy regarding the locust army could be mistaken for the demonic locust connected to the fifth trumpet, greater support suggests the army described by Joel is the sixth trumpet and the second woe of the Tribulation.

When considering the compatibilities of Joel's prophecy and chapter nine of the book of Revelation, there are four associated characteristics with the fifth trumpet and first woe and five with the sixth trumpet and second woe. The first and second woe likewise share some similar traits; for example, the power of both is in their tails (9:3, 5, 10 & 9:19). Although they are similar, as seen in the chart below, they are not the same. Joel makes a distinction when describing the powerful army, supporting that the locust army (1:4) is literal and not insect locusts. This literal army is of men, not natural locust, or of the demonic kind, which is to be released on the sound of the fifth trumpet (Rev. 9:1-11).

Joel	1:4	1:6	1:6	2:2	2:3, 5	2:4	2:5	2.5, 11	
	Locust	Nation	Teeth lions'	Powerful people	Fire	Horses	Chariots	Army	
Rev.	9:3, 7	9:1-2, 11	9:8	9:5, 10		9:11	9:11	9:7, 9	9:9
	Locust	Demon leader	Teeth lions'	Power in tales		Horses	Chariots	Battle	Breastplate
Rev.	9:16	9:14, 16:12	9:17	9:19	9:18	9:16, 17		9:16	9:17
	Mounted horses	Demonic leader and Kings of the East	Heads lions'	Power in tails	Fire	Horses		Troops	Breastplate

As stated above, Joel's prophetic insight is arguably the same as what John saw, confirming the army is literal. It is a literal, great and powerful army of people like never before, nor will be again through the years of all generations (Joel 2:2). The army is a literal army having supernatural ability to kill with fire (Joel 2:3a, Rev. 9:18), and nothing escapes them (Joel 2:3b). Their appearance will be of horses, like war horses they run (Joel 2:4), leaping on top of mountains, like the crackling of a flame of fire (Joel 2:5a). They are a formidable army drawn for battle (Joel 2:5b); like warriors, like soldiers, they scale the wall (Joel 2:7). They march (Joel 2:7-8) and burst through weapons and are not halted (Joel 2:8). They leap upon cities, run upon walls, climb up into houses, enter through windows, like a thief (Joel 2:9). They kill with fire coming out of their mouths and have serpent (poison) power in their tails (Rev. 9:18-19). So powerful is this army that the earthquakes before them, and the heavens tremble (Joel 2:10). The army is exceedingly great, executing the word of God (Joel 2:11, 3:25b).

Although the army is heathen, it belongs to God (Joel 2:11, 3:25b), which is to say, it is released on God's say-so (Rev. 9:15) to do as God prepared and commands. Some say the army represents China, which fits with Revelation 16:12. Interestingly, years ago, Red China claimed to have an army of 200 million (cf. Time, May 21, 1965, p. 35), perhaps prophetically fulfilling Revelation 9:16.

While some may take issue with God using a heathen army to do as He commands, it is not the first time. God did the same with Nebuchadnezzar, calling him, 'My servant' (Jer. 27:6, 43:10), and with Cyrus (Isa. 44:28, 45:1). The same will be true of the army released on the sixth trumpet, which is sent by God to produce repentance (Joel 2:20-21). Despite the anguish causing people's faces to grow pale (Joel 2:2), on the great and awesome (fearsome) day of the Lord, none can endure (Joel 2:11b, Rev. 6:17); yet still, they refuse to repent. Again, repentance is the tribulation's point and purpose (Joel 2:12-13, 15-17).

In conclusion, the sixth trumpet and second woe are most likely the same events described by the prophet Joel in chapter two of this book. This event of an invading demon-led army in itself is the sole and terrifying judgement of Joel's prophecy that will see in the return of Jesus (3:18-21). Just before Jesus returns to strike down the powerful force (Rev. 19:11-21), He offers one final alter call: "Multitudes, multitudes, in the valley of decision! For the day of the Lord is near in the valley of decision" (Joel 3:14).

Even at this late hour, God is STILL seeking to save the lost:

> "Yet even now, declares the Lord, return to Me with all your heart, with fasting, with weeping, and with mourning; and rend your hearts and not your garments. Return to the Lord your God, for He is gracious and merciful, slow to

anger, and abounding in steadfast love; and He relents over disaster" (Joel 2:12-13, cf. Acts 2:20, 21).

The call to salvation is as true today as it will be during the Tribulation:

> "Everyone who calls on the name of the Lord will be saved" (Rom. 10:13). The urgency to respond and accept the invitation to salvation has never been more apparent! 'Today, if you hear His voice do not harden your hearts as in the rebellion" (Heb. 13:5).

CHAPTER TEN

(vv. 1-11)
The Little Scroll

Closing in on the tribulation's halfway point, the message is: 'There would be no more delay,' meaning; there is no time left (cf. 1:1b, 3, 7, 22:7, 12, 20). Due to the shortness of time, the last remaining mystery would soon be revealed or unveiled through the seventh trumpet. Until then, it is concealed: "Seal up what the seven thunders have said, and do not write them down" (v. 4). The same words were given to Daniel (8:26, 12:4, 9); only in that time, Daniel was told to seal up the words due to the judgement being many days from his own. Again, with John's revelation, there is a sense of urgency; time is running out. That is not to say there is no time left, but rather, there is little time left. At this point in the Tribulation (chapter 10), there are still at least 42 months remaining in the seven-year period (11:3), yet still, the mystery remains concealed for many until the seventh trumpet is blown.

Not only does the seventh trumpet contain the third woe, but a mysterious component that will be both bitter and sweet (vv. 9-10). The mystery is concealed in a little book (vv. 2, 8, 9) until revealed for the bulk of the remaining, and left behind, the population of the world (v. 11). Until the revealing and fulfiling of the mystery through the seventh trumpet (v. 7), most are still spiritually asleep to the times and the sign of the times, being blinded by the god of this world (2 Cor. 4:4).

Even confessing Christians fall into this category due to not studying God's word for themselves, instead, scoffing at prophecy concerning the return of Christ (2 Pet. 3:3, Jude 1:8). Subsequently, they have been deceived (1 Tim. 4:1, 2 Tim. 4:3) by the antichrist's spirit (1 Jn. 4:2-3) operating through many preachers. The Antichrist's spirit has brought about this age of apostasy (2 Thess. 2:3), which is conditioning the sleepy church (Rev. 3:3) for the strong delusion to come (2 Thess. 2:11). The current apostasy is the fulfilment of the prophesied great falling away before the Tribulation commences, which coincides with the removal of the Bride of Christ. The falling away is not a departure from religion, but rather a departure from Jesus where entire churches and dominations continue to gather for worship in His name yet are void of His presence and His leading (Rev. 3:17, 20).

For those looking to Jesus, the mystery is no mystery at all, for it has previously been revealed through God's servants, the prophets (Rev. 10:7). The prophecy is straightforward and refers to Jesus (Rom. 16:25, Eph 1:9-10, 3:2-11, 5:32, 6:19, Col. 1:27), who is the blessing of the revelation (Rev. 1:3) and the prophecy of the book (Rev. 19:10b). Through Jesus, salvation is gained and proclaimed (Rev. 6:9-11, 7:9-17, 14:12, 20:4). Again, as for the perishing, the mystery of Jesus will be made known through the seventh trumpet, ushering in His return (Rev. 1:7, 16:17, 19:11-21).

To reiterate, leading up to Jesus' return, the mystery is revealed through the seventh trumpet, the third woe of the Tribulation (11:15-19). The return of Jesus will be both bitter and sweet (vv. 9, 10). Bitter for those rejecting and or disobeying Him, but sweet for those accepting, looking for, and living for Him. Isaiah also references the bitter/sweet idiom (Isa. 5:20), addressing those who twist scripture by calling right wrong and wrong right. Remember, Isaiah addresses religious Israel, who 'think' they are following God, just like many in the church today. The evidence of truly following God follows, gaining a revelation of the mystery of Christ. Once you have indeed received a revelation of Christ, you will no longer call right wrong and wrong right; instead, you will walk in the light and be transformed by the light, evidently living for Him and living like Him (1 Tim. 3:16). This transformation is contrary to those confessing Christ yet lack devotion to Him (1 Tim. 4:1-2).

For those who genuinely come to Christ (and endure for Christ), it will come at a cost (Lu. 14:25-33, Jn. 16:33). During the tribulation, the cost to follow Christ will be so much greater than this side of the seven-year ordeal. During the Tribulation period, the left behind will come to Christ through the ministry of the 144,000 (Rev. 7, 14), the two witnesses (Rev. 11), and even through ministering angels (14:6-7). Following conversion, they will suffer terribly for the purpose of testing and separation, having failed to count the cost on this side. However, when Jesus returns (as long as they endure until the end (Matt. 24:13, Rev. 14:12)), they shall then be rewarded beyond measure.

During the Tribulation, the 'blessed ones,' however, die early (Rev. 14:13, 20:6) rather than endure all seven years of the judgement. Blessed moreover, are the ones who escape the time of trial all together through the resurrection (Rev. 3:10), which is the rapture of the living saints (Rev. 4:1, Luke 21:36, 1 Thess. 1:10, 4:15-17, 5:9), being the Bride of Christ.

Regarding the return of Jesus at the end of the Tribulation period, the passage opens up with the introduction of 'another' mighty angel. This angel is different from the seven blowing the trumpets; he comes down from heaven, wrapped in a cloud, with a rainbow over his head, and his face was like the sun and his legs like pillars of fire (v. 1). Furthermore, his voice is likened to a roaring lion, calling out the seven thunders. Notice also the angel has one foot on the land and another in the sea, symbolic of great authority. The imagery here is descriptive of judgement, not dissimilar to Revelation, chapter one with the introduction of Jesus; however, the angel IS NOT Jesus, as some suggest. The angel is 'another' angel like the previous and could be Michael, who is known to be exceedingly powerful. Whoever he is, and as powerful as he is, it should be noted, he is submitted to God (v. 5), recognising His authority, alone (v. 6). The acknowledgment infers that God alone is the Creator (4:11, 14:7), and He alone has absolute authority over His creation, including angels, demons, and us.

During the tribulation, God is still sovereign; every judgement and every creature is under His absolute authority, including Satan, the Antichrist, and the False Prophet. Satan and company are only 'allowed' power for a while, but the time will soon end (Rev. 12:12b, 20:1-3, 10). If the strong angel is Michael, then it is probably this angel (chapter 10) who throws Satan into the bottomless pit (Rev. 20:1) when Jesus returns, the angel being the only one who has contested against him (Jude 1:9), and other powerful demons as well (Dan. 10:13). Either way, the strong angel submits to Jesus and points to His return, concerning the bitter and sweet mystery (10:11). The angel then tells John to prophesy concerning the effect on every person and nation, of every language and every kingdom (10:11, cf. 6:15, 19:15, 18).

Before the completion of the mystery through the sounding of the seventh trumpet, in the same way, we saw the sealing of God's servants for evangelism following the sixth seal; the same is repeated following the sixth trumpet judgement. Here, the two witnesses are revealed, preaching repentance for 42 months (11:2-3). At the three-and-a-half-year mark of the Tribulation, they are killed by the Antichrist—this is the first half of the

Tribulation period. After lying dead in the streets for three and a half days, they are resurrected and raptured into heaven (Rev. 11:12). The whole world will see this event, which coincides with a great earthquake, drawing many more to God, resulting in godly fear and repentance (11:13). This period concludes the second woe (Rev. 11:14), and now the seventh trumpet will be blown, revealing the mystery and containing the seven bowls.

Remember, Revelation chapter 8 introduced the seventh seal, which is the most severe of the judgements to date, indicated by silence in heaven for about half an hour (v. 2a). Within the seventh seal are the seven trumpets (v. 2b), and the same is true of the seventh trumpet regarding the seven bowls (15:7). Said another way, the seventh judgement contains the next seven to come, only intensified. Each set of experiences progress in time and increase in severity. The seventh trumpet is the third woe, and it also reveals the mystery of Christ's return to an unprepared and perishing world. The return of Christ, for the majority of humanity, will be a very bitter day.

In conclusion, with little time left, the strong angel, probably Michael, points to the return of Christ, which is the concealed mystery for those both rejecting Him and disobeying Him. The secret will be revealed through the blowing of the seventh trumpet, which contains the seven bowls. The seventh trumpet also includes the third woe, which is Christ's judgement on a rebellious world. With the worst of the tribulation yet to come, the experience will become increasingly bitter, especially for those now confessing Christ, however sweet upon His return. The opposite will be right for those still rejecting Jesus, living in the hope of their 'best life now, or at least to come.' What may seem to be sweet for a moment (Rev. 18) will end abruptly on the day of judgement.

CHAPTER ELEVEN

The Two Witnesses (Lampstands)

Chapter eleven of the book of Revelation is said to be one of the most challenging chapters to interpret, which is evident in the various understandings and applications. However, when sticking to the three main rules of biblical interpretation: 1). Literal, before allegoric interpretation; 2). Context, context, context, and, 3). Applied systematic theology, the meaning is exact. The best way to approach any portion of scripture is literally, first and foremost. When the literal understanding makes no sense, then (only then) look for some other reason; otherwise, you will end up with nonsense.

While the book of Revelation holds a great deal of symbolism where allegoric interpretation is required (i.e., Rev. 11:8), chapter eleven, as a whole, does not need to be treated that way. When considering the chapter literally, contextually, and systematically, it is not difficult to understand. The reason many fail to interpret scripture correctly is due to not following the mentioned three simple rules. When applied to Revelation chapter eleven, it will lead you to Zechariah chapter four. There, the prophet Zechariah introduces the two witnesses who appear around the same time the Temple is rebuilt.

Before we go on to identify the two witnesses, or olive trees (v. 3), being the two anointed ones (v. 14), it is necessary to first focus on the topic of the Temple (v. 9). In Zechariah's account, the angel made the point; the Temple will be rebuilt before the witnesses are revealed, proclaiming the gospel from within the Temple courts. Revelation chapter eleven also makes that clear, introducing the Temple in the first verse. Despite the numerous challenges that stand in the Temple's way being rebuilt, God will remove every 'mighty mountain' (Zech. 4:7) or challenge any obstacle, supernaturally, to establish it. Zechariah (4:7) reveals God is personally project managing this divine event. Although the prophecy was fulfilled, in part, with the rebuilding of the second Temple, it is yet to be fulfiled, in full, concerning the third Tribulation Temple. The fulfilment with the third Temple is why the angel in Zachariah's account had to address the Temple rebuild first before the two anointed ones could be revealed, for their end-times ministry will coincide with this event.

The Temple's significance is the place of worship and the place where God is known and made known. The same is true of the Body (Temple) of Christ (1 Cor. 3:16, 6:19) through whom the gospel is purposed to go out into the whole world. The lampstands (two witnesses) will fulfil that same mandate as representatives of God and Israel and as a light to the nations (cf. Isa. 42:6; 49:6) during the Tribulation. Therefore, the two witnesses are Jewish, anointed, and priestly prophets who will preach the gospel of repentance to the world in the future, fulfiling Matthew 24:14.

While we know the actual identity of one of the two through the prophet Malachi, being Elijah (Mal. 4:5-6), the other one is suspected to be Moses. Moses is most likely to join Elijah due to the similarity of the plagues on Egypt with the tribulation plagues, the Law being preached in the Tribulation, and accompanying Elijah at the Mount of Transfiguration (Matt. 17). Nothing more is said of the two witnesses other than what is found in the book of Revelation. From there, we learn they will appear during the first half of the Tribulation period (Rev. 11:3–6, esp. v. 4). During the Tribulation, the two witnesses stand by the Lord of the whole earth (Rev, 11:4, Zech. 4:14), preaching repentance.

The two witnesses are dressed in sackcloth, which represents repentance. Therefore, their gospel message will be calling the Jews first back to God, and then the world, which is why the world will hate them, and even be tormented by their message (Rev. 11:10). Adding to the torment, these two lampstands will operate in unstoppable power through signs and wonders (Rev. 11:5-6), due to being anointed by God (Zech. 4:14). They will preach for three-and-a-half years, which is the same timeframe Jesus preached, and then, after their ministry is complete, the Antichrist will kill them (Rev. 11:7-8). The world will rejoice over their deaths, and they will even exchange gifts (vv. 9, 10). But like Christ, the two witnesses will rise again three days later (Rev. 11:11), even from the same place Jesus was crucified (Rev. 11: 8). Then, 'great fear' will come over all that see them (Rev. 11:11, 13), which will be everyone on the planet due to live Internet streaming.

After a short time, the witnesses will be raptured (Rev. 11:12). The words, "Come up here" are a repeat of Revelation chapter four (v. 1), which is symbolic of the Bride of Christ being raptured just before the Tribulation commences (Rev. 3:10). The whole world will witness their ascent into heaven (Rev. 11:12), which will also be the case for the waiting, watching, praying Bride, who escapes the things to come (Lu. 21:34-36).

Again, the two witnesses will be present in the first part of the Tribulation (Rev. 11:3), departing just before Satan is cast to the earth (Rev. 12:12), which is another sub-woe between the second and third woes of the seven-year event (Rev. 8:13). From the time Satan is cast to the earth, the Jews will suffer the most significant persecution ever experienced by the devil (Rev. 12:15, Matt 24:9-12, 17-22).

When comparing the two passages (Zechariah 4, and Revelation 11), the connection is clear, and so is the interpretation of the prophecy. The two witnesses will appear after the third Temple has been built (Zech. 4:6-10, Rev. 11:2-3), which will be overrun (trampled) by the nations (Rev. 11:2). The Temple will also be where the Antichrist announces that he is God at the halfway point of the Tribulation (Dan. 9:27, 11:31, 12:11, Matt. 24:15, 2 Thess. 2:1-11).

Within this section we have seen something of what will take place in the not so distant future; but, 'what about the here and now?' While the lampstands or two witnesses are specific to the Tribulation period, there is also an application for the church today. The lampstands are first introduced in chapter one of the Revelation, symbolic of the church (1:12, 13, 20), and again in chapter two, when addressing the church of Ephesus (2:5). The church address (2:5) is one of rebuke, with a command to repent, or else the lampstand will be removed. Like the two witnesses dressed in sackcloth, the message connected with the lampstand is one of repentance and returning (2:4). Furthermore, within the seven letters to the churches (Rev. 2-3), there is a prophetic parallel with the two witnesses. The seven churches represent seven types and seven conditions. They represent seven types of churches in existence throughout the entire church age. The evidence is seen with the statement: "He who has an ear, let him hear what the Spirit is saying to the CHURCHES" (Rev. 2:7, 11, 17, 29, 3:6, 13, 22). Each church received the same announcement, both literal for them, then, and prophetic for us today.

Further evidence for these churches representing our current time is seen through references to the Tribulation (2:22, 3:3, 3:10). These verses are an end-times warning to the church living in the last days (US!). Five of seven churches received warnings: Repent, or else… The 'Or else' is always significant in salvation.

The five conditions of the end-time church are as follows:

- Abandoned first love (Ephesus)
- Holding to false prosperity teaching and lording it over others (Pergamum)
- Tolerating Jezebel (Thyatira)
- Being spiritually dead, and in need of waking up (Sardis)
- Being lukewarm (Laodicea)

The two churches doing well are charged to remain:

- Be faithful unto death, and I will give you the crown of life (Smyrna)
- Hold fast to what you have so no one can seize your crown (Philadelphia).

As seen clearly with the two churches, salvation is conditional on being faithful, holding fast, and keeping the commands. Also seen with the five churches, salvation depends on required repentance, then holding fast, remaining, and enduring until the end (Matt. 10:22).

While only two of the seven churches receive no rebuke from the Lord, they are slandered by the religious. On both occasions, the 'Jews', who are said to be from the synagogue of Satan (2:9, 3:9) are those attacking the true Church. These Jews represent the religious, thinking they are of God but are, in reality, from Satan. These Jews are no different from the Pharisees of Jesus' days. The link between the two witnesses, seen through the two churches, represents God's approved people, preaching repentance and holiness to others. Both are situated outside the Temple, or organised religious institutions, in the same way Jesus was. The above-mentioned suggests that not all who call themselves believers are approved or empowered by God, which is evident with the five churches in need of repentance.

Furthermore, only two of the seven churches are rightly positioned, therefore appointed and anointed for ministry. The others are in danger of losing their salvation. These findings suggest that only thirty percent of confessing Christians are genuinely saved. These same findings reflect the world's current population of seven billion, with an estimated two billion confessing to being Christian. Again, thirty percent are 'supposedly' saved. Realistically, thirty percent of the thirty percent might be.

The point here is: only a minority, or remnant, are actually saved, against the majority who are not. The conclusion is that this generation will see the fulfilment of Jesus' words, "The majority (from the church) will say to Me on that Day, Lord, Lord…" to which Jesus will respond: "I never knew you, depart from Me, you workers of lawlessness" (Matt. 7:21-23).

To clarify the above - the two candlesticks represent the remnant, both within the church and of Israel. Further support is seen where only two millions Jews (2.4m) exiting Egypt entered the Promised Land, being Joshua, and Caleb (Joshua 2, 6). The application today is that we are all wandering through the desert (earth), towards the Promised Land (heaven), albeit, only a remnant will make it in, thus and thereby are saved (Rom. 9:27). These findings support that you cannot live faithlessly by continuing in sin and expect to be saved and or used by God, for God will only seal, secure, and operate through vessels walking in repentance. Repentance is critical to salvation! Repentance is a way of life, not a once-off and one-time confession, as many suppose.

In Sum: The true church will be likened to the two lampstands, dressed in sackcloth, walking in, and calling for repentance. The true church will also operate in power, not needing worldly means to attract and retain (Rev. 3:17). The true church will be criticised from within by the false, liberal, and legalistic confessing believers for their stance on repentance and holiness.

Following the witness of the two-lampstand churches (Smyrna and Philadelphia), after being taken out of the way (Rev. 4:1, 3:10), the remaining five churches (unless repentance comes first) will be left behind and cast into the Great Tribulation (Rev. 2:22, 3:3). From there, the remaining five churches, along with the Jews, and the rest of the world, will come into direct contact with the message of repentance, preached through the two witnesses (Rev. 11:1-13). The two witnesses will preach repentance for the first half of the tribulation before being raptured (Rev. 11:12). Coinciding with the two witnesses preaching repentance is the rebuilt Temple, from which the antichrist will announce he is God at the halfway point of the seven-year event.

The message of repentance to be announced during the Tribulation by the two witnesses is being proclaimed here and now through the two faithful lampstand churches, just as it was through Zechariah (1:3). The question remains: Will you hear and respond to the message now, then, or never?

"He who has an ear let him hear what the Spirit is saying to the CHURCHES."

The Seventh Trumpet, and the Third Woe
What will you do when the end comes?
(11:15-19)

Following the second woe of the tribulation is the mystery of chapter 10 (v. 7), which is the revelation of Jesus Christ. Jesus is the revelation (1:1), blessing (1:3), and the prophecy of the book (19:10b). In short, the book of Revelation is the testimony of Jesus (1:2), who is the Almighty God (1:4, 8, 4:8, 11:17, 16:15), who will reign (1:5, 5:10, 11:15, 17) in His coming kingdom (11:15, 17). The book is all about Jesus, who was, is, and is to come (1:4, 8, 4:8, 11:17). The seventh trumpet completes the trilogy; He HAS come!

When Jesus arrives back on the scene, the question previously asked of the false preachers and prophets by Jeremiah now needs to be answered: 'What will you do when the end comes?' (Jer. 5:31). Indeed, the end has come, which is the beginning of believers 'best life now' and the unbelievers 'worst life now.' The unbelievers include preachers who scoffed at the prophecy (Jer. 4:10, 5:12, 6:14, 14:13, 23:17, cf. 2 Pet. 3:3, Jude 18), especially those who indulge in lust, greed, defiling passions, and who despised (godly) authority (2 Pet. 2:10). The authority being despised by the false prophets is that of Jesus (2 Pet. 2:1). They twist the scriptures (2 Pet. 3:16) to suit themselves, and namely, to fill their pockets (Jude 11-12).

The question raised is - 'What will you do when the end comes?' was directed at false prosperity preachers (14:13) who said that God will not judge us (Jer. 4:10, 5:12, 6:14, 14:13, 23:17). But, He did, and He is about to do it again, for the same reason - to understand why Jeremiah chapters three to eight are worth reading alongside Revelation 11 (vv. 15-19).

An interesting observation is also found with the mention of the Ark of the Covenant (Jer. 3:16, Rev. 11:19). For Judah, the reference refers to a coming day when they would no longer trust in religious rituals and relics but in Jesus. The context of the passage points to Jesus' return, as with Revelation 11 (vv. 15-19).

The reference to the ark in Revelation, chapter 11 (v. 19), refers to the covenant with Jesus. Besides the book of Revelation, there is only one other place in the NT mentioning the Ark of the Covenant, which is in Hebrews (9:4). Similarly, the reference to the Temple (11:19) refers to Jesus (21:22), not a physical building. Physical buildings were done away with through the new covenant (1 Cor. 3:16, 6:19). That said, the only approved and authorised 'building fund' today would be that of the great commission (Matt. 28:18-20), seeking first God's kingdom (Matt. 6:33).

The writer of Hebrews picks up on something of the same: "We (the church) are His (Jesus') house if indeed we hold fast our confidence and our boasting in our hope" (Heb. 3:6). As mentioned earlier, the author also references the Ark of the Covenant, describing the first covenant, then points to the second, being Jesus (9-10). Again, the covenant is conditional and met with another warning for those who enter but do not remain (10:26-39). It will be worse for those who do and then walk away (v. 29); worse again in fact than it was for Israel and Judah. Peter picks up on something similar (2 Pet. 2:21).

Contrary to popular belief, God will treat us more severely than He did Israel and Judea for doing the same thing. The sins of Judah were rejecting and replacing God with 'stuff.' The church of Laodicea, prophetically representing us, was guilty of this sin and was called to repent before it was too late.

Another section of scripture worth considering regarding the Ark of the Covenant is Joshua's book, chapters three to eight. There, numerous references are made of the Ark of the Covenant (3:3, 6, 8, 11, 14, 17, 4:7, 9, 18, 6:6, 8, 8:33), but perhaps more interesting is the paralleled pattern provided through these chapters.

The pattern is as follows:

- Israel crosses over (chapter 3)
- Twelve stones, a memorial of deliverance (chapter 4)
- New generation (chapter 5)
- Conquering (chapter 6)
- Conquered, due to sin (chapter 7)
- Reconquering (chapter 8a)
- Renewed covenant (chapter 8b)

Consider the pattern and the parallel of the believer:

- Crossing over (spiritually before literally) into the Promised Land (Matt. 8:11)
- Given a white stone (delivered), crossing over from death to life (1 Cor. 15:54-57, Rev. 2:17, innocent)
- New generation (creature), in Christ (2 Cor. 5:17)
- Conquering and overcoming this world (1 Jn. 5:3-4)
- Sometimes conquered by the world due to sin (1 Jn. 19, 2 Jn. 2:1)
- Reconquering through repentance, and overcoming sin (Rev. 2:7, 11, 17, 26, 3:5, 12, 21)
- Entering into the fullness of the new covenant when Jesus returns (22:17)

In sum, the Ark of the Covenant, seen from the heavenly Temple (Rev. 11:19), is the covenant with God, through Jesus Christ. The Christian journey stems from this world to the next, as seen in the pattern reflected in chapters three to eight of Joshua's book.

Speaking again on the seventh trumpet - this event is the same as the seventh bowl (16:12-17), which is Jesus returning to judge the nations. Remember, within the book of Revelation, the story told is retold three times. The seventh seal (8:1-5), seventh trumpet (11:15-19), and seventh bowl (16:17-21) are one in the same event. The sixth seal (6:12-17), alongside chapter one (vv. 9-17) and chapter nineteen (vv. 11-21), should also be treated in the same manner. Many more supporting sections of scripture point to this same prophetic event, such as Isaiah 2 (vv.6-22) and 66 (vv. 15-24), Jeremiah 10 (vv. 23-25), Daniel 12, Zechariah 14, Joel 2, and 3, Matthew 24:29-30, and 2 Thessalonians (1:5-12), among many others.

Although the above-mentioned sections of scripture, pointing to the return of Jesus, are sobering, on each occasion that the event was referenced, indicating the day is drawing near, or here, by the twenty-four elders in heaven, they rejoiced (4:4-5, 5:9-14, 11:16-19, 19:1-5). Now, the mystery has been revealed (Rev. 10:7), He who was, and is, has come (Rev. 1:4, 8, 4:8 = 19:6). The righteous will stand triumphant on that day, while the wicked will fall and faint with terror (Joel, 2:11, Nam. 1:6, Mal. 3:2, Rev. 6:17). Indeed, through the prophet Jeremiah, the question raised by God, directed at the false prophets, has been answered: "What will you do when the end comes?" What will you do…? You will faint in terror (Luke 21:26); that is what you will do!

CHAPTER TWELVE

The Seven Personages Part One

Following the seventh trumpet, Revelation, chapters twelve and thirteen should be considered together regarding the seven personages of the Tribulation. The seven personages are as follows:

- The women clothed with the sun (Israel)
- The red dragon (Satan)
- The male child (Jesus)
- The archangel (Michael)
- The offspring of the woman (believers)
- The first beast (Antichrist)
- The second beast (false prophet)

Similar to chapters twelve and thirteen are chapters seventeen and eighteen:

- The great prostitute (one world religion)
- The beast (false prophet)

- The saints (believers)
- The merchants (rejecting Jesus)
- Angels
- The mighty angel (Michael)
- Jesus

Chapters twelve and seventeen also reference the ten kingdoms, which will make up the Antichrist's alliance in the New World Order (Rev. 12:3, 13:1, 17:3, 7, 12, 16). Daniel also mentions the ten nations, which are the end times' coalition (Dan. 7:7, 20, 24).

Interestingly, within the book of Revelation, there are two women referenced; one representing Israel (the woman clothed with the sun), and the other, Jezebel (2:20), which is also the harlot church (chapter 17). As a result of tolerating Jezebel, church members are threatened by Jesus; that they would be thrown into the great Tribulation unless they repent (2:22). While in the Tribulation, they can either continue to tolerate Jezebel's teachings and practice false worship (chapter 17), or they can repent and follow Jesus (12:11). Choosing to follow Jesus will cost the majority of them their natural lives, having failed to take up their cross this side of the Tribulation. Some, however, will survive, albeit a few. The remnant survivors will then be expected to endure until the end (Matt. 24:13, Rev. 12:17, 14:12). The 'blessed' ones will die early in the tribulation (14:13). They will be blessed through the escape of death in the tribulation due to the longer it goes, the worse the judgements become.

During the Tribulation, Satan will pour out all that he has on Israel (Rev. 12:15). It is not the first time Satan has tried to destroy Israel, but it will be the last. Satan attempted to keep Israel bound by killing Moses (Ex. 1-2), then, failing that, he got Israel into sin (Num. 22-24), which has been continued until this day. Satan repeated a similar event to Moses with Jesus

(Matt. 2:16-18). Satan also attempted to get Jesus into sin (Matt. 4:1-11) and then tried to kill Him again through the crucifixion, which backfired badly. Satan wanted to kill Moses and Jesus, knowing 'salvation is from the Jews' (Jn. 4:22). If he could destroy the cause of salvation, he would have prevented the effect, claiming victory over God.

Revelation twelve reveals that Satan was ready to kill Jesus at birth (12:3), but God delivered Him by leading His parents to Egypt. God will likewise deliver a remnant of Israel during the Tribulation; a third (Zech. 13:8), supernaturally (Rev. 12:6-14), by hiding them away (Zep. 2:3). At that time, many believe that Israel will flee to Petra (Isa. 2:19, 21). Regardless of the location, Satan will pursue them, pouring out water, after them, like a river (Rev. 12:15). At the end of the tribulation, God will come to Israel's aid, like a raging flood (Isa. 59:19, cf. 17:13).

In the case of Satan pouring out a river or flood after the woman (Rev. 12:15), it is symbolic of warfare (12:17). Through the Antichrist, who commands the army of the New World Order (Rev. 12:3, 13:1, 17:3, 7, 12, 16), Satan will seek to destroy Israel; however, unsuccessfully. As Israel's offspring, other nations will come to her aid (12:16), which will draw fire away from Israel unto themselves. The Antichrist will then be fighting against an army protecting Israel and the two-hundred million mounted troops (Rev. 9:13-19). Those protecting Israel, being her offspring (Abrahamic covenant), are likely to be a nation of believers who have repented during the Tribulation. During this period, those coming to Christ must then keep the commands and hold fast to the testimony of Jesus until the end (12:17).

Remember, the woman clothed with the sun is Israel, who, according to verse one, is a 'great sign' of the Tribulation, alongside another sign, which is the dragon (12:3). The whole book of Revelation is made up of symbols, sigifying the things to come. To 'signify' is to have an idea or meaning of something expressed by a sign. Revelation chapter one (v. 1) states the signs of the book reveal Jesus and the nearness of His return: "The Revelation of Jesus Christ, which God gave unto him, to show unto his servants things which must shortly come to pass; and he sent and signified it by his angel unto his servant John" (KJV). Each sign, revealing and unveiling the things to come, contains a prophetic warning and an opportunity to repent before it is too late. Even during the Tribulation, salvation is on offer and will be right up until the end.

Once more, the woman clothed with the sun, and with the moon, having a crown of twelve stars on her head, is Israel and is a great sign of the Tribulation, which is the fulfilment of Joseph's dream (Gen. 37:9-11), and the Abrahamic covenant. During the Tribulation, Israel and her offspring will be greatly persecuted (12:13-17); Israel's oppression will be Satan's main priority during the last three and a half years of the ordeal (12:6, 14). Again, the reason Satan will seek to destroy Israel, above all else, is that without her, Jesus could not come and will not return. Jesus made it clear; He will not return before the Jews say: "Blessed is He who comes in the name of the Lord" (Matt. 23:39, cf. Zech. 12:10, 13:6). If Satan can wipe out Israel beforehand, he will prevent Jesus from returning; therefore, he will escape imminent judgement (Rev. 20:1-3, 10).

Although the scriptures reveal that Satan has already been defeated by Jesus (Col 2:15), he still operates in the heavenly realm today (Eph. 6:12, Rev. 12:10), and will do so until he is cast to the earth (Rev. 12:7-10, 12-13). Despite false preterist theology suggesting Satan is bound, he is very active (Acts 5:3, 1 Cor. 5:5, 7:5, 2 Cor. 2:11, 11:14, 12:7, 1 Tim. 1:20, 1 Pet. 5:8). And, soon, he will be very present when cast to the earth, which will occur at the midway point of the Tribulation, 42-months into the 84-months of trouble. At the halfway point (42-months), all hell breaks loose (Rev. 12:13), and Israel will flee for their lives. Until then, Israel will be saying 'peace and security' (1 Thess. 5:3, cf. Jer. 6:14) due to the signed peace treaty (Isa. 28:15, 18, Dan. 9:27).

The false peace treaty will be broken three and a half years into the Tribulation, where the Antichrist announces from the Third Temple, he is God (Dan. 11:31, 12:11, Rev. 13:5, 19:20, Matt. 24:15). When the Antichrist declares he is God, he will be empowered and possessed by Satan (2 Thess. 2:9), just after Satan is cast down to the earth. When Satan is cast down, the martyred tribulation saints (Rev. 6:9-11, 7:13-14) will rejoice (Rev. 12:10). While heaven rejoices, the world will mourn! (Rev. 12:13). For the slain believer, who has conquered this world and sin through repentance, by not loving their lives until death (Rev. 12:11), their best life has just begun (Rev. 15:2-4). As for those seeking 'their best life now,' their worst is yet to come (Rev. 11:13, 17).

In conclusion, Revelation chapter twelve, leading into thirteen, provides an overview of Christ's first appearing (v. 5a), leading to His next (v. 5b). In doing so, the chapter focuses on Israel's ongoing persecution, from Satan, due to salvation (Jesus) coming from the Jews. Chapter twelve also reveals that Satan will be defeated and frustrated during the Tribulation period, albeit he will claim many lives and many more souls. Those who perish naturally, for the sake of Christ, shall live eternally. As for those seeking to save their natural lives, they shall perish forever. Alongside Israel, Satan, Jesus, and Michael the archangel are referenced in chapter twelve, referencing Israel's offspring, making up five of the seven personages. The remaining two personages are the Antichrist, and the false prophet, who are introduced in chapter thirteen.

CHAPTER THIRTEEN

The Seven Personages – Part Two
The Antichrist

Throughout chapter twelve of the book of Revelation, we identified five of the seven personages. Chapter thirteen presents the remaining two. The first of which is the first beast, who is the Antichrist. Verses 1-10 provide a detailed account of the Antichrist; however, this is not the first time he is referenced through John's vision.

Having established the revelation is not primarily about the Antichrist, it is still important to note he is a significant player in the end times with over one hundred scripture references provided. In the book of Revelation, he is introduced in chapter six as the rider of the white horse (6:2). The Antichrist is in the company of the red (v. 4), black (v. 6), and pale horses (v. 8). Collectively, they kill one-fourth of the population (v. 8). Alongside, millions more are martyred by the following fifth seal for their belated testimony of Jesus Christ (v. 9). Their testimony was belated on the grounds it came on the wrong side of Jesus returning for His bride, subsequently leaving them behind to endure the things to come.

Following the Antichrist's introduction through the seal judgements, he is referenced again amidst the trumpet judgements in chapter eleven. In chapter eleven, the Antichrist kills the two witnesses (11:7). Here, the Antichrist is described as the beast that rises from the bottomless pit. The book of Revelation provides six references to the bottomless pit (9:1, 2, 11, 11:7, 17:8, 20:1). Each describes who has the keys to release what is bound in the pit, what comes out of the pit, and what goes back into the pit. Needless to say, nothing good comes out of the pit, and nothing good goes back there.

The next reference to the Antichrist brings us back to our opening passage, Revelation thirteen. From there, we learn that he gathers ten nations (ten horns) and seven heads (leaders), which will represent the new world order. We also understand the Antichrist is Antichrist in every way, indicated by his blasphemous nature. He is empowered by Satan and even resurrected, or resuscitated, by Satan after receiving a mortal wound to the head. Whichever way it is he will be supernaturally and spectacularly revived, causing the whole earth to marvel, follow and worship him. Actually, they worship Satan in and through him.

The issue of worship, is found in chapters thirteen and fourteen, where humanity will either worship God or Satan.

Worship is the central theme of the entire Bible, which was the cause of Satan being cast out of heaven (Isa. 14:12), and the cause of Adam and Eve's being cast out of the garden (Gen. 3), and is the cause of every other sin following. Essentially, how the story starts, it ends. Worship is perhaps the most important theme within the Bible, resulting in either eternal life or eternal death. Again, it was due to false worship that Adam and Eve fell, as did Israel, as it is with the church.

Chapters two-three of the book of Revelation address the churches, representing every church throughout the entire church-age. Five of seven were rebuked due to false worship and warned to repent, or else! The same warning is extended to those left behind, enduring the Tribulation. Even, through angels flying overhead, the message is proclaimed, "Fear God and worship Him" (14:7). Despite the warnings, like today, most will fail by refusing to obey. Instead, they will have itching ears desiring to be tickled by what they want to hear. And, the Antichrist will accommodate them, as will God, for that matter (2 Thess. 2:9-10). As for the few with listening ears (13:9), they are called to endure in their sufferings until the end (13:10b, 14:12), that they may be saved (Matt. 24:12-13). Their persecution will be by the hand of the Antichrist (v. 7). So severe will that persecution be, the blessed ones will die early (14:13). And, death will come to many, if not most, through the sword (13:10) and guillotine (20:4).

Additional information about the Antichrist from chapter thirteen reveals he will rise out of the sea, which is the Mediterranean Sea (Dan. 7:2). From Daniel, most accept the Antichrist is a Gentile rising out of the revived Roman Empire (Mediterranean region). However, the Jews are looking for a descendant of David (Jer. 33:14-16, Eze 37:24-25), therefore, a Jew. The Antichrist then could be of Jewish origin, rising from, and out of a Gentile nation. Nevertheless, whoever he is, he will be recognised through the fulfilment of prophecy, which will include the following: He will:

- Make Jerusalem the capital of Israel
- Establish peace in the Middle East
- Rebuild the Temple
- Gather the Jews back to Israel
- Rule over the Jews

When this man, the Antichrist, does appear, the Jews will accept him as their messiah. In fact, according to Sanhedrin, he is well overdue. They are looking and longing for him now.

Also, from chapter thirteen, we learn that following the established new world order, the Antichrist will force the whole world to receive his mark (666). Without the mark, no one can buy, sell, trade, or even operate and function in society. The high-tech future will be both cashless and keyless. Motor vehicles and machinery, including computers, will not be operatable without access to blockchain technology, which will only be available through an implanted chip in your hand or forehead. Those who receive the mark are unredeemable (14:9-11). Those who don't are executed (13:15, 20:4).

Alongside Revelation thirteen, Daniel chapter seven needs to be taken into consideration. From Daniel (name meaning: God is my judge), we gain further insight revealing that the Antichrist will initially appear as a little horn, meaning someone insignificant (v. 8), yet he will rise to power quickly. His term, however, will be short, lasting just seven years, and only three and a half years at its peak (Dan. 7:25c, 13:5). At the end of his appointed term, Jesus will defeat and destroy him (Dan. 7:11, Rev. 19:20, 20:10). His appointed time is granted by God, indicating the authority and sovereignty of God over him.

While there is much more that could be said about the Antichrist, the following list summarises his characteristics:

1. He comes from among ten kings in the restored Roman Empire; his authority will have similarities to the ancient Babylonians, Persians, and Greeks [Dan. 7:24; Rev 13:2 / Dan. 7:7]
2. He will subdue three kings [Dan. 7:8, 24]
3. He is different from the other kings [Dan. 7:24]
4. He will rise up from obscurity… a 'little horn' [Dan. 7:8]
5. He will speak boastfully [Dan. 7:8; Rev 13:5]

6. He will blaspheme God, [Dan. 7:25; 11:36; Rev 13:5] slandering His Name, dwelling place, and departed Christians and Old Testament saints [Rev 13:6]
7. He will oppress the saints and be successful for 3 ½ years [Dan. 7:25; Rev 13:7]
8. He will try to change the calendar, perhaps to define a new era, related to himself [Dan. 7:25]
9. He will try to change the laws, perhaps to gain an advantage for his new kingdom and era [Dan 7:25]
10. No other earthly ruler will succeed him but Christ [Dan. 7:26-27]
11. He will confirm a covenant with 'many,' i.e., the Jewish people [Dan. 9:27] this covenant will likely involve the establishment of a Jewish Temple in Jerusalem [see Dan 9:27; Matt 24:15]
12. He will put an end to Jewish sacrifice and offerings after 3 ½ years and set up an abomination to God in the Temple [Dan. 9:27, Matt. 24:15]
13. He will not answer to a higher earthly authority; "He will do as he pleases" [Dan. 11:36]
14. He will show no regard for the religion of his ancestors [Dan. 11:37]
15. He will not believe in any god at all [except for himself] [Dan. 11:37]
16. He will have 'no regard for the desire of women': The fact that he has no regard for the one desired by women suggests he repudiates the messianic hope of Israel. [Dan 11:37]
17. He will claim to be greater than any god [Dan. 11:37; 2 Thess. 2:4]
18. He will claim to be God [2 Thess. 2:4]
19. He will only honour a 'god' of the military. His whole focus and attention will be on his army. He will conquer lands and distribute them [Dan. 11:39-44]

20. His arrival on the world scene will be accompanied by miracles, signs, and wonders [2 Thess. 2:9]
21. Either he or his companion [The False Prophet], will claim to be Christ [Matt. 24:21-28]
22. He will claim that Jesus did not come in the flesh, or that Jesus did not rise bodily from the grave [2 John 7]. He will deny that Jesus is the Messiah [I Jn. 2:22]
23. He will be worshipped by many people [Rev. 13:8]
24. He will hate a nation that initially will have some control over his kingdom, but he will destroy this nation [Rev 17:16-18]
25. He will appear to survive a fatal injury [Rev. 13:3; 17:8]
26. His name will be related to the number six hundred and sixty-six—but not necessarily in a prominent fashion [Rev 13:17-18].
27. He will be empowered by the devil himself [Rev. 13:2]

From the list above, clearly, the Antichrist is yet to come, despite preterists claiming Antiochus IV Epiphanes (Greek: "God Manifest") fulfilled the prophecy (Dan. 11:28-32), or that the book of Revelation was fulfiled in 70 A.D; both notions are ridiculous! For starters, the book of Revelation was not written until 95 A.D, the opening statement being, 'The things that must soon take place' disqualifies any previous event. Apart from that obvious insight, no one has ever fulfiled the yet to be fulfiled prophecies revealing the coming Antichrist, such as:

- Rule the entire world (Dan. 7:23, Rev. 7-8)
- Followed and worshipped by the whole world (Rev. 13:8)
- Haled by the whole world: "Who is like the beast!" (Rev. 13:4)
- Subdue 3/10 kings at once (Dan. 7:24)
- Persecute Israel for precisely 42 months (Dan. 7:25)

- Control the world economy (Rev. 13:16-17)
- Demand the whole world take his mark (Rev. 13:16-18)
- Thrown alive into the lake of fire (Rev. 19:20, 20:10)

Further evidence for a futuristic event is seen in Revelation, chapter seventeen (vv. 8-14). To claim verses 9-11 have been fulfiled demonstrates a lack of historical understanding. At the time of writing, John states there are to be seven kings (world powers), five have fallen (Egypt, Assyria, Babylon, Persia, and Greece), and one is (Rome). A seventh is yet to come (none have), and out of the seventh (the new world order) will rise another, the eighth who is the Antichrist.

In sum, chapter thirteen provides in-depth detail of the first beast, who is the Antichrist. The Antichrist is yet to be revealed and will be revealed through the fulfilment of prophecy. The Jews are expecting him to appear any day now; however, most of them will not recognise that their appointed messiah, is Satan incarnated. For the few who do, unmatched persecution awaits, not just for the Jews, but for all and any refusing to worship him by receiving his mark (666). At the midway point of the Tribulation, the pressure to renounce God for Satan will be at its peak, which is why there is a call for the endurance of the saints (13:10c, 14:12). HANG ON, holdfast and remain faithful is the message… "Anyone who has an ear let him hear" (13:9).

The closing statement: It is important to remember, John's vision is not the revelation of the Antichrist, but the revelation and the testimony of Jesus Christ (Rev. 1:1, 19:10). Jesus Christ is the blessing of the book (1:3). And, although the Antichrist is significant, he will be effortlessly defeated by Jesus on His return. But, even during the Tribulation, Jesus will still give the Antichrist a taste of the hell to come (16:10).

The Seven Personages – Part Three
The Second Beast

As mentioned earlier, chapter thirteen introduces the sixth and seventh personage of the book of Revelation. The sixth personage is the first beast, who is the Antichrist. The seventh personage is the second beast, who is the false prophet. Although the false prophet is only mentioned a few times in the book of Revelation (19:20, 20:10), and only in the book of Revelation, the Bible is loaded with references warning about false prophets and false teachers. When Jesus gave the list of signs of the times, leading toward His return, an increase of false prophets, teachers, and teachings was number one on the list, repeated several times (Matt. 24, Mk. 13, Lu. 21). Paul, Peter, and Jude likewise focus on this topic with many warnings that the last days will see an increase of false teaching (i.e., 1 Tim. 4:1, 6:3—5, 2 Tim 4:3-4, 2 Pet. 2, Jude). The rise of false teachers is a repeat of what took place with Israel and Judah and will be responded to by God in the same way.

False teachers/prophets major on three things:

1. Hyper grace
2. False peace
3. Prosperity

False prophets deceive their audience into believing, "You can do whatever you like, and it will be alright; that, there is no judgement; and, God wants you to be happy, healthy, and wealthy." Of course, the scripture makes no such provision for this teaching; on the contrary, it condemns it. Spurgeon put it this way: "It was never said, 'Whom the Lord loveth, He enricheth," but it is said, 'Whom the Lord loveth, He chasteneth." Evidence in support for Spurgeon's statement is found in the book of Hebrews (12:6), and the book of Revelation (3:19), as well as Proverbs 3:12 and Psalms 94:21, 118:18. God chastening His people to bring about repentance is a common theme throughout scripture.

The prophet Jeremiah also confirms Spurgeon, prophesying, "I (God) will discipline you in just measure and by no means leave you unpunished" (30:11c, 46:28). The reason, Judah was a rebellious people (30:8, 9), unwilling to hear the instructions of the Lord. Instead, they preferred to listen to 'smooth things' (talk), despising God's word (vv. 10-12). In other words, they favoured the teachings of the false prophets over instruction from God. The rebellious favoured lying prophets (Jer. 5:31) who deal falsely (Jer. 8:10), filling them with vain hope (Jer. 23:16), by proclaiming peace, peace (Jer. 4:10, 6:14, 14:13, 23:17), when there was no peace. In sum, the false prophets promised cheap grace, false peace, and prosperity, at the expense of their followers, to fill their own pockets (Jer. 5:27, 6:13, 22, 14:18). And, nothing has changed up until this day.

False teachers within the church do the same thing, deceiving and conditioning lukewarm liberal and lazy churchgoers in preparation of the ultimate false teacher to come, the false prophet. Moreover I would argue he is already among us, fulfiling prophecy (2 Thess. 2:3), deceiving billions in preparation for the Antichrist. Like the Antichrist, the false prophet will come out of the church (1 Jn. 4:1), abandoning truth (not religion) to head up a global ecumenical system. This is a one-world religion where all paths (supposably) lead to God. The false prophet will appear to be Christlike, even operating in signs and wonders (Rev. 13:13). However, he will be empowered by and speak for Satan (Rev. 13:11, 12), not God. His purpose will be to prepare the way and promote the Antichrist and to set up the

Antichrist's image, forcing the global population to worship him, and his image (Rev. 13:14-15, 14:9, 11, 15:2, 16:2, 19:20, 20:4).

Interestingly, the image receives more attention than the false prophet, and like the false prophet, the image is only mentioned in the book of Revelation. Much speculation has circulated over the image, regarding what it is and how it is given breath and to speak (Rev. 13:15). With the advancements of modern science, a clone would perfectly fulfil this prophecy. Effectively, the image could be a clone of the Antichrist, in his precise image. It is also likely the image would have A.I incorporated, giving it the ability to control who can buy and sell (Rev. 13:17) in an age where trade will be almost impossible without cryptocurrency. A.I will connect every human being on the planet bearing the mark (666) to the image. The mark (666) is what connects humanity to the beast through its image.

The image's ability to financially control people will place great pressure on them to receive the mark of the beast (666), not to mention its ability to kill those who resist (Rev. 13:15). Like the Antichrist, but unlike the false prophet, the image is worshipped (Rev. 13:14-15, 14:9, 11, 15:2, 16:2, 19:20, 20:4). A powerful demon undoubtedly inhabits the image in the same way the false prophet is possessed (Rev. 16:13). The Antichrist is also possessed, only by Satan (Rev. 13:4). The Antichrist is probably possessed by Satan when resurrected after receiving a mortal wound (Rev. 13:12, 14). Needless to say, when the false prophet and the Antichrist appear, they will be incredibly convincing, deceiving most into following and worshipping Satan through them. Today, there are many false preachers standing behind pulpits preparing the way (2 Cor. 11:13-15, cf. v. 4).

Chapter seventeen of the book of Revelation speaks of the harlot that rides the beast. The harlot is the religious system in the Tribulation, made of the billions worshipping Satan, deceived and led by the false prophet. Instead of being the body of Christ (1 Cor. 12:27), the harlot will represent the Antichrist, with every member baptised into Satan, eternally sealed by the mark (666). The harlot church is carefully described in chapter seventeen, "Arrayed in purple and scarlet and adorned with gold and jewels and pearls, holding in her hand a golden cup full of abominations and the impurities of her sexual immorality" (v. 4). Only one existing religious system qualifies to fit this description.

Furthermore, the same system is guilty of shedding the innocent blood of the saints (v. 6). This is the same system located on the seven mountains (v. 9) located in Rome. This religious system has and will continue to deceive billions from every nation and of every language (v. 15), headed up by the false prophet, who rises out of the earth (Rev. 13:11). Rising out of the earth refers to being connected to everyone, everywhere. During the Tribulation, the harlot will have dominion over the kings of the earth (Rev. 17:18), which is essentially what another group known by the doctrine of dominionism, teaches today, stating they will have dominion over the seven mountains.

Dominionism teaches that the seven mountains are:

1. Education
2. Religion
3. Family
4. Business
5. Government/Military
6. Arts/Entertainment
7. Media

Of course, dominionism is false teaching designed to distract and deceive deluded people into having an earthly focus by building an earthy kingdom instead of a heavenly one. False teachers always focus on an earthly kingdom with statements like, "Bringing heaven down to earth." Instead of praying, "Your kingdom come, Your will be done" they essentially claim, "My kingdom come, My will be done." This is idolatry and a form of self-worship.

Worship is what chapter thirteen is all about. Chapter fourteen contests the unholy trinity (Satan, the Antichrist, and the false prophet) by saying, "Fear God and worship Him" (alone). In sum, how the story begins (Gen. 3) it ends, where the universe and everything in it revolve around worship, either worshipping God or Satan. Satan's ability to deceive humanity has always been impressive. However, during the Tribulation, it will be even more so; so much so, few will escape (Matt. 24:24). Again, for this reason, when Jesus was asked about the signs of the end times, He listed deception as number one (Matt. 24, Mk. 13, Lu. 21).

In conclusion, false teaching is always wrapped in empty earthly promises of cheap grace, false peace, and prosperity; as it was for Eve (Gen. 3:5) and Jesus (Matt. 4:1-12), the same applies to us (1 Thess. 5:3). False teaching is on the increase, and it is so bad now that many churches are no longer safe, which is why we need to be extra vigilant, examining doctrine, testing spirits, and judging fruit. In these last days, it is more important than ever to make sure we are not deceived by false teachers, and nor tolerating them.

The spirit of deception is alive and well, operating freely within the organised, institutional church today, which will evolve into the harlot that rides the beast. Most churchgoers are asleep and utterly ignorant of prophecy being fulfilled right under their noses. The same was true for the church of Sardis that had a reputation of being alive but was dead. They were asleep and were warned by Jesus to, "Wake up and repent." Otherwise, He would come like a thief (rapture), leaving them behind to endure the Tribulation (Rev. 3:1-6).

CHAPTER FOURTEEN

Part One
Bringing Heaven Down to Earth

As mentioned in the previous section, chapter fourteen of the book of Revelation is in direct contrast to chapter thirteen. Chapters thirteen and fourteen centres on worship and chapter thirteen addresses the Antichrist's false worship and his image, which is directed by the false prophet. Chapter fourteen focuses on true worship and the true worshippers of God, the 144,000. The reintroduction of the 144,000 is followed by an angelic invitation for any with an ear to hear to respond. The required response is to Fear God and Worship Him (alone, v. 7). Following the one proclaiming the eternal gospel, two more angels warn that time is short, that the hour of judgement has come (vv. 8-12). Then, following the three angels' warning, three more angels call for the end-time judgement where sinners would be reaped from the earth with a sharp sickle (vv. 14-20). The latter will be addressed in the next section (14b).

In the previous section, in chapter thirteen, it was stated false prophets are known to have a worldly focus and obsession over a heavenly one. Essentially, they look back at Eden, seeking to recreate, or re-establish what was lost in the here and now, instead of looking to Jesus' return. Dominionism, promoted through the New Apostolic Reformation (NAR), is perhaps best known for the false teaching of recreating or reconstructing paradise lost in preparation for Jesus' return. An example of this is with one of the most recognised NAR movement leaders, famous for claiming to 'Bring heaven down to earth.' In other words, God's glory as it is in heaven, to be established here and now on the earth, by us. While what the NAR movement is claiming is false, there is, however, evidence in chapter fourteen for a more accurate application, albeit during the Tribulation. What chapter fourteen presents with heaven being brought down to earth during the tribulation is a far cry from what dominionism teaches.

Again, chapter fourteen (vv. 1-5) reintroduces the 144,000 who are Jewish evangelist (7:4-8), which presents another problem for dominionism, which subscribes to replacement theology. The 144,000 were first mentioned in chapter seven, where God seals them on their foreheads in preparation for their Tribulation ministry. Through their powerful evangelistic testimony of Jesus Christ, they lead a multitude to faith from every nation, from all tribes and people, and languages (7:9).

Effectively, seen through chapters seven and fourteen is the unfulfiled prophecy of the greatest revival yet to be known to man, taking place in the worst possible time yet to be known to man. As the 144,000 witnesses to every nation, tribe, and people of every language, they do so alongside the heavenly angels (14:6). During the Tribulation, flying angels are visible, proclaiming the eternal gospel (v. 6), which is the best example of heaven being brought down to earth; heavenly beings ministering to earthly (human) beings.

Heaven is also brought down to earth through the 144,000 Jewish evangelists, evident that while Jesus is in heaven, He is standing with the 144,000 (v. 1). And, while the 144,000 are on earth, they are singing a new song before the heavenly throne, before the four living creatures, and before the elders (vv. 1-3). In other words, the gap between heaven and earth has been closed. Not literally closed, but spiritually for the 144,000, where, like Jesus (Jn. 5:19-20), their communion with God is precise and unhindered, which is why their ministry is so powerful amidst a time of unprecedented persecution.

Persecution and power are inseparable, albeit power is quashed and lost through prosperity. The 144,000 are so powerful due to fulfiling the requirement of Christ (Mk. 8:34-35). In doing so, they are sealed by Jesus (7:), standing with Jesus (14:1), singing before Jesus (v. 3), they are pure (v. 4) and blameless before God (v. 5), and they follow Jesus wherever He goes (v. 4). In the same way, Jesus ministered when on earth (Jn. 5:19-20, Matt. 4:17, Mk. 1:5, Matt. 5:10), the 144,000 will do, doing and saying whatever Jesus is doing and saying.

As stated in chapter thirteen, Satan tried hard to crush the early church through persecution during the first and second centuries. However, the more he persecuted it, the faster it grew and more powerful it became. In the third century, Satan changed his tactic; instead of persecuting the church, he prospered it.

Through an exchange of persecution for prosperity, the church became powerless and apostate, which is why most churchgoers will find themselves 'waking up' in the Tribulation. However, during the Tribulation, those coming to genuine faith in Jesus through real repentance will again suffer terrible persecution and also experience the power of God. Essentially, they will experience 'heaven brought down to earth' in a time when the hordes and horrors of hell are unleashed. Adding to this, there will be unprecedented natural catastrophes, fulfilling Acts, chapter two.

In sum, chapter fourteen provides insight into the coming persecution for those left behind to endure the Tribulation. The insight comes through the

144,000 and the three angels proclaiming the eternal gospel, warning, and encouraging believers to endure (vv. 6-13). The warning is aimed at those tempted to 'take the easy way out' by receiving the mark of the beast (666). Those who do are eternally damned (vv. 9-11). There is no possible means of redemption left for anyone who receives the Antichrist's mark. By refusing his mark (666), those rejecting the Antichrist will be slain (13:15), and in being slain, will be considered blessed. "Blessed are the dead who die in the Lord from now on" (v. 14). The words 'from now on' indicate there may be as much as three and a half years left of the seven-year ordeal at this point in the Tribulation. Further evidence for the suggested timeline is based on the beast's mark only now becoming mandatory, which will be enforced under the threat of the penalty of death, triggering intense persecution for those rejecting it.

In conclusion, worship is the 'big idea' of chapters thirteen and fourteen. During the coming Tribulation, there will be no lukewarm and compromising believers, no one will be sitting on the fence; everyone will be either worshipping God or worshipping Satan through the Antichrist and his image. The penalty for worshipping Satan, by receiving the mark of the beast, is unredeemable, eternal damnation. The punishment is severe due to the unprecedented revelation of God, affording none to have an excuse.

During the tribulation, the 144,000 will operate with great power. Also the two witnesses with signs and wonders (Rev. 11), and even angels will be seen and heard preaching the eternal gospel as they fly overhead. As a result of the collective evangelistic effort, there will be no atheists during the Tribulation, but only those either accepting or rejecting Jesus Christ.

Through the powerful Pentecostal proclamation, heaven will be brought down to earth; meaning, God's will, will be made known, and His presence will be experienced by everyone, everywhere. For a minority, heaven brought down to earth will result in salvation; however, heaven brought down to earth will result in eternal damnation for the majority.

CHAPTER FOURTEEN

Part Two
Heaven on Earth

Following the three angels calling and warning humanity to Fear God and Worship Him (vv. 1-13), there are three more angels calling for judgment (vv. 15-20). Within the passage, verse fourteen is somewhat different, where it introduces a figure seated on a cloud, 'one like a son of man, with a golden crown on his head.' While the references to the three angels (vv. 15, 17, 18) are obvious; verse fourteen needs more work. The description of the one seated on the cloud is the same as chapter one (vv. 7, 13), seen again in Daniel (7:13). The controversy arises as to whether the one seated in the cloud is Jesus or not, due to verse fifteen, where an angel is instructing Him. The same is seen again in verse eighteen, where another angel instructs an angel with a sharp sickle to reap the harvest referring to the angel of verse seventeen.

In sum, the one like the son of man has a sharp sickle, and so does an angel. Two have sickles, and two more are calling for those with sharp sickles to reap the harvest. The objection is that angels do not instruct Jesus and will not be reaping alongside Him (Isa. 63:3, 5). However, angels are seen reaping alongside Jesus at the end of the Tribulation in Matthew's account of the parable of the weeds (13:39). Angels are also involved in gathering the elect (Matt. 24:31).

Another objection is, the one seated on the cloud is 'like' the son of man, but he is not 'the' son of man, being Jesus. However, Revelation, chapter one introduces Jesus as 'one like a son of man' (v. 13), in the same way, Daniel (7:13) does, 'one like the son of man.' The term 'Son of Man' is commonly used for Jesus, seen thirty times in Matthew's book, alone. But, then again, it is also used for Ezekiel, seen eighty-two times in the book of Ezekiel. The term is not just used by Ezekiel, referring to himself or humanity, but also by Daniel (8:17). However, the term is not used to describe angels, for they are known as 'sons of God' (Gen. 6:2, 4). Although some do state Daniel's description (7:13-14) is referring to Michael, the archangel, which is flawed because Michael, or any angel, is not served by humanity and is not given a kingdom or everlasting dominion (v. 14).

Based on the above mentioned, the conclusion is, the one seated on the cloud is Jesus, which means, chapter fourteen (vv. 14-20) is the same event described in chapters six (vv. 14-17) and nineteen (vv. 11-21) of the book of Revelation.

In short, chapter fourteen is prophesying that Jesus will return at the end of the Tribulation to judge the nations by way of reaping a harvest of sinning souls. Joel chapter three describes the same event, specifically referenced through verses twelve to twenty-one, as does Isaiah (63:1-6). Joel and Isaiah describe the same event yet differently. Some state Revelation fourteen reveals two separate harvests, one of the righteous and the other of the self-righteous, which is why two individuals carry sharp sickles (vv. 14, 17). Both are reaping a ripe (ready) harvest from the earth; the only difference is the latter (v. 18) where the angel gathers from the vine, reaping 'grapes.' The 'grapes' are then thrown into the winepress of the wrath of

God. Clearly, the latter refers to judgement, where the blood will run for 180 miles. While the former lacks the reference specifically to judgment, it also lacks any connection to harvesting the righteous. While there is scriptural support for angels reaping and gathering both the righteous and the self-righteous (wicked) at the end of the age, it does not seem to be apparent here.

When Jesus returns, He will separate the just from the unjust. Luke seventeen (vv. 34-36) addresses the same, albeit many present these verses in reference to the rapture: "In that night there will be two in one bed: the one will be taken and the other left. Two will be grinding together: the one will be taken, and the other left. Two will be in the field: the one will be taken, and the other left." However, the verses (34-36) fall within the greater context of judgement (vv. 20-37) and should be interpreted within that setting. Regarding these verses (vv. 34-36), when the disciples asked where the 'one taken' would go (v. 37a), Jesus answered by saying, "Wherever the body is there, eagles will be gathered" (37b). Some say the word 'eagles' could be better translated as 'vultures,' which is how the New American Standard Version presents it. The inferred meaning is that the dead body will attract scavengers (Job 39:30; Matt. 24:28; Rev. 19:17-19). That said, the 'one taken' clearly does not refer to a believer going up in the rapture, but rather the unbeliever being taken into judgement.

To understand the passage correctly, one needs first to consider additional verses (vv. 20-21), where the Pharisees ask about the coming Kingdom of God. Jesus told them that it is already here, in part. The translation "within you" would be better said, "within your midst." Otherwise, Jesus would have been saying the Kingdom of God was within the Pharisees, which was not the case. On the contrary, Jesus told them, "For all your study, you'll never see the Kingdom" (v. 20b; Jn. 5:39). The reason is, the self-righteous refused to accept Jesus as their Messiah (v. 25; Jn. 5:40), being instead lovers of themselves and this world (vv. 27a, 28, 32). Verse thirty-three, in response, comes as a stern warning, "Whoever seeks to save his life will lose it." The warning highlights the danger of loving worldly possessions (vv. 28, 31), the very thing that caused the Pharisees to stumble (Lk. 16:14). The same caused Lot's wife to 'look back' (v. 32). Therefore, the message in context (vv. 20-37) is straightforward; you can't serve two masters! (Matt. 6:24). Those who love their lives or the things of this world (materialism) won't take part in the coming kingdom (Jn. 2:15-17), but instead, they will be judged (Lk. 12:20) as the 'one taken' (vv. 34-36). Something similar is seen in Matthew's account (24:40-41).

Although, some say these verses support the rapture, however, the context (cf. vv. 36-39) is talking about judgement, where one is separated from the other. The one taken is eternally separated, cast into a place of torment. Matthew's gospel speaks more on this than the other synoptic gospels (Matt. 8:12, 13:42, 13:50, 22:13, 24:51, 25:30). Matthew also warns more about hell than the others (Matt. 5:22, 29, 30, 10:28, 18:9, 23:15, 23:33). On each occasion, the warnings were aimed at the religious, as with all the parables, all sharing the common theme of being separated, one from the other; the religious (self-righteous) from the righteous.

In sum, the doctrine of separation is common within scripture, where Jesus will separate the wheat from the chaff (Matt. 3:12) and the goats from the sheep (Matt. 25:31-46). Matthew, chapter twenty-five, is very similar to Revelation fourteen with the introduction of Jesus, who comes with His angels to judge (v. 31). When Jesus returns, He will separate one from the other (v. 32); one being prepared for reward (v. 34) and the other for judgement (vv. 41, 46). Those going into judgement do so due to their self-righteousness and vested interest in themselves.

Instead of looking out for the well being of others, they pursue their own pleasure and prosperity. Again, here lies the warning; you cannot serve two masters (Matt. 6:24), which is precisely the message of Revelation, chapter fourteen. You will either worship the beast for temporary gain resulting in eternal loss (chapter 13), or you will fear and worship God (14:7), thereby reap the eternal reward. Instead of reaping the eternal reward, those who compromise in any way will be harvested for the purpose of eternal judgement at the close of this age. Not just by Jesus, but also by the heavenly angels. Once again, when heaven comes down to earth, God's will – will be done (Matt. 6:10), which will be vastly different from what most are expecting.

Thus, when heaven comes to earth, it will come out from the temple of God, in heaven, wherefrom two of the three angels depart (14:15, 17). When heaven comes to earth, it will not be by or through man's efforts and achievements as dominionism teaches. Besides the angels coming out of the temple, another angel comes from the altar (v. 18). The reference to the alter is interesting because the altar is a place of mercy, mentioned seven times in the book of Revelation. The verses of particular interest refer to the tribulation saints under and before the altar (6:9, 8:3), avenged by the angel of God, who comes from the altar. God avenging His people will be the fulfilment of Romans chapter twelve (v. 19).

Alongside the angel avenging the Tribulation martyred saints, another angel joins in having authority over the fire (v. 18). The joining angel is possibly the same one mentioned earlier (8:5) who filled a censer with fire from the altar and threw it on the earth. The fire hurling the angel's judgment was in response to the prayers of the martyred tribulation saints (8:3-4).

As written above, the end times judgements on the wicked are activated through the saints' prayers, and they are celebrated when poured out; celebrated by the heavenly saints and the angels (11:17-18, 15:3-4, 16:5-7, 19:1-3, 6-8). When the judgement does come, it will be exceedingly great. Nothing close to the forthcoming event has ever occurred on the planet before now, nor will again (Jer. 30:7, Dan. 12:1, Matt. 24:21). The judgements lead to the battle of Armageddon (Isa. 63:1-3, Jer. 25:15, Dan. 11:40-45) where Jesus completes what He began (Lk. 3:17), which is the second part of His ministry (Isa. 61:1-2, cf. Lu. 4:18-19). When Jesus appeared the first time, it was to proclaim the good news and to set the captives free (Isa. 61:1-2, Lk. 4:18). When Jesus appears the second time, it will be to judge the nations, proclaiming the day of vengeance of our God (Isa. 61:2).

The day and the hour have come; even now, saints and sinners are fully ripe (14:15, 18) and ready for harvest. The word 'ripe' means 'overdue.' In other words, God's patience has run out for the wicked, and the delayed judgement is well overdue. God has delayed His judgement long enough, wanting all to be saved, that none would perish (2 Pet. 2:9). But, like God's patience, the time has also run out, and when judgement does come, it will come like a thief (2 Pet. 2:10), catching many by surprise, including confessing Christians (Rev. 3:3). On that day, sinners will be gathered up like 'grapes' and thrown into the great winepress of God (14:19), where their blood will rise as high as the horse's bridle and will flow for 180 miles (v. 20). While the reference of 180 miles is descriptive, it demonstrates an unprecedented level of destruction. Nothing remotely close to this event has been seen in the past, which again debunks preterist thinking.

In conclusion, chapter fourteen is possibly the most graphic of any passage in scripture, painting a very different picture of Jesus. One in direct contrast to the Jesus many worship today (cf. 2 Cor. 11:4). As mentioned earlier, the reason for the severity of judgement is due to the unprecedented revelation of Jesus. The book of Revelation is the revelation of Jesus, where He is unveiled and revealed uniquely. Still, many refuse to repent and worship Him (Rev. 9:20-21, 16:8, 10), and now their end has come. Instead of having ears to hear what they need to hear (Matt. 13:43b), they opt for teachers telling them what they want to hear (2 Tim. 4:3).

Once more, we are reminded of Jeremiah's words to the false prophets who proclaimed that God would not judge them. Instead of warning, they announced peace, peace, grace, and prosperity: "The prophets prophesy falsely, and the priests rule at their direction; my people love to have it so, but what will you do when the end comes?" (Jer. 5:31). Indeed, what will the self-righteous do when the end comes - when the Son of Man returns?! (Matt 6:10). Revelation, chapter six, answers that question (vv. 14-27).

CHAPTER FIFTEEN

The Wrath of God is Finished

Chapter fourteen's opening sentence contained the words "I looked," and now in chapter fifteen are the words, "I saw." What John saw in chapter fifteen was 'another sign.' In chapter twelve, the first sign seen was the woman (Israel); the second was the red dragon (Satan). This time, the sign relates to seven angels (15:1). In the previous chapter, six angels were referenced, three calling and warning regarding salvation, and three more calls for judgement. While chapter fourteen reveals the harvest of sinners and possibly saints, chapter fifteen introduces the final set of judgements leading up to Jesus' return. Chapter sixteen provides the details of the judgements introduced in chapter fifteen. The judgements of chapter sixteen are the bowl judgements, following the seal and trumpet judgements. Essentially, the same story is retold three times. The evidence is seen with Jesus returning in chapter six (vv. 12-17), chapter fourteen (v. 14), and chapter nineteen (vv. 11-21). Jesus does not return three times, but rather the story is being retold three times.

Following the second announcement of Jesus' return (14:14), chapter fifteen introduces the final set of judgements, and acknowledges the conquering saints. In verse one, John saw the seven angels carrying seven plagues, and in verse two, John saw those who had conquered the beast and its image and the number of his name. In other words, John saw the saints who refused to accept the mark of the beast (666). "They have conquered the beast by the blood of the Lamb and by the word of their testimony, for they loved not their lives even unto death" (12:11).

The conquering saints were before the throne, standing beside the sea of glass (15:2, cf. 4:6), with the harp of God in their hands, singing the song of Moses, and the song of the Lamb (Jesus). The music is a victory song, similar to that of Exodus, chapter fifteen. The 144,000 are also singing the victory song, accompanied by heavenly harpists (14:2-3); only the 144,000 are still on earth, while those who had conquered the beast are now in heaven (15:2-4). Those in heaven are the 'blessed ones' who died in the Lord for refusing to bow down to the Antichrist (14:13). They were slain by the sword (13:10, 15) and beheaded for their testimony of Jesus (20:4). The next 'blessed' group is still on the earth, enduring by staying awake during the Tribulation (16:15), refusing to bow down and accept the mark (666). Seven times the word 'blessed' is used in the book of Revelation (1:3, 14:13, 16:15, 19:9, 20:6, 22:7, 14), each reference points to those who, without compromise, worship God alone.

At this point, think back to the letters addressed to the seven churches (2-3). Five of the seven churches were in trouble (70%) and in need of repentance due to compromised worship. Only two (30%) were given a commendation, without rebuke, yet they were told to be faithful unto death (2:10) and to hold fast to what they have (3:11). Faithfulness and steadfastness are the conditions for receiving and holding onto the crown of life (2:10, 3:11). Each church was told, "Those (alone) that conquer (the world, corruption, false worship) would receive the reward and avoid judgement" (2:7, 11, 26, 3:5, 12, 21).

As mentioned above, the reference to Moses's song is interesting in that it could be supportive of the argument that Moses is one of the two witnesses (Rev. 11). Elijah is the other witnesses, confirmed by the prophet Malachi (4:5-6). The other suggested witness is Enoch. Enoch and Elijah are thought to be the possible pair because they are the only two humans who have not experienced physical death. The reasoning is based on the book of Hebrews (9:27), which says, "It is appointed for people to die once--and after this, judgement." So again, Enoch and Elijah did not die but instead were 'taken' by God. However, Moses is also a good candidate alongside Elijah at the Mount of Transfiguration (Matt. 17).

Furthermore, support is seen with the similarity of Egypt's plagues to the plagues of the Tribulation. The plagues of Egypt are recorded in the book of Exodus, chapters seven to eleven. There are ten plagues, eight of them are seen again in the Tribulation, and five of the eight are seen in the final judgements, described in chapter sixteen of the book of Revelation.

Egypt (Exodus)	Tribulation (Revelation)	Revelation, chapter 16
Blood 7:20	Blood 8:8-9, 11:6, 16:3-6	Blood
Frogs 8:6 (natural)	Frogs 16:13-14 (demonic)	Frogs (demonic)
Pestilence 9:1-3	Pestilence 6:8	
Boils 9:8-9	Boils 16:2	Boils
Hail and Fire 9:22-24	Hail and Fire 8:7	Fire
Locusts 10:4-5	Locust 9:3-4	
Darkness 10:21	Darkness 16:10-11	Darkness
Passover (first born) 11:4-5	Passover 15:5-8	

Adding to the plagues listed above, God's glory is also paralleled. Exodus 40:34-38 should be compared with Revelation 15:5-8. Both come after the story. Following the Tribulation, God's glory will be known and experienced on the earth throughout the millennium (Hag. 2:1-9). The prophet Haggai's announcement of the latter glory, being more significant than the former, takes place after the Tribulation (2:6, cf. Matt. 24:29, Lu. 21:26, Heb. 12:26), the double reference of Haggai's prophecy relates to the second and the millennial temple (Hag. 1:8). Ezekiel also has much to say about the millennial temple (40-48), including that God's (Shekinah) glory will fill it (43:5) because God is there (48:35b). To this day, we have not seen anything like what Ezekiel was predicting for the future millennial temple. In the OT, the shekinah glory filled the original temple (2nd Chronicles 7:1).

In the NT, the shekinah glory was made manifest in the announcement of Christ's arrival (Lu. 2:9), seen again through the Transfiguration (Matt. 17:2), and will also be seen when Jesus returns and dwells with His people (Rev. 21:3). The word shekinah is from the Hebrew word shākan, which means to reside or to stay permanently. The Shekinah glory departed (Ichabod) due to Israel's disobedience, and it has not remained with man to this day due to man's desire to rule and reign in replacement of God. Do you remember the final church, Laodicea, which prophetically speaks of us? Laodicea means: 'People ruling.' Ichabod means: 'Where is the glory?' The glory has departed and remains with God, in heaven, and it will return with Jesus when He returns. Then, everyone will bow down and worship Him. Then, Jesus will be reigning, not man.

Like John (Rev. 6:17), when Ezekiel had a vision of God's future glory, he fell on his face (43:3). The same will result when this generation truly encounters God; when we encounter God, the next thing we will encounter will be the ground. In short, a genuine experience of God will change you! Isaiah is another example of someone who had an encounter with God, where the house was filled with smoke (glory), resulting in a similar response to that of John and Ezekiel (Isa. 6:4-5).

Again, the shekinah glory will return with Jesus, filling the millennial temple as described by Ezekiel. Additional evidence for the temple Ezekiel speaks of, being the millennial temple, is made clear where the one (Jesus) Ezekiel was talking to stated that He will dwell amid the people of Israel forever and that they will no more defile His name (43:7). Israel will no more defile the Living God because the Living God changes them (Ezek. 11:19, 36:26). Ezekiel's prophesy is still yet to be fulfilled and will not be fulfilled until Jesus returns to rule and reign on the earth.

Ezekiel, chapter forty-seven, also provides evidence for the prophesied temple being fulfiled in the millennium, evident by the river's reference. The river flowing from the temple will breed and sustain life. As a result the millennium fisherman will reap a bountiful harvest (v. 9-10), whereas today, they are lucky to get a single bite due to the rivers and oceans being over-fished.

Some confuse the millennial temple with the church, stating the prediction has been fulfilled by the church, which is ludicrous for more reasons than I can express here. The main reason is Ezekiel's specifics, which are impossible to be applied to anything else other than a literal temple. Within scripture, there are seven earthly temples mentioned:

1. The Tabernacle (Ex. 25:8)
2. Solomon's Temple (2 Chron. 7:1)
3. Zerubbabel's Temple (Zech. 4:9)
4. The Church (2 Cor. 6:16, Eph. 2:21, 22)
5. Individual Believers in Christ (1 Cor. 3:16, 17)
6. Tribulation Temple (Rev. 11:1, 2, cf. Dan. 9:27, 12;11, Matt. 24:15, 2 Thess. 2:4)
7. Millennial Temple (Ezek. 40-48, Rev. 3:12)

Another temple mentioned in scripture, refers to a heavenly temple, which we have been discussing for the last few chapters (Rev. 7:15, 11:19, 14:15, 17, 16:1, 17). After the millennial dispensation, in the 'Eighth-Day,' there will be no more temples: "And I saw no temple in the city, for its temple is the Lord God the Almighty and the Lamb" (Rev. 21:22).

The next earthly temple we should be looking forward to is the millennial temple, which will be filled with God's glory because He (Jesus) is there. During the millennial reign, life will be better due to the whole world worshipping God, confirmed through John (Re. 15:4). Zechariah confirms the same; however, some will rebel, albeit their rebellion will be short-lasting (Zech. 14).

During the millennium, the rebels will make up Satan's final army after his release from the pit. The army will rise and march against Jesus at the close of the millennium. They rise, and they fall; they are quickly and effortlessly destroyed (Rev. 20:7-9). In the end, all nations will worship God (Dan. 7:14, Zeph. 2:11, Zech. 19:9, Rev 15:4). On this subject, the prophet Isaiah has plenty more to say (e.g., 2:2-4, 9:6-7).

Furthermore, in just a few short verses, Isaiah foretells the final events concluding the tribulation and following the millennium (66:15-24). The last verse refers to the 'eighth day' where all things are made new—the eighth day following the millennial reign is covered in chapter twenty-one of John's revelation. But, before we will see all things restored and worldwide worship of God, the world will be becoming increasingly hostile towards the one true God, especially during the Tribulation (Rev. 11:18, 9:20-21, 16:8-10). Again, the delusion of dominionism is evidence by this fact alone; things are getting worse, not better. This evidence also debunks preterist ideology. Increasing wickedness is predicted by scripture leading to Jesus' return (2 Tim. 3:4, 12-13), which is contrary to the false claims of the groups mentioned above. As a result of increasing wickedness, God responds with unprecedented judgement.

Contrary to the millennium temple where everyone worships God, most will follow the Antichrist during the Tribulation. In response, angels will come out from the heavenly temple, seen in chapter fourteen, announcing judgement (vv. 15-20), seen again in chapter fifteen, executing judgement. Consequently, the wrath of God that has been stored up (Rom. 2:5) is now being poured out (Rev. 15-16). While the kindness of God was meant to lead sinners to repentance (Rom. 2:4), the hardness of man's heart has almost dared God to pour out His final judgement (15:1, 8) on the remaining population of the earth. Again, the judgement is triggered by the prayers of the saints (6:9-11, 8:3-5). At the beginning of the Tribulation, the martyred saints asked Jesus, "How long before you will judge and avenge our blood on those who dwell on the earth?" (6:10). Jesus replied, "Not until the number of the [your] fellow servants and their brothers are complete, who were to be killed as you have been" (6:11). Now that the number is complete, the full and overflowing cup of God's wrath is poured out upon the planet (15:7).

Interestingly, during the exodus account, God's judgements were designed to free God's people from slavery at the Egyptians' hands. During the Tribulation account, God's judgements are to free people from the deception and slavery of sin through repentance, thereby saving humanity from the wrath of God. The wrath of God is a common theme throughout scripture (Matt. 3:7, Jn. 3:36, Rom. 1:18, 2:5, 8, 5:9, 9:22, 12:19, 13:5, 1 Thess. 1:10, 2:16, 5:9, Heb 3:11, 4:3), referenced eleven times in the book of Revelation, alone (6:16, 17, 11:18, 12:12, 14:10, 19, 15:1, 7, 16:1, 19, 19:15). Yet, few talk about it today. The wrath of God is first and foremost designed to bring people to repentance; the threat of judgement is purposed to save, not destroy. Those who refuse God's free gift of salvation by rejecting Jesus Christ and preventing others from receiving Jesus subject themselves to God's wrath (1 Thess. 2:16). Those who do respond to God's free gift of salvation, they (alone) will be delivered from the wrath to come (1 Thess. 1:10, 5:9, cf. Rev. 3:10).

In conclusion: John received a revelation of the end; the final judgement poured out on the Tribulation population due to refusing to worship Him. Instead, they bowed down and worshipped Satan by following the Antichrist and his image and accepting his mark (666). Amidst the greatest calamity the earth has ever seen, John also saw the Tribulation saints singing a song of victory. The victory was that of Jesus Christ's victory over Satan; with the announcement, He is returning soon to rule and reign on the earth. Once He has returned, Jesus will set up the millennial temple wherefrom the whole world would worship Him, being freed from sin and the power thereof. God's glory will then fill the millennial temple because God will be there. Never before have we seen what is set to take place.

In sum, the millennial dispensation will be the believers 'best life, then,' contrary to false teachings of the seven mountain, hyper-faith camp, claiming their 'best life now.' Indeed, when the wrath of God is finished, the best to come will come for those that lose their lives here and now. The worst to come is yet to come for those who attempt to save their lives here and now (Rev. 20:11-15).

CHAPTER SIXTEEN

The Bowls

"And then I heard a loud voice from the temple telling the seven angels, 'Go and pour out on the earth the seven bowls of the wrath of God'" (v. 1). As mentioned in the previous chapter, chapter fifteen announces the last seven judgements, which will finished the wrath of God (vv. 1, 8). Chapter sixteen reveals the seven judgements that have completed the wrath of God (16:17b) and describes each of them in rapid succession. Also, as previously mentioned, the bowl judgements seem to repeat the seal and trumpet judgement. The judgements also describe what Jesus predicted, as recorded by Matthew (24).

Matt 24	Matt 24	Matt 24	Matt 24	Matt 24	Matt 24	Matt 24
Deception vv. 5, 11, 24	War vv. 6-7, 22	Famine vv. 7b-8	Pestilences v. 7	Martyrdom v. 9	Earthquake vv. 7	Cosmic events vv. 29
Seal 1	Seal 2	Seal 3	Seal 4	Seal 5	Seal 6	Seal 7
White Horse 6:2	Red Horse 6:3-4	Black Horse 6:5-6	Pale Horse 6:7-8	Martyrdom 6:9	Earthquake 6:12	Cosmic events 8:5 (cf. 6:12)

The seal judgements are repeated twice more through the trumpet and bowl judgements, almost in the same order.

Trumpet 1	Trumpet 2	Trumpet 3	Trumpet 4	Trumpet 5	Trumpet 6	Trumpet 7
Hail and Fire, mixed with blood, 1/3 of earth destroyed 8:7	1/3 of the Sea becomes Blood 8-9	Nuclear Warfare, 1/3 fresh Water Poisoned 8:10-11	Sun struck, resulting in Darkness, 1/3 of natural light affected 8:12-13	Demonic Locust 9:1-11 Painful Stings' unless sealed 9:5-6, 10	Fallen Angels 9:13-15 Dem-Army (killing 1/3) 9:15-16 Earthquakes 11:13	Loud Voice in Heaven 11:19 Satan cast down 12:7-8 (3.5 years left)
Bowl 1	Bowl 2	Bowl 3	Bowl 4	Bowl 5	Bowl 6	Bowl 7
Painful Sores for Follower the Beast 16:2	Sea became Blood 16:3	Fresh Water became Blood 16:4	Sun given Power to Scorch 16:8	Darkness / Painful Sores 16:10	Kings / East 16:12 Spirits 16:13-14	Loud Voice came out of the Temple 16:17-20

When comparing the three sets of judgement (seals, trumpets, bowls), the repetitiveness of them is hard to ignore, arguably, the same story is being retold three times over. The same applies to Jesus' return referenced three times over (Rev. 6:12-17, 14:14, 20, 19:11-21).

Leading up to Jesus' return, some claim to be the returned Christ (Matt. 24:5, 11, 24), while others claim to speak on behalf of Him. The ultimate fulfilment of the prophecy (false Christs) is fulfilled with the Antichrist (first seal), and the false prophet (Rev. 13), resulting in masses of people being deceived into following Satan. As a result of mankind rejecting Jesus, God will respond first with hail and then boils (first trumpet and first bowl).

As mentioned earlier, deception is the foremost end times sign, which will trigger a divine stoning (Rev. 8:7, 11:19, 16:21). God will stone the

Tribulation population due to rejecting His Son, for worshipping the beast, and for blasphemy (Rev. 16:10-12). The penalty for blasphemy is death by stoning (Lev. 24:10-23).

Evidence for deception being a leading sign of the end times is seen with the first seal, which introduces the beast. The first trumpet is God's response to the deceived that continue to reject God during the Tribulation, in favour of the beast. The first bowl is God's judgement on those that have received the mark of the beast. The next warning from Jesus relates to war (Matt. 24:6, 7, 22). The second seal releases the red horse, symbolic of war. The second trumpet speaks of a third of the ocean turning to blood, as does the second bowl judgement. The reference to 'something like a great mountain burning with fire, thrown into the sea (8:8), causing a third of it to turn to blood' could refer to modern warfare. Daniel supports the idea, predicting that during the tribulation there will be a continuous time of world war (Dan. 11:36–45). Notice the words of chapter sixteen, "The sea became like the blood of a corpse, and every living thing died that was in the sea" (v. 3). The dead would include every navy sailor on every battleship, millions of them. For example, there are up to 500,000 enlisted sailors (including reserves) in the US navy alone, and China's navy boasts even greater numbers than the US. When you consider worldwide war, where every nation has its troops engaged at sea and on the battlefield, it is not hard to imagine the seas and the land turning to blood, as will be the case at Armageddon (14:20, 19:15).

The next sign Jesus gave relates to famine (Matt. 24:7b-8). The third seal is the black horse (famine), the third trumpet and third bowl judgment relate to the water being poisoned. Without clean water, nothing survives, neither crop nor livestock, resulting in famine. However, the difference between the trumpet judgments and the bowl judgements, is that with the trumpet judgements a third of the earth, sea, etc., is affected. While with the bowl judgements, the entire earth, sea, etc., is affected.

Chapter sixteen reveals that the sea became like the blood of a corpse (v. 3) in response to shedding the blood of saints and prophets (v. 6): "An eye for an eye, a tooth for a tooth, and blood for blood" (Ex. 21:24). Under the Law, the shedding of blood requires the shedding of literal blood. Those following the beast will pay for their sins with their own blood because they refused the literal sacrifice of Jesus Christ (Matt. 26:28), where His blood was shed for the sins of all (Heb. 9:22). Now, their own blood is required of them, where they will be made to drink of the cup of the wine of the fury of God's wrath (Rev. 14:10, 16:19), in double portion (18:6). The cup of wrath is the very cup of suffering that Jesus asked the Father (God) to take away from Him, if possible (Matt. 26:39).

Nevertheless, Jesus drank the cup that we would not have to. Those who refuse Jesus, refuse His once and for all sacrifice (Heb. 7:27), therefore will have to pay the price for sin themselves. The penalty for sin is death (Rom. 6:23). Following the famine is pestilence. War naturally results in famine and famine in pestilence. Worldwide sickness will be an ongoing plight throughout the Tribulation period. Regarding pestilence, the third seal and the third trumpet judgements do not directly correlate; however, the third trumpet and third bowl judgements do. Regarding the trumpet and bowl judgements in one instance, the sun is stuck resulting in darkness (8:12-13), in the next the sun is given power to scorch (16:8). Although it could be argued without a balanced distribution from the sun, either way, sickness will result, perhaps gaining some correlation, at a stretch.

Martyrdom is next on the list of Jesus' end times signs.

Chapter sixteen seems to focus on martyrdom where God takes revenge on those responsible for the death of the saints and the prophets (v. 6). Chapter six sets the theme with the opening of the fifth seal, resulting in countless millions martyred for their newfound faith in Jesus (6:9). The fifth trumpet and fifth bowl judgement are aimed at those who follow the beast (9:4, 16:10-11), and those who killed the saints (an eye for an eye).

The next sign of the end times is earthquakes (Matt. 24:7), seen in the sixth seal (6:12). The sixth trumpet and sixth seal, however, focus on a demonic army led by powerful demons (9:13-16, 16:12-14); therefore, no correlation is found, albeit, between the sixth and seventh trumpet there is a great earthquake (11:13). The next earthquake is seen in chapter sixteen (v. 18) in the seventh bowl judgement.

Finally, the seventh sign of the end times is cosmic events (Matt. 24:26, Rev. 6:12, 8:5, 11:19, 16:17-21). The cosmos events conclude the Tribulation period, confirmed by the words: "It is done" (16:17), similarly to Christ's words on the cross "It is finished" (Jn. 19:28-30). In chapter ten, the angel announced, "There would be no more delay" (v. 6) that the mystery of God would be fulfiled (v. 7); and now it has been fulfiled. The wrath of God is finished (15:1), and the mystery revealed, as to who is Jesus? (Rev. 6:12-17, 14:14, 20, 19:11-21). Jesus is the mystery (15:1), the blessing (1:3), and the prophecy (19:10b).

At this stage of the Tribulation, those remaining faithful are encouraged to keep on keeping on (16:15). By now, believers in the Tribulation will know that the end is in sight due to the gathering at the place called Armageddon (v. 16). They will also know that the end is near due to the Tribulation only lasting seven years (Dan. 7:24-27, Rev. 11:2, 3, 12:6, 7, 14, 13:5). Also, the judgements are in succession; therefore those familiar with scripture will know where they are within the eschatological calendar by which judgement is being poured out at the time. Quite possibly, of the seven judgements (repeated three times - seals, trumpets, and bowls), there will be one main judgement per year for seven years. Chapter nineteen narrows in on the final judgement (vv. 11-21). Few will make it this far, and even less will remain faithful to Jesus (Matt. 24:24), deceived by false teachers, the Antichrist, the false prophet and, demons (16:13-14).

In conclusion, at the beginning of this section, the leading sign of the end times is deception, which will be the main reason so many will end up in the Tribulation. Deception results from an increase of false teachers (and false worship), even in the church, conditioning people for the Antichrist to come. False teachers are conditioning their hearers (who cannot endure sound doctrine) for the 'strong delusion' to come. God sends the strong delusion (Antichrist) to those (including churchgoers) who did not love the truth, but instead had pleasure in unrighteousness (2 Thess. 2:10-12).

The letters to the seven churches (Rev. 2-3) addressed this very issue, five of seven receive a bad report, failing the test, and unless repentance came first, judgement was imminent. The seven churches are symbolic of the church throughout the entire church age whereas, every condition (good and bad) is readily seen. The warnings to five of the seven churches apply just as much to the collective church today, as they do to individual believers. Again, people fail the test due to deception; they 'think' they are saved when they are not. Sadly, billions of believers will wake up in the Tribulation, 'thinking' they are alive in Christ when they are dead (Rev. 3:1). Unless they wake up (spiritually) this side of the Tribulation (Rev. 3:2) they will wake up in the Tribulation.

Today, billions of believers have been deceived by a false gospel of 'peace and security' (1 Thess. 5:3), including a doctrine of hyper-grace and prosperity. Even while in the Tribulation, many will still be blinded by Satan (2 Cor. 4:4), and his doctrines of demons (1 Tim. 4:1); therefore, they will be subject to the judgements and finally, to the eternal Lake of Fire (20:11-15).

CHAPTER SEVENTEEN

The Woman who Rides the Beast

In chapter fifteen, through the bowl judgements came the announcement: "The wrath of God is finished (v 1), and 'The seven plagues of the seven angels were finished" (v. 8). In chapter sixteen, following the seventh angel pouring out his plague, a loud voice came out of the (heavenly) temple, from the throne, saying, "It is done" (v. 17).

Now, in chapter seventeen, verse one, it is revealed that one of the seven angels is announcing yet another judgement. This time the judgement is on the great prostitute (v. 1). The great prostitute is the woman sitting on a scarlet beast full of blasphemous names (v. 3). The beast has seven heads and ten horns (vv. 3, 7). From the beast's blasphemous nature and the description of having seven heads and ten horns, we know straight away that this is the Antichrist (13:1, 5, 6), as previously discussed.

Further confirmation of the beast being the Antichrist is seen in verses eight to thirteen. Throughout these verses, we identify the beast as the Antichrist who comes out of the seventh kingdom, making the eighth. Before the seventh, there have been five kingdoms that have fallen (Egypt, Assyria, Babylon, Medes Persian, Greece), and one at the time of John's writing (Rome). The one to come will be the Revived Roman Empire or the New World Order. The book of Daniel (chapters 2 & 7) is commonly used to support the coming seventh kingdom's idea, or new (one) world order - also, the book of Revelation (13:1). The reference to the ten kingdoms and seven heads refers to the coming seventh kingdom, consisting of ten nations and seven leaders/kings. As quickly as they form a new world order, they surrender their power to the eighth (v. 12). The eighth kingdom will come out of the seventh with a one world leader, the Antichrist, although his term is short lasting (v. 10). The seventh and eighth kingdom's demise will result from making war against the Lamb (Jesus), who will effortlessly conquer them (v. 14).

As previously written, we already know who the beast is, but who is this mystery woman (vv. 5, 7), the great prostitute, who rides the beast? (17:3) Within the book of Revelation, there are two women mentioned. The first is Israel (12:1, 4, 6, 13, 14, 15, 16, 17), and the other rides the beast (17:3, 4, 6, 7, 9, 18). The first (Israel) is persecuted by Satan (Rev. 12), the next is Satan's whore (the harlot church) who persecutes believers (17:6). There is one other woman mentioned in the book of Revelation who is the same as the second. That woman is Jezebel (2:20), who will be readdressed shortly. Before then, verse eighteen should be considered providing another clue as to who the mystery woman who rides the beast is. She is, "The great city with dominion over the kings of the earth. (v. 18). She is the great city (v. 18), the great prostitute (v. 1), and the great mother of prostitutes" (v. 5). Further insight is provided in verse four, "She is dressed in purple and scarlet, adorned with gold and jewels, and pearls, holding in her hand a golden cup."

The true church (the bride of Christ) is the other woman, not mentioned after chapter four, or again until chapter nineteen, due to being raptured. (4:1, cf. 3:10). The harlot church is left behind, where she will lead the kings of the earth into immorality and adultery (v. 2), as with the whole world, which is drunk with the wine of sexual immorality (14:8). The harlot is also drunk with the blood of the martyrs of Jesus (v. 6). She is a blasphemous church (17:3), linking her directly to the Antichrist (13:1, 5). Satan's Babylonian whore rides his son of perdition, the Antichrist.

The reference to Babylon is essential, adding further symbolic support of the false religious system (Gen. 10-11); the word 'Babel' means 'confusion' (Gen. 11:9). Babylon was both religious and political and has been the root of every false religion, producing harlotry. Harlotry was the main problem for Israel, causing God to judge them. The central theme of the book of Hosea is spiritual harlotry. God illustrates Israel's spiritual harlotry through physical whoredom.

Today, we see the same through the likes of the RCC. Like the Babylonian cult, the Catholic cardinals wear crowns in the shape of a fish head, worn by the Babylonian cult's chief priests to honour the fish god. On this subject, Walvoord states the crowns bore the words, "Keeper of the Bridge," symbolic of the 'bridge' between man and Satan. This handle was adopted by the Roman emperors, who used the Latin title Pontifex Maximus, which means "Major Keeper of the Bridge." And the same title was later used by the bishop of Rome. The pope today is often called the pontiff, which comes from pontifex.

When the Babylonian mystery religions' teachers later moved from Pergamum to Rome, they were influential in paganizing Christianity. They were the source of many so-called religious rites, which have crept into ritualistic churches. Babylon then is the symbol of apostasy and blasphemous substitution of idol worship for the worship of God in Christ.

The church in Pergamum is where Satan dwells (2:12, 13), where a remnant of believers was holding fast, by not denying the faith, despite persecution (2:13). The shared problem for the church of Pergamum and those influenced by the woman who rides the beast (chapter 17) is sexual immorality (2:14). Sexual immorality is mentioned nine times within the book of Revelation (2:14, 20, 21, 9:21, 14:8, 17:2, 4, 18:3, 9). Sexual immorality is referenced to Babylon five times and twice within the letters to the churches. Joining Pergamum is the church of Thyatira.

The church of Thyatira's problem is that of Jezebel. Jezebel represents false religious doctrine and practices. Interestingly, Jezebel does not stop the church; she joins it and leads it. The issue for Pergamum was similar, only instead of Jezebel, it was the teachings of Balaam and the Nicolaitans. Balaam led Israel into sexual sin, bringing God's judgement upon them (Num. 22-25). The Nicolaitans refer to 'clergy lording over the laity.' Jesus hated the work of the Nicolaitans (2:6). Jezebel, on the other hand, means 'unhusbanded,' and is guilty of teaching that 'you can do whatever you like, and you will be alright' (hyper-grace), including sexual sin. God addressed both churches, warning them that judgement would come, just like it did for Israel unless repentance came first.

Today, many believers have an issue with God judging the church in the same way He did Israel. However, Paul made it clear, He would, if the church repeated Israel's blind and proudful ways (Rom. 11:19-24). An example of this is seen with Pergamum's church that was threatened with the sword of Jesus' mouth (2:16), executed after the Tribulation (19:15). The church of Thyatira was also threatened with being thrown into the great Tribulation (2:22), that they would know that Jesus is the one who searches mind and heart (v. 23). Throughout the Tribulation, God is searching the minds and hearts of humanity, identifying and revealing their true adulterous and idolatrous nature.

As mentioned earlier, the woman who rides the beast is often thought to be symbolic of the RCC, which is directly responsible for the deaths of millions of martyrs (v. 6), with numbers even exceeding fifty million according to Foxe's Book of Martyrs. If the woman is the RCC, then the pope is the false prophet (Rev. 13). However, the end times religious system is bigger than the RCC but undoubtedly incorporates it.

Recently, popular Word of Faith preachers were seen to be showing solidarity with the pope, stating the reformation was over and that we are all now one Catholic (universal) church, again. 'Solidarity' is precisely what the end times ecumenical system will promote; unification of denominations and all faiths who practice false worship. On one hand, spiritual adultery will be committed by those professing to know and follow God. On the other hand, spiritual fornication will be committed by every other faith rejecting Jesus Christ as God. During the tribulation, there will be no atheists; everyone will either accept or reject Jesus Christ. This is why the woman is called the great mother of prostitutes. Every false religion that has been birthed from her will come back to her during the Tribulation. During the Tribulation, the great harlot's influence will dwarf anything of the past, including her murderous history, killing millions of God-fearing and worshipping Christians.

During the Tribulation, the harlot church will be a controlling religious system, operating by Satan's power, alongside the Antichrist (vv. 7-8, 13:4). The whole world will marvel significantly at her - the revived religious Babylonian system (v. 6, 13:3), led by the false prophet, which promotes the Antichrist. The worshippers of the false religious system are those whose names are not found in the book of life (v. 8). The book of life is mentioned six times in Revelation (3:5, 13:8, 17:8, 20:12, 15, 21:27). The references to the book of life serve as a warning; anyone found guilty of false worship will not have their names written in the book of life. Only those who do not compromise will remain, according to Jesus: "The one who conquers will be clothed thus in white garments, and I will never blot his name out of the book of life. I will confess his name before my Father and before His angels" (3:5).

Note, the reference is given to the church of Sardis, the reverse is just as valid, 'If you fail to conquer, your name will not remain.' Sardis was a church having a reputation of being alive but was dead, and unless she repented, Jesus would come like a thief (3:3). The reference to coming like a thief refers to the tribulation. When Jesus returns, He will only come for His own (rapture), leaving the rest behind (cf. Lu. 21:24-26).

Once more, during the Tribulation, the woman will play a significant part, both politically (v. 18) and religiously (v. 5), deceiving most (v. 8) into following and worshipping the beast (cf. Rev. 13). She will be instrumental in setting up the seventh kingdom, with an alliance of shared power; though, an eighth kingdom will emerge from the seventh (v. 11). Again, the eighth kingdom is the Antichrist's global government, where the beast will not share his power with any other, including the woman. He will break up with her and even turn on her (v. 16). The breakup will occur around the halfway point of the Tribulation, whereas the worldwide harlot church will be destroyed by the Antichrist, who puts himself on the throne, to be worshipped alone (cf. Dan. 11:36–38; 2 Thess. 2:4; Rev. 13:8, 15). The false prophet will also abandon the harlot church in full submission to the Antichrist (Rev. 13:12). Throughout the Tribulation, the false prophet and the Antichrist are of one mind, united together (17:13, 17), carrying out God's purposes (v. 17) until the end (19:20). Then, in the end, together, they will be conquered by Jesus (v. 14), who will cast both of them alive into the lake of fire (19:20), where they will remain together in torment for all eternity (20:10). After one thousand years, they will have not one less day to stay, forever suffering, alongside Satan (20:10) and those that followed them (14:11, 20:11-15).

In sum, chapter seventeen is God's judgement on the false religious system (the harlot church), led by the false prophet. At the halfway point of the Tribulation, the Antichrist will turn on the whoring church, taking its power for himself (vv. 16-17), fulfiling God's purpose and words (17:17).

Remember, the book of Revelation commenced with an introduction to Jesus returning to judge the nations. The book then proceeds with the letters to the churches, warning of imminent judgement for seventy percent of them. When comparing the churches alongside chapter seventeen, something of the same is seen. False worship is the problem, separating one from the other. Only those remaining loyal to Jesus, without compromise, are kept from the hour of trial (Tribulation) coming to test the whole world (3:10). Only those remaining faithful, even until death, receive the crown (2:10). The rest are in danger of the judgement.

During the Tribulation, those caught up in the false worldly (whoring) church will have one last opportunity to repent or else join her in the final judgement (18:4). Remember, only two (30%) of the seven churches addressed (Rev. 2-3) by Jesus received a faultless report and were without the need for repentance.

Regarding the last, being Laodicea, Jesus has nothing good to say about her, other than He loved her and invited her to receive Him through repentance (3:19-20). The church of Laodicea prophetically represents the last church before Jesus returns, being us. But, we shared the same conditions of every church referenced and the same odds; just thirty percent of the church is considered to be doing well, without the need for correction. The poor (Smyrna) and the weak (Philadelphia) church were the two churches whose only requirement was to remain faithful (2:10) and to hold fast (3:11). The other churches, seemingly doing well by the world's standard, were in big trouble.

CHAPTER EIGHTEEN

Come out of her My People

Following one of the seven angels who judged the woman of chapter seventeen, another angel with great authority announces Babylon's fall: "Fallen, fallen is Babylon the great" (18:2, cf. Isa. 21:9, Jer. 51:49, Rev. 14:8). For a while, Babylon, the great mother of prostitutes (religious system), and the great city (political and economic system) assume great authority. Still, the genuine authority of God judges it.

While some confuse chapters seventeen and eighteen as the same event, they are not the same; although, Isaiah and Jeremiah's accounts are the same as chapter eighteen when applying the principle of double referencing. The difference between chapters seventeen and eighteen is, that the kings of the earth morn the judgement of Babylon (vv. 9, 19); however, in chapter seventeen, there is no evidence of mourning. Instead, the ten horns (nations) turn on (17:15) Babylon, the great mother of prostitutes (v. 5), in total submission to the Antichrist. Unbeknownst to the ten nations, they turn on the prostitute, fulfiling God's purpose and word (17:17). On every occasion, God is sovereign; Jesus is Lord and King (17:14); Satan and his Antichrist are not.

The prophecy of the destruction of the harlot church is fulfilled at the midway point of the Tribulation. In contrast, the collapse of the economic and political Babylonian world system, which incorporates a new/one world religion, comes at the close of seven years. Again, God is the one who caused the ten nations and the Antichrist to turn on the harlot church in chapter seventeen, and it also is God who overthrows Babylon in chapter eighteen, this time through a mighty angel (18:21).

For comparison purposes, John previously addressed Babylon's destruction through the fourteenth chapter (v. 8), and the seventh bowl (16:19:21); the seventh bowl judgement is the final judgment aimed at the world economic system. Again, Jeremiah prophesied of the same event (50-51). In Jeremiah, take special note of 50:8, 27, 51:6, 9, and 45 in consideration of Revelation, chapter eighteen, verse four. The Babylon Jeremiah refers to is both the literal Babylon of his time and the future Babylon of Revelation eighteen; hence, the principle of double referencing is applied.

Again, seen through chapter eighteen is the one-world Antichrist religion, merged with political and economic policy and ideology (Babylon), that has produced the most extraordinary global economy ever seen. For some (just a few), great wealth is now the focus of the final Tribulation judgement. Those who acquire great wealth during the Tribulation will do so at the expense of others (as always). However, during the Tribulation, the great divide between those who have and have not will widen, for most will experience unsurpassed poverty (6:6). In chapter eighteen, the love of money is the primary problem - such as it was for the church of Laodicea who had no glory (God) but plenty of gold (3:14-22). The reverse was true of the church of Philadelphia; they had no gold, but they did have God (3:7-13).

Just like the Christless church of Laodicea (3:17, 20), the harlot church (chapter 17) and the prosperous city (world system) will be full of demons

(18:2). Take note: Satan will use prosperity to produce spiritual poverty; he attempted this tactic with Jesus, replacing persecution with prosperity (Matt. 4:8-9). Where Satan failed with Jesus, he was successful with Judas (Matt. 26:14-16), and Demas (2 Tim. 4:10), and again with the church of Laodicea (prophetically speaking of us). Matthew (4) is the first place the prosperity gospel is seen in the NT, and Revelation (18) is the last place we see it. On every occasion, Satan is behind it.

As seen today, the prosperity gospel is the prophetic fulfilment of the Laodicean church, and a cause of those left behind enduing the Tribulation (18), all sharing the same spiritual condition as the last church (3:14-22), and people (chapters 17 &18), before Jesus returns. In these last days, believers need to be aware of deceptive doctrines of demons (1 Tim. 4:1) promoting prosperity over persecution, flowing from preachers full of greed (1 Tim. 6:5, 10, 2 Tim. 3:2, 2 Pet. 2:2, 3, 14). Prosperity preachers follow the same path as the false prophets of Jeremiah's day (6:13, 8:10). Believers need to flee from such preachers and churches promoting the prosperity gospel, pursuing their own passions, lest they become like them (2 Tim. 4:3). Similarly, announced five times in Jeremiah's prophecy against Babylon (the city of prosperity), "Flee!" (50:8, 27, 51:6, 9, & 45). The same announcement is made during the Tribulation from a voice in heaven, "Come out of her My people!" (Rev. 18:4). The reference to 'My' people would suggest the voice from heaven belongs to Jesus. The application today would be, 'Leave Laodicea, My people!' Flee from the institutional, prosperity-driven (Babylonian) church.

Again, in chapter eighteen, verse four, a voice from heaven says, "Come out of her My people." If they had listened to God in the first place, they would not have been there (cf. Isa. 48:18-21). Relating to the same, as seen through the prophet Isaiah, the command from God is to 'Flee' (Isa. 48:20). The question you might be asking at this point is, "What on earth are God's people still doing in Babylon at this late stage of the tribulation?" Some say Babylon refers to Babylon's literal city, as referenced five times (vv. 10, 16, 18, 19, 21), but the problem with that interpretation is, sin is not isolated to a single city; neither does it flow from a single city. Another obvious problem with Babylon being a literal city is that literal Babylon (Iraq) has been devastated by war, leaving it anything but prosperous. In this late eschatological hour, it is unlikely, if not impossible, for Babylon to recover economically; therefore, Babylon refers to a system, not a location.

Further support for an allegoric understanding and application is where God uses the term Babylon, in the same way, He used the name Sodom and Gomorrah, referring to Israel (Isa. 1:9-10). Israel was not literal Sodom and Gomorrah, but instead, they behaved like them; therefore God called them by the same name. Consider another reference in Zechariah, chapter fourteen, where God calls the rebels in the millennium, Egypt (vv. 18, 19); the rebels are not literal Egypt, but instead, they behave in the same way.

Regarding Isaiah, the warning to Israel acting like Sodom and Gomorrah is repent or else be destroyed (vv. 18-20). The literal place called Sodom is where Lot (Gen. 19) was told to flee (v. 15), to escape (vv. 17, 19, 20), that his life would be saved (v. 20). The same application is used with the allegoric understanding of Babylon; FLEE! The word Babylon is also used in the NT with the same allegoric application, referring to a system or political rule. Peter (1 Pet. 5:13-14) confirms this to be true when using Babylon as a code for Rome. When

Peter wrote his letter, he was nowhere near Babylon; he was in Rome, and therefore referred to Rome as Babylon.

Rome was the new Babylon that would seduce people away from worshipping God. Revelation seventeen and eighteen also refers to postmodern Babylon succeeding Rome (17:9-12). The sixth kingdom at the time of John's writing is literal Rome, the seventh kingdom is the new world order, and the eighth comes out of the seventh. The seventh and eighth kingdoms are an end-times Babylonian system (the new world

order), as described by Isaiah (47). In an allegoric sense, Babylon even exists today, known for its riches, power, influence, education, innovation, and false worship. The Babylonians worshipped Murduk, the storm god. The Babylonian system is what believers are called out of during the tribulation (18:4) or else perish with her.

Interestingly, after the tribulation, God destroys the god of storms with a storm of His own (16:18-21), which is precisely what He did with the Egyptians. Each plague was targeted at a particular Egyptian god (Exod. 7-12). God will do the same to the Antichrist, who proclaims to be God. God will pour out a plague on the throne of the Antichrist, demonstrating he is no God at all (16:10).

Tribulation Babylon will not be a place of just one false god, but many, for it will be a place where demons openly rule and reign (18:2-3), where all nations, kings, and merchants are seduced and drunk with sin (v. 3), they are seduced by demons and the Antichrist. The Tribulation will see hordes of demonic activity unleashed upon the earth to test and separate. Remember, though, God is sovereign over the entire Tribulation period, like any other time. God is also responsible for sending the Antichrist, the 'strong delusion' (2 Thess. 2:11). God will send the Antichrist so those left behind would believe what is false to be condemned because they did not love the truth (vv. 11-12).

Throughout the entire book of Revelation, God is separating one from the other by making a show of Satan, exposing him for the liar that he is. Yet still, most will not see it, being blinded by the god of this world (2 Cor. 4:4). Once again, the big idea of Revelation chapter eighteen is to Flee, "Come out of Babylon," and anything, everything representing it, or associated with it, including the 'harlot church.'

Today, many churches look no different from the world (Babylon); they imitate the world because they have so much of the world within them. Paul condemns such behaviour, stating believers should not be yoked with the world, or have partnership or fellowship with the world and what it offers. We are to be separated from it (2 Cor. 6:14-18). The Greek word for 'church' is ekklesia, which means 'to call out.' To call out of the world is the literal application. Those who come out of the world, separating themselves from the world, are partnered with God. Those who do not will get a firsthand experience of Revelation, chapter eighteen, if they make it that far, that is, for most will not.

People finding themselves in this predicament - the Tribulation, include those who did not heed the warning, who did not have ears to hear; deceived churchgoers, blinded by the prosperity gospel promising they can have their 'best life now.' Some may even achieve such worldly wealth, albeit short-lasting. Satan will always give you the desires of your heart to keep you where he wants you long enough to destroy you. When at the peak of riches and luxurious living (18:3, 7, cf. 1 Thess. 5:3), judgement will then come, suddenly. In a single day (v. 8), and in just one-hour (vv. 10, 17, 19), Babylon (the great world system) will be found no more, no more, no more, no more, no more, no more (vv. 21-23). Following the judgement, six times, God states, Babylon will be no more! The very thing that held those judged by God has now been taken away from them. The fruit their soul longed for is gone, gone forever, and never to be found again (v. 14).

In sum, for the great sins of Babylon (18:4, 5) her judgement will be severe, in double portion (v. 6), producing torment and mourning (v. 7), weeping and wailing (v. 9), weeping and mourning (v. 11), fear and torment (v. 15), and mourning and crying (v. 19). The same arrogant Babylonian whore who sits as a queen and says, "I am no widow, and mourning I shall never see" (v. 7), now comes crashing down, fallen, fallen, in a single day, in a single hour. Death and mourning and famine (v. 8) will replace her riches, power, and luxurious living (vv. 3, 7, 9, 12-16, 19). While sinners mourn, saints rejoice (v. 20) over fallen Babylon (vv. 22-23). The same system that killed the prophets and the saints (v. 24) has itself now been destroyed. Those who were slain in the world by the world rejected Babylon and all it had to offer, unlike Judas, Demas, and Laodicea's church.

CHAPTER NINETEEN

After This

Chapter nineteen starts with the words 'after this' supporting the book's chronological order and structure of the prophecy. As stated in my book, 'The Revelation The Revival,' the Greek word for 'after this' is meta tauta. Meta tauta is used seven times within the book of Revelation (1:19, 4:1, 7:1, 9, 15:5, 18:1, and 19:1). The use of meta tauta in chapter four marks the distinguishing point between the church age and Tribulation. Revelation (4:1) begins with meta tauta, indicating the completion of "what is" and the commencement of 'what is to come.' Daniel likewise uses meta tauta when describing the four beasts in Daniel's book (Dan. 7:6a, 7a), predictive of the then-coming and conquering Roman Empire.

Daniel's prophecy was fulfiled in part yet consists of three: The first is the original Roman Empire; the second (ten horns) will be the revived Roman Empire, which is fulfilled during the first half of the Tribulation period; and the Antichrist fulfils the third midway through the Tribulation, where he takes the dominant role as the world leader. The difference between John's vision to that of Daniel's is where meta tauta is used seven times (heptadically) to introduce something positive. Five of the seven times refer to the saints (Rev. 4:1; 7:1, 9; 15:5; 19:1), and three speak of the saints in heaven during the Tribulation period (Rev. 4:1; 7:9; 19:1). Again, the importance of identifying the prophetic structure of the book of Revelation enables the reader to interpret its purpose and meaning properly and to understand the biblical calendar of events.

The seven churches fall within the initial use of meta tauta (Rev. 1:19) as, in part, 'things to come'. Although each church mentioned was a literal church at the time of John's writing, there were many more. Sixty-three years after Pentecost, over one hundred churches existed. These include the church of Jerusalem, Antioch, Colossae, Philippi, Galatia, Iconium, Lystra, Derbe, Miletus, Hierapolis, and Troas, to list just a few. As for the literal seven churches addressed in the book of Revelation, the letters address serious problems of every church and extend to all churches collectively throughout every century.

Therefore, the seven churches are prophetic of the church age, pointing to false worship and the increasing problem of false worship nearing Christ's return. If the letters to the seven churches were in any other order, the claim of being a prophetic blueprint for the church age would not be valid; but because they are presented in the exact order they are, it can only be true. The order as outlined is noted and agreed to by various serious scholars of eschatology:

- Ephesus, the Apostolic Church (AD 30–100).
- Smyrna, Roman Persecution (AD 100–313).
- Pergamum, Age of Constantine (AD 313–600).
- Thyatira, Dark Ages (AD 600–1517).
- Sardis, Reformation (AD 1517–1648).
- Philadelphia, Missionary Movement (AD 1649–1900).
- Laodicea, Apostasy (AD 1900–present-day).

Again, the church age ends when the bride of Christ is raptured (4:1). The removal of the church releases the Antichrist (2 Thess. 2), who is also revealed as the one successfully initiating the signing of the Middle East Peace Treaty (Dan 7:24, Isa. 28:15, 18). The Middle East Peace Treaty will trigger the Tribulation.

Following the church's removal (Rev. 4:1), Revelation chapter seven is the third time we see the words 'after this' (7:1), with the sealing of the 144,000 witnesses who bring about the greatest revival known to man, during the Tribulation. The fourth time 'after this' is used is to describe the great multitude coming to faith in Jesus through the testimony of the 144,000 Jews (7:9). Those coming to faith in Jesus during the Tribulation will be mostly slain (7:13-14, 12:11, 13:15, 14:13), and they will be the same singing the song of Moses from heaven (15:3). The fifth use of 'after this' follows the reference to the slain saints singing Moses' song in heaven (15:5), referring to God's judgement on those who killed the Tribulation saints.

Revelation chapter eighteen is the same event described in chapter fifteen, unpacked further in chapter sixteen, seen explicitly through the seventh bowl judgement. The seventh bowl judgement is the same event described in chapter eighteen, and it is the sixth time we see the phrase 'after this' (18:1). After God's wrath is finished (15:1, 7) and done (16:17), the tribulation period is complete. 'After this' (19:1), THEN, Jesus returns to the earth to set up His kingdom (1:6, 5:10, 11:15, 19:6). Chapter nineteen is the last and seventh time the phrase 'after this' is used.

Following the words 'after this,' the next that should catch our attention is 'great multitude' (19:1, 6). Twice John gives reference to the great multitude, describing two separate groups. The first refers to those saved, through martyrdom, out of the Tribulation (6:9-11, 713-14, 13:15, 14:12-13, 17:6). The second reference refers to the collective saints and or friends of the bride, who are announcing and celebrating the bride's wedding (the church) to Christ. While many confuse the bride of Christ and the wedding guests as the same, they are not. The bride and the wedding guests will be addressed in the next section, under the heading of 'The Marriage Supper of the Lamb.' But, for now, it is worth noting the blessing in verse nine, "Blessed are those who are invited to the marriage supper of the Lamb." Like the words 'After this,' there are seven blessings in the book of Revelation (1:3, 14:13, 16:15, 19;9, 20:6, 22:7, 14). The blessings refer to those who obey and endure, who stay awake and remain pure, and to those (alone) who keep the words of Jesus. Nothing less than absolute dedication and devotion to Jesus will qualify for the blessings. Without the endorsement, none will be invited to the marriage supper of the Lamb.

Following the wedding and the marriage feast, there is more cause to celebrate, a celebration of victory. Throughout the book of Revelation, there are fourteen shouts of praise to God led by saints, angels, the twenty-four elders, and/or the four living creatures (4:8, 11; 5:9–10, 12–13; 7:10, 12; 11:16–18; 15:3–4; 16:5–7; 19:1–4, 6–8). Each occasion points to Jesus' return, His rule, and reign singing hallelujah, meaning, 'praise Yah' (Yahweh). Yahweh is a name for God, meaning, 'He brings into existence whatever exists'. The word 'hallelujah' is only seen four times in the NT, and all four times are found in Revelation, chapter nineteen (vv. 1, 3, 4, 6). The shouts of hallelujah are directed at the one true and Creator God. The angel flying overhead proclaiming the eternal gospel referenced the one and only Creator God by saying, "Fear God, give Him glory, and worship Him (alone) who made heaven and earth and the sea the spring water" (14:7). Another angel announced something similar in chapter ten (v. 6).

Simply said, God is the Creator of all things, and nothing in existence exists without Him. God has absolute power and authority over everything, including the Tribulation. Isaiah narrows in on the same, stating God is the

Creator, who created humanity (43:1), the nations (43:15), the earth and the heavens (45:12, 18), light, darkness, wellbeing, and calamity (45:7), forming all things for Himself (43:21). Simply put, God is God, and there is no other God (43:10-11). He is the first and the last; besides Him, there is no other god (44:6, 8, 45:5, 14b, 18, 21, 22, 46:9, 47:10b, 48:12)

Following the proclamations of God's absolute sovereignty over all of His creation (including Satan, demons, the Antichrist, the false prophet, and their followers), chapter nineteen reveals that God will execute justice with true and eternal judgements (vv. 2-3). As shown in chapter nineteen, Jesus will return and judge this world, and then He will set up His kingdom.

Today, many confuse the church age with the kingdom age, but the book of Revelation clarifies, the coming kingdom (Matt. 6:10) will come when Jesus returns (1:6, 5:10, 11:15, 19:6). Currently, Satan is the god (2 Cor. 4:4) and the ruler of this world (Jn. 14:30). Soon, however, he will be cast down to the earth (Rev. 12:12-13), having only three and a half years left before Jesus returns (12:6). When Jesus returns, Satan is then cast into the bottomless pit for one thousand years (20:1-3). After one thousand years, he will be released for a short time and then cast into the lake of fire for all eternity (20:7-10).

Now that the end is in sight, alongside the great multitude (vv. 1, 6), the twenty-four elders and the four living creatures (v. 4), shout hallelujah, with another voice coming from the throne, saying, "Praise God all you servants, you who fear Him small and great" (v. 5). Not only are they all praising God over His victory through true and just judgements, but they also celebrate the marriage of the Lamb and His bride, who has made herself ready (v. 7). Due to the bride's faithfulness and her righteous deeds, she is now clothed in fine linen. The words 'fine linen' are found four times in the book of Revelation (18:12, 16, 19:8, 14). In chapter eighteen, the reference to fine linen refers to the merchants who rejected God for material wealth, somewhat like Laodicea's church. However, the connection to fine linen in chapter nineteen relates to the saints, who rejected worldly wealth for God. Fine linen for the saints refers to salvation and purity (2 Cor. 11:2), reserved alone for the conquering bride of Christ (Rev. 3:4-5).

In sum, unless the believer conquers this world, they will have no part with Christ. The church is told to conquer this world seven times throughout the letters (2:7, 11, 17, 26, 3:5, 12, 21). Contrary to the false teachings of dominionism, or reconstructionism 'kingdom now' theology, biblical conquering does not refer to dominating this world by conquering the supposed seven mountains. The seven mountains, according to dominionism are:

1. Religion
2. Family
3. Education
4. Government
5. Media
6. Arts and Entertainment, and
7. Business

As mentioned earlier, dominionists are false teachers, looking back, trying to recreate what was lost in the garden of Eden, rather than looking forward to what Jesus is going to re-establish on His return.

In sum, victory and conquering are the themes of Revelation, in chapter nineteen, where Jesus, and His spotless bride, dressed in white linen (3:4, 4:4, 19:14), return to earth to set up His kingdom. Jesus returns to earth to set up His kingdom 'after this,' referring to the church age, followed by the tribulation. Halleluiah!

The Marriage Supper of the Lamb (vv. 6-9)

When considering the chiastic structure of the book of Revelation to pinpoint the 'big idea' in a single verse, chapter twelve, verse twelve is at the heart of the chiasmus. Chapter twelve, verse twelve, draws our attention to Satan being 'cast out.' When the book is considered more holistically, still within the chiastic structure, chapters eleven, (v. 19) to fourteen (v. 20) narrows in on Satan's demonstration of power (11:19-13:18) versus God's demonstrations of power (14:1-20). Again, chapter twelve identifies Satan as the loser and God as the winner of the age-old cosmic battle. When considering chapter nineteen's chiastic structure, through to chapter twenty-one, we see something of the same; Revelation chapter twenty (vv. 1-7) marks the point and purpose contrasting the millennial reign of Christ and the saints versus the binding of Satan. Once again, Satan loses, and God wins. The chiastic structure of chapter nineteen to twenty-one is as below:

A. 19:1-10 The Marriage Supper
B. 19:11-16 Jesus Appears to Judge the Nations
C. 19:17-21 Jesus Defeats His Enemies
D. 20:1-7 **The Reign of Christ and Defeat of Satan**
C. 20:8-10 Defeat of God's Enemies
B. 20:11-15 Jesus Appears to Judge the Wicked
A. 21:1-8 Consummation of the Marriage

Note that the marriage supper and the marriage's consummations are the starting and finishing points of the chiastic structure. The fourth hallelujah of the book of Revelation, chapter nineteen accompanies the announcement of Christ's reign (v. 6) and the marriage supper of the Lamb (v. 7) to the bride (the church) who has made herself ready (v. 7). Due to her readiness, she is clothed with fine linen, representing her righteous deeds (v. 8). Following the proclamation of the great multitude (v. 6), an angel says, "Blessed are those who are invited to the marriage supper of the Lamb" (v. 9). The wedding ceremony and the Lamb's marriage supper will be the focus of the remainder of this section.

Regarding the marriage supper of the Lamb, Matthew chapter twenty-five should be taken into consideration. Still, before we go there, it is necessary to have a Jewish perspective of a traditional marriage ceremony. A standard Jewish wedding consist of four steps:

1. The arrangement of payment
2. Upon the father's direction, the son is sent for the bride
3. The son returns with the bride, who undergoes a ritual cleansing
4. The marriage feast lasts for seven days

It is important to note, there is a distinction between the wedding ceremony and the marriage feast. Not all who attend the wedding feast are included in the ceremony.

The same pattern of a Jewish marriage applies to the church, the bride of Christ. First, Jesus makes the payment for His bride through the cross (1 Cor. 7:23). Second, The Father-God sends Jesus for His bride (the Church), returning to a place provided in heaven for her (Jn. 14:1-3). The Father-God will send Jesus at a time of His choosing (Matt. 24:36, 44, 1 Cor. 15:50-58, 1 Thess. 4:13-18). When He returns with His raptured bride, the cleansing ceremony occurs, which is the believers' judgment (Rom. 14:10-12, 1 Cor. 3:10-15, 2 Cor. 5:10). During the cleansing ceremony, the believer is tested by fire (1 Cor. 3:13, 1 Pet. 1:7) and then fitted with white garments (Rev. 3:4, 5, 18, 4:4, 7:9, 19:8). The believer is fitted with a white garment in preparation for the marriage, which takes place in heaven (19:6-9). The fourth step of the wedding takes place on earth when Jesus returns with His bride (now wife), the church. When Jesus returns to the earth with His bride, following the judgement, the marriage supper begins. Matthew, chapters twenty two (vv. 1-14) and twenty-five (vv. 1-13) should be considered at this point.

Again, the church is the bride of Christ, which distinguishes her apart from the friends of the bride and the wedding feast's guests; the bride, the friends of the bride, and the guests are not the same. The friends will be made up of the OT saints (Jn. 3:29), and the guests will be the virgin Jews (Matt. 25:4, Rev. 14:4), and the Tribulation saints (Rev. 7:9, 13-16).

If the friends of the bride and the marriage feast guests are made up of the OT saints, the virgin Jews, and the Tribulation saints, then only those who have died as believers in Christ under the new covenant and those raptured will qualify as the bride of Christ. Said another way, many 'believers' left behind to endure the Tribulation, who could have qualified to be the bride, never will be. Unless they repent and remain during the tribulation, neither will they be invited to the marriage feast. Matthew, chapter twenty-two (vv. 1-14), makes it clear, only those clothed with the wedding garment will qualify, although many will be called, few are chosen (v. 14).

During the tribulation, many will exchange their filthy rags (Isa. 64:6, cf. Rev. 3:4) of self-righteousness for God's righteousness (2 Cor. 5:21), and in doing so will wash their robes, made white in the blood of the Lamb (Rev. 7:14, cf. 12:11). These will be the blessed ones invited to the wedding feast (19:9) and the blessed ones who have the right to eat from the tree of life (22:14).

The tree of life is mentioned four times in the book of Revelation (2:7, 22:2, 14, 19). The first was in the letter to the church of Ephesus, which was called to repent or lose their candlestick (2:5). On the condition that they repent, they will be granted access to the tree of life (v. 7). If they do not repent, they will not be granted access; therefore, they will not enter the paradise of God (v. 7). The paradise of God is where the marriage supper will take place. Revelation, chapter two describes the paradise of God, where the tree of life is located. The mention of the candlestick in the letter to the church of Ephesus is also worth noting, for, without it, none will access paradise. Matthew, chapter twenty-five should be considered regarding the candlestick.

In Matthew, chapter twenty-five (vv. 1-12), Jesus tells the story of the ten virgins, who also had candlesticks (lanterns) filled, or not filled, with oil. Those failing to keep their lamps filled were shut out of the marriage supper (v. 11). They started in the same way as the rest who entered in, having the same opportunity but, they did not remain in the same way, therefore, missed out. Jesus closed this story with the words, 'Watch, therefore, for you know neither the day nor the hour (v. 13). In other words, the bride must keep watch and be prepared. Luke records something similar in chapter 21 of his book (vv. 34-36), saying, "Watch yourselves lest your hearts be weighed down with dissipation (overindulgence) and drunkenness and care of this life, and that day comes upon you suddenly like a trap" (v. 34). The remaining verse says to "stay awake at all times, praying that you have the strength to escape all things that are going to take place" (v. 36). Verse thirty-five tells us the things that are going to take place will affect the whole world. Jesus says something similar to the church of Philadelphia (Rev. 3:10). To understand the parables properly, one needs to understand a Jewish wedding, more specifically, a Galilean wedding. When you compare a Galilean wedding to Jesus returning for His bride (the church), they are an exact fit.

Remember, every story Jesus told was culturally relevant for His hearer, based on the life and location He and they lived. Jesus was a Galilean, living in Galilee for the best part of His ministry, drawing from the Galilean culture when talking in parables. When talking about the marriage supper, He based His teachings on a Galilean wedding, which was even unique within Jewish culture. For a more in-depth study of the above mentioned four steps of the Jewish wedding, there are seven specific steps to a Galilean marriage, as follows:

1. An agreeable price must be paid for the bride to be. For the bride of Christ, the shedding of Jesus' blood was the price paid.
2. The bride must accept the groom's marriage proposal, in full agreement with the terms and conditions, and by drinking from the cup of joy. At this point, the bride has total authority whether she accepts or rejects the groom. If she rejects, she pushes the cup away. If she accepts, and drinks, then the groom also drinks from the cup, signalling the covenant. Neither the groom nor the bride drinks again until they are reunited. Jesus touched on steps one and two at the Last Supper (Matt. 26:26-29).
3. After drinking from the cup of joy, the groom departs, with a promise to return for his bride at a time only known by the father. While away, the groom prepares a place for his bride in his father's house. While the groom is away, the bride also has responsibilities. She has to prepare herself for the groom's return. She has to make sure she has her wedding dress on; she must remain faithful, and awake, she must have oil, and be occupying. The groom will return on a day and in an hour unknown to her, although one year is the general timeframe.

4. Once all the preparations are made, the son returns for his bride on the day of the father's say-so. "Go get your bride, son!" The wedding feast is prepared, and the bride is waiting, looking, loving, and living for her groom.
5. On the father's say-so, the son blows the shofar, waking the wedding party and any others waiting and watching for the special day. The wedding party joins the groom, sounding the shofar repeatedly as he goes to fetch his bride. For those not ready, the son will pass them by like a thief in the night. The reference to the 'thief in the night' is significant as the groom sets off to collect his bride in the middle of the night when most are sleeping. The need for oil-filled lanterns also fits in with this understanding. The groom comes in the middle of the night; however, the bride must be dressed and ready, even sleeping in her wedding dress.
6. Once the groom arrives at the bride's house, she greets the groom by stepping into a chair lifted up and carried to the father's house. This is called 'flying the bride to the father's house.' The bride is caught up in the air (rapture). All that is required is that she be ready, waiting, watching. After the bride has been flown to the father's house, the wedding feast begins, and the bride and groom share a cup of joy once more.
7. Those who are not ready for the day and hour will be shut out of the wedding feast that lasts for seven days, paralleling the seven-year Tribulation. They are shut out and left behind. As for those who could have partaken in the cup of joy, they will now partake of the cup of suffering, which is the wrath of God being poured out during the Tribulation. Remember, believers are not destined for the wrath of God (1 Thess. 1:10, 5:9, Rev. 3:10). Isaiah (26) prophecies the same, making a clear distinction between those

removed and those left behind. God's purpose in the judgements (tribulation) for those left behind is that they would find/learn righteousness through favour (v. 9b-10). God's favour during the Tribulation is evident by offering the left behind an opportunity to repent that they can be counted among the 'blessed' that will be invited to the marriage supper of the Lamb.

In sum, the pattern of the Galilean wedding mirrors that of pre-Tribulation theology. Only those who have either died in Christ under the new covenant or are raptured can be the bride of Christ. If you are left behind, and then come to faith through repentance during the tribulation, you can never be the bride but instead guests of the marriage supper.

Following the wedding ceremony in heaven, the marriage supper occurs on the earth, where wedding guests then have an opportunity to participate. The wedding ceremony takes place in heaven while the whole earth goes through the Tribulation for seven years. The marriage supper takes place after the judgement of this world and before the establishment of the millennial kingdom. That being the case, I would strongly argue that only those attending the marriage supper will enter into the millennial kingdom.

The marriage supper and the marriage's consummations are the starting and finishing points of Revelation, chapters nineteen to twenty-one's chiastic structure. The overall story throughout these chapters, the book of Revelation, and the entire Bible is one of victory, God wins, and Satan loses. Hallelujah!

CHAPTER NINETEEN

Part Two (vv. 11-21) Jesus Returns, Satan Loses, and God Wins

As stated previously, the single 'big idea' of the book of Revelation is that Satan loses, which means God wins. The big idea of Satan losing and God winning revolves around worship. Those that worship God alone are on the winning side. Those guilty of false worship, compromised or corrupt worship, lukewarm worship, or any other form of worship will be judged; first, through the tribulation and secondly, failing to repent during the trial, they will be judged before the great white throne (Rev. 20:11-15). The fact is, the entire book of Revelation could be summed up with just one word, 'Worship.' The seven churches were addressed over the single issue of worship, likewise, are those going through the tribulation for failing to worship God, alone. Even John, the revelator, fails by falling down, worshipping an angel. Twice he was rebuked by an angel for doing this (19:10, 22:8), demonstrating how easily we can be deceived, therefore the need to be extra vigilant. Remember, when Jesus was asked what the signs of His return would be, He indicated false teachers and teachings would be the number one sign of the end times (Matt. 24:5, 11, 23-26). False teachers and false teachings are addressed in every N.T. book, except for Philemon. Every prophet of the O.T., major and minor, likewise focuses on false teachers and false teachings, which is the very thing Jesus is coming back to judge (2 Pet. 2). Chapter nineteen of the book of Revelation provides detailed insight of what Christ returning to judge false worship and false worshipers looks like, with the opening scene of heaven opening up.

Heaven opened, revealing Jesus (19:1), the Lamb of God (cf. 6:12-17). Previously mentioned, the return of Jesus is the seventh trumpet (11:15-19), which is the third woe (8:13). The seventh trumpet is the same as the seventh bowl judgement (16:17-21). Following the completion of the wedding ceremony in heaven, lasting seven years, Jesus returns to the earth with His bride, the church. The second coming of Christ is a prominent doctrine in Scripture (Ps. 2:1–9; 24:7–10; 96:10–13; 110; Isa. 9:6–7; Jer. 23:1–8; Ezek. 37:15–28; Dan. 2:44–45; 7:13–14; Hos. 3:4–5; Amos 9:11–15; Mic, 4:7; Zech. 2:10–12; 12; 14:1–9; Matt. 19:28; 24:27–31; 25:6, 31–46; Mk. 13:24–27; Lk. 12:35–40; 17:24–37; 18:8; 21:25–28; Acts 1:10–11; 15:16–18; Rom. 11:25–27; 2 Thess. 2:8; 2 Pet. 3:3–4; Jude 14–15; Rev. 1:7–8; 2:25–28; 16:15; 22:20).

When taking the vast amount of supporting verses pointing to the return of Christ, anything other than pre-millennial theology simply does not work. In the same way, Jesus appeared the first time, He will reappear the second time; physically, and literally. Anyone suggesting the prophecy foretold in the book of Revelation was fulfilled in 70 A.D. overlooks the obvious – Jesus is not yet ruling and reigning on the earth, and neither are we.

Further to the return of Christ, the armies in heaven follow Him to the earth (v. 14), which includes the raptured church. Post-Tribulationists state the church is delivered at the end of the seven-year event; however, there is nothing in chapters nineteen to twenty supporting that view. Furthermore, post-Tribulationists confuse the church for Israel, thereby are guilty of adopting and promoting replacement theology. Replacement theology is a deceptive doctrine of demons. On the other hand, mid-Tribulationists claim the church will be raptured at the mid-way point of the Tribulation, stating the seal and trumpet judgements are not the same as the bowl judgements and that the church will be removed before the bowl judgements.

As previously illustrated, the three sets of judgements are the same, retold three times. Post-trib and mid-trib *theology* (ideology) lack biblical support, as well as customary and chronological alignment. The original first century position of pre-Tribulation theology not only mirrors a customary Jewish wedding ceremony (as explained in the previous section), it also works chronologically. Further to the pre-Tribulation position mirroring a Jewish wedding, the following seven reasons support and confirm that the church will not take part in the seven-year ordeal:

1. The church meets Jesus in the air, not on the ground (1 Thess. 4:17)
2. The church is not appointed to wrath (Rom. 5:9, 1 Thess. 1:10, 5:9).
3. The church is removed before the Tribulation commences (Rev. 3:10, 4:1)
4. Revelation (19:7-9) portrays the church as pure before Christ returns.
5. Christ's judgment seat must previously occur, where believers are judged and rewarded according to their works before Jesus returns (2 Cor. 5:9-11).

6. The marriage supper of the Lamb takes place before Christ returns (Rev. 19:7-10), requiring the church to be purified ('in white garments').
7. There is the need for non-glorified saints to populate the millennial kingdom, to account for death (Isa. 65:20) and apostasy (Rev. 20:7-9) in the millennium. But if all believers are raptured and glorified at the end of the Tribulation, and all unbelievers are killed at the return of Christ (Rev. 19:17-21), then there is none left to enter the millennium in non-glorified bodies.

Adding to the above-mentioned, verse eleven reveals Jesus riding a white house, returning to judge and make war. While some have confused the white horse rider of chapter six (v. 2) to be Christ, he is the Antichrist. The Antichrist cannot be revealed until after the church has been removed (2 Thess. 2:7-8). If either mid or post-trib positions were correct, the Antichrist would be announced at either the halfway point of the Tribulation, having only three and a half years, or at the end, having only minutes before Jesus kills him (v. 8).

However, scripture reveals the Antichrist will be given power for seven years (Dan. 7:24-27, Rev. 11:2, 11, 13:5). Going by the above theory, the order is exact, the church is removed, the Antichrist is revealed, and the Tribulation commences. Seven years later, Jesus returns, and the Antichrist is defeated. The return of Christ is the focus of chapter nineteen.

John describes Jesus as Faithful and True, the Word of God, having eyes like a flame of fire, wearing many diadems, and clothed in a robe dipped in blood (vv. 11-13). Chapter nineteen's description of Jesus should be compared to chapter one. This same imagery was presented to each of the seven churches addressed in chapters two and three. The words Faithful and True are in the introduction to the letter to the church of Laodicea - a very fitting introduction due to the worship of this lukewarm church being anything but faithful and true. Chapter one, verse twelve, says Jesus has eyes like the flame of fire, which was also in the introduction to the church of Thyatira, the corrupt church (2:18). If Thyatira's church did not repent, they would be cast into the great Tribulation (2:22), similar to the church of Sardis, which would be left behind due to being asleep (3:2). Because Sardis was asleep spiritually, albeit having a reputation of being alive (3:1), Jesus would come as a thief in the night (3:3, cf. Matt 24:43, 1 Thess. 5:2, 2 Pet. 3:10, Rev. 16:15), leaving them behind to face the tribulation. The church of Ephesus would find themselves in the same predicament, having no lampstand, therefore no oil, thus they would be 'shut out' of the wedding ceremony (cf. Matt 25:10) and consequently left behind. Worst of all is the church of Laodicea, which had nothing good going for it; this church is in danger of being vomited out of Jesus' mouth, therefore vomited into the great tribulation (3:16).

While one church is vomited out of Jesus' mouth, another is in danger of being slain by the sword that comes out of His mouth (3:16). The image of Jesus with a sword coming out of His mouth was presented to Pergamum's church. Jesus is the one with the sharp two-edged sword (2:12), which can either save or slay. Unless this compromising church repents, Jesus will war against her with the sword of His mouth (2:16).

The purpose of chapters one, two, and three, and chapter nineteen's introduction of Jesus is to reintroduce Him to the churches. That is, reintroduce them to the real and returning Jesus, due to seventy percent of them having replaced the biblical Jesus with another, just like today (2 Cor. 11:4, cf. Gal. 1:8-12). The biblical and returning Jesus is the King of kings and the Lord of lords (1 Tim. 6:5, Rev. 17:14, 19:16). Now, and up until the close of the Tribulation, Satan is the ruler (Jn. 12:31) and god of this world (2 Cor. 4:4). During the Tribulation, Satan and his Antichrist will present as the ruling king, wearing (diadems) crowns (12:3, 13:1); however, when Jesus returns, He will be wearing many diadems, which translates, royal headband (19:12). The returning, ruling King (Jesus) is very different to the one presented from most pulpits today; returning to strike the nations with the sword of His mouth, to rule over them with an iron rod, and to tread the winepress of the fury of God (19:15, 14:19, 20).

Again, remember the warning given to the church of Pergamum, that was guilty of compromising God's word. They were told to repent or else Jesus would fight against them with the sword of His mouth (2:16). Chapter nineteen reveals what it would look like with Jesus fighting against you with the sword of His mouth! Jesus was warning the church, repent, or else!

Jesus is still warning the church today, in the same way. The 'or else' is graphically illustrated in verses seventeen to twenty-one of chapter nineteen, resulting in Jesus' robe being dipped in blood (19:13; cf. Isa. 63:2–3; Rev. 14:20). Because false worshipers failed to Fear God and Worship Him (14:7), alone, by trusting in Christ and His finished work, alone, now instead of being saved by His shed blood, alone (1:5, 5:9, 7:14, 12:11), their own blood will be required of them (14:20, 19:13, 21). Only those who trust in Christ, conquer, and are dressed in white robes and fine linen (3:4, 4:4, 7:9, 19:14), thereby avoiding the judgement, and instead, rule and reign with Jesus (12:5, 19:15) in the millennium. The promise of ruling and reigning was given only to the weak and poor churches of Smyrna and Philadelphia, and a faithful few members of Thyatira's corrupt church (2:24-28), and a few more from the dead and soiled church of Sardis (3:4). The rest of the addressed seven churches and the majority of the members of Thyatira's church were in danger of being thrown into the great Tribulation (2:22).

For summarization, refer to the grid below showing the introduction of Jesus in chapter one, alongside the image of Jesus presented to the churches and the imagery of the returning Christ.

Introduction, chapter 1	The churches, chapters 2 & 3	Return of Christ, chapter 19
Holding seven stars and seven lampstands	Ephesus and Sardis: Holding seven stars, lampstand (Eph)	(cf. 22:6, 22:13)
First born of the dead	Smyrna: Who died and came to life	The Lord God Almighty (lives and) reigns
Before His throne	Laodicea: Sit with Me on My throne	Seated on the throne
Faithful Witness	Philadelphia and Laodicea: The True One, Faithful and True Witness	The Word of God, Faithful and True
Eyes like fire	Thyatira: Eyes like flames of fire	Eyes like fire
Voice like roar of many waters	Laodicea: Hears My voice	Voice like roar of many waters, loud voice
Sharpe two-edge sword	Pergamum: Sharpe two-edged sword	Sharp sword
Long (white) robe, (priestly garment)	Sardis and Laodicea: White garment	White linen
The Almighty	Thyatira: Rod of iron	The Almighty reigns, Rule with an iron rod

Remember, so frightening was the image of Jesus that John fell as a man dead (1:9). In other words, he was terrified to death. The same imagery seen in chapter one was represented to the churches to produce godly fear (2:23), which was evidently lacking then, as it is today, replaced by false worship. Once more, the same imagery is seen again with the return of Christ (chapter 19). So, the returning Christ is not the Jesus most worship today, having replaced Him with 'another' Jesus by preaching a 'different' gospel through a 'different' (demonic) spirit (2 Cor. 11:4). The 'other' Jesus being preached today is conditioning hearers for the coming false-Christ, who is the Antichrist. Jesus will deal with the counterfeit Christ and those who follow him, at Armageddon's battle (16:16, 19:19).

Armageddon's battle (16:12-16) occurs at Megiddo, in Israel; contrary to the term, 'battle', this event is no battle at all, but rather a slaughter. Millions of deceived followers of the Antichrist follow him to make war against Christ (v. 19, cf. 16:14-16, 17:14, Ps. 2:2). However, they are effortlessly struck down, lying dead in the plains of Megiddo. From kings and captains to commoners, free and slave, small and great, their slain and lifeless bodies feed the birds flying overhead (19:17-18, 21, cf. Rev. 6:15, 16:16, Matt. 24:28, Ezek. 39:4, 17-20).

At the battle of Armageddon, none will escape the sword of Christ, including the Antichrist, the false prophet (19:20, 20:10, Dan. 7:11), and everyone else who has followed them (19:21, 17:14, cf. 2 Thess. 2:8, Isa. 11:4). Instead of being among the blessed invited to the Lamb's marriage supper (19:9), the wicked are the great supper of God (19:17). Following the slaughter, the Antichrist and the false prophet are thrown alive into the lake of fire (v. 20).

Notice that verse twenty also mentions the Image given life, causing humanity to worship the beast and receive his mark (13:14-16), yet says nothing of the Image being eternally judged. In chapter thirteen, I stated the Image could be a clone, being the Antichrist's literal Image, yet inhabited by a powerful demon, thus given life. If that is the case, it would explain why it is not mentioned alongside the Antichrist and the false prophet when cast alive into the lake of fire. The Image does not have a soul; therefore, it does not go into eternal punishment, but rather it is destroyed. The soul cannot be destroyed; thus, the wicked must be eternally imprisoned.

Contrary to liberal theology promoting instant annihilation, hell is eternal; it is never-ending and everlasting. It is the place where the wicked are tormented, finding no rest, day and night, forever and ever (14:9-11, 19:20-21, 20:10, 14). Those slain by the sword that came from the mouth of Jesus (v. 21) are held in hades, awaiting judgement, set to take place in one thousand years from now, following the release and rebounding of Satan (20:7, 11-14). Following the great white throne of judgement, the rebels and Satan join the Antichrist and the false prophet in the lake of fire. The Antichrist and the false prophet have already been in the lake of fire for one thousand years and have not one less day to stay.

That fact alone debunks the idea that the judgement of the wicked is temporary suffering. The great white throne of judgment follows a time of imprisonment in hades, where the unjust will be resurrected and then eternally cast into the lake of fire. The great white throne judgement will be covered in part three of chapter twenty.

In sum, Jesus' return will be equally the saint's best day on earth as it will be the sinner's worst. Contrary to preterist theology claiming the book of Revelation was fulfiled in 70 A.D., it is still to be fulfiled and will be in the not-so-distant future. If the prophecy was fulfiled in 70 A.D., the obvious questions in need of answering are:

1. Where is Jesus, considering every eye will see Him?
2. When were the nations judged?
3. When did the marriage supper of the Lamb take place?
4. From where is Jesus ruling and reigning on the earth right now?
5. If the Antichrist and the false prophet were judged, who were they?

6. If Satan was cast into the pit, and Jesus is now ruling and reigning, why is there still so much evil in the world, and increasing, including saints being martyred?
7. How are any of the millennial passages of scripture being fulfilled today?

Simply put, if Jesus is ruling and reigning on the earth right now, and the devil is in the pit, then Jesus' rod of iron is either too short or too soft, and the devil's chain is way too long. On the contrary, Jesus will soon rule and reign on His return, and Satan, who is the current god, and ruler of this world, will be cast into the pit for one thousand years. The defeat of Satan will be discussed in the following section.

CHAPTER TWENTY

(vv. 1-6)
One Thousand Years

Following the capture of the false prophet and the Antichrist (19:20), Satan is captured and bound for one thousand years (20:2) and then thrown into the bottomless pit until one thousand years were ended (v. 3). Now that the ruler (Jn. 12:31), prince (Jn. 14:30), and god (2 Cor. 4:4) of this world has been removed and replaced by the true King, Jesus, the saints begin their rule and reign on the earth, under the kingship of Christ (Rev. 1:6, 5:10, 11:15).

The saints return to the earth with Jesus after the Tribulation (Rev. 19:14). Until then, anyone truly following Christ can expect tribulation in this world (Jn. 15:20, 16:33, Rev. 1:9, 2:10). We are destined for tribulation (1 Thess. 3:3, 2 Tim 3:12), and it is through many tribulations that we must enter the kingdom of God (Acts 14:22) on the condition we endure (Rom. 5:3-4, Rev. 2:10). If we do not suffer with Christ, we will not reign with Him (Matt. 10:38, Rom. 8:17, 2 Thess. 1:5, 2 Tim. 2:11-13). When Christ returns, we shall be delivered from the present sufferings (1 Pet. 5:6-11). Not just us, but the entire planet also (Rom. 8:18-24).

The doctrine of suffering is a forgotten fundamental doctrine, whereas most now are surprised by it, as were some confused believers in the first century (1 Pet. 4:12). Test and trials are necessary, producing the genuineness of our faith (1 Pet. 1:7); therefore we should rejoice in it. It produces endurance (Rom. 5:3-5), and patience, establishing our hearts on the coming of our Lord (Jam. 5:7-8). So much more could be said about the doctrine of suffering, but in sum, the fact that believers will and do suffer in this world is evidence enough. We are not ruling and reigning in it; not right now anyway.

Under the current world ruler (Satan), this world is not our home (Heb. 13:14); while we are in it, we are not of it (Jn. 15;19, 17:14-16). We are passing through it (1 Chron. 29:15, 1 Pet. 2:11), for our citizenship is in heaven (Phil. 3:20), a better and heavenly country (Heb. 11:16). Anyone caught up with this world or who is loved by it (cf. Jn. 15:18, 1 Jn. 2:15, 3:13) is evidently of it and therefore, has no part in the next (Jn. 8:22-24, 1 Jn. 2:15-17, cf. Rev. 18).

Again, as previously mentioned, the danger of loving this world is the focus and error of dominionism, also known as seven mountains, kingdom now, and reconstruction theology. Dominionism is a false teaching that many biblically illiterate charismatics subscribe to, which is promoted primarily by the New Apostolic Reformation (NAR). The NAR is a new movement of confused charismatics that cannot distinguish between Israel and the church; neither do they understand Bible prophecy, or dispensationalism. NAR leaders are mostly without formal evangelical theological training and education, better known for editing the Bible, rather than their exegesis. They edit the Bible by taking one verse out of context, joining it to another. They literally 'lift' verses by 'copying and pasting' them from one section of scripture to another, which is the only way they can form and support their erroneous doctrines, at best: doctrines of demons in the worst case.

Contrary to the false teaching that believers are to rule and reign in this life, verse four tells us that the persecuted believers (cf. Matt. 24:9-13, cf. Matt. 23:34-25, Rev. 2:10, 6:9-11, 7:13-14, 12:11, 13:10, 15, 14:13) will reign with Jesus when He returns (Rev. 1:6, 5:10, 11:15-16). Therefore, the only thing a true convert should expect to be ruling and reigning over right now, in this life, is sin (Rom 5:17).

Another problem with the kingdom now theology is their amillennial eschatological position. Amillennialism teaches that Jesus bound Satan at His first appearance and that Satan has been bound ever since. Charismatics apply Satan being put to open shame (Col. 2:15), defeated and under our feet to mean, believers are now ruling and reigning on the earth (Rom. 16:20). As stated in the last section of this work, if the charismatics interpretation is correct, and Satan is currently bound, then his chain is too long! Therefore, the correct interpretation is that Satan has been disarmed - having no claim over true believers' souls (cf. 1 Cor. 15:55). And soon (Rom. 20:16), Satan will be judged, which takes place when Jesus returns. Until then, he will continue to cause divisions and create obstacles for believers (Rom. 16:17), through others sown among us teaching false doctrines, which should be avoided (16:18).

Simply put, Satan is very active in the world and church today. Satan will continue to exert great power against the world and against Christians (Acts 5:3; 1 Cor. 5:5; 7:5; 2 Cor. 2:11; 11:14; 12:7; 1 Tim. 1:20) until Jesus returns. Peter confirms that Satan is very active in the world today by saying, "Be self-controlled and alert. Your enemy, the devil, prowls around like a roaring lion looking for someone to devour." (1 Pet. 5:8). Satan is 'prowling around' not bound! As this age draws to a close, we will see an increase, not decrease, of satanic activity (Rev. 13:4). Once cast out of the heavenly realm (Eph. 6:12) at the mid-way point of the Tribulation, Satan will be more active on the earth than ever before (Rev. 12:9, 13, 15, 17).

Adding to the above mentioned, 'kingdom now' amillennialism faces another problem in that Satan will be released after one thousand years to deceive the nations once again (20:3, 7-9). In the same way, the nations are being deceived today; they will be again. Zechariah provides some insight into John's statement of Satan deceiving a great many from the millennial period. Zechariah, chapter fourteen (vv. 18-19) references those within the millennial dispensation who refuse to worship God. These will be the same who make up Satan's great army (Rev. 20:8), who march against the New Jerusalem, and who are quickly destroyed by fire that comes down from heaven (v. 9). Further examination of Zachariah fourteen will be conducted in the following section of this work.

Again, Satan is very active in the world today, evident by the increased level of deception. Evidently, things are getting worse, not better (1 Tim. 4:1, 2 Tim. 4:3, 2 Thess. 2:3-9, Lu. 18:8). While 'kingdom now' subscribers are claiming to recreate what was lost in the Garden of Eden, in preparation for Jesus' return, they are oblivious to and are a part of the most significant sign of the end times, which is deception. They are deceived, and they are deceiving others as well.

As earlier written, Jesus said that in this world we will have Tribulation. Tribulation will only increase for the remanent who hold fast to God's word, without compromise. That fact is true today, and it will be even more so during the Tribulation (Rev. 7:13-14). Many will lose their lives during this seven-year period for refusing to bow down to the Antichrist and receive his mark (13:15). Those refusing to follow the Antichrist will fear and worship God alone (14:7) during the Tribulation and will most likely perish (14:13) by the sword (13:10) or by beheading (20:4a). However, for their sacrifice and commitment to Christ, alone, they will live again, ruling and reigning with Him in the millennium (v. 4b).

Notice that these martyrs (20:4) are resurrected at the end of the Tribulation period. The resurrection of the Tribulation slain saints is singled out, standing alone and apart from the raptured saints (1 Cor. 15:50-51, 1 Thess. 4:16-17, Rev. 4:1), which took place seven years earlier (Rev. 3:10, 4:1) before the wrath commenced (1 Thess. 1:10, 5:9, Rev. 3:10). Until Jesus returns, the bodies of the Tribulation, saints are not resurrected, but in the meantime, their spirits will join those seated on thrones, around Jesus in heaven (Rev. 20:4).

Luke records the words of Jesus (22:29-30) regarding those seated with Him in heaven, which will be made up of the raptured bride (church), and the friends of the bride, who are the OT saints. Those who followed the Antichrist by receiving his mark (20:5) shall be imprisoned for one thousand years before facing the final judgment (20:11-15). Those facing the final judgement will go into eternal suffering where they will be tormented with fire and sulphur, where the smoke of their torment will go up forever and ever; they will have no rest day or night (14:10-11). The order of the final judgement is as follows:

1. Following the tribulation, the nations are judged (Matt. 25:31-46)
2. The false prophet and the Antichrist are cast alive into the lake of fire (Rev. 19:20)
3. Satan is bound and thrown into the pit (Rev. 20:1-3)
4. Satan is released after one thousand years and then recaptured and thrown into the lake of fire where the false prophet and the Antichrist have been for one thousand years (Rev 20:3b, 7, 10).
5. The unjust are resurrected at the end of the one thousand years to face the great white throne judgement, from where they too will join Satan in the lake of fire (Rev. 20:5, 11-15).

At the close of the great Tribulation, the just are rewarded, trading their worst life then for their best life now, and the unjust are judged (trading their best life then for their worst life now).

Again, 'kingdom now' theology has this fundamental biblical doctrine the wrong way around, believing that they are to rule and reign here and now. If, in fact, you are ruling and reigning in this life as dominionism suggests, the chances are, you are not following the biblical Jesus, but rather another Jesus (2 Cor. 4:11). So, you will not take part in Jesus' coming kingdom (cf. Lu. 21:34-36), which means you will miss the rapture of the church, unless repentance comes first. The same applies to the resurrection of the slain saints; unless those left behind to endure the Tribulation come to repentance, they too will miss the final resurrection of the just, leaving them to face the last resurrection of the unjust.

The resurrection topic has been a point of confusion for many, and chapter twenty, verse five, of John's revelation has been a point of great controversy, even for serious Bible scholars. Post-Tribulationists have used verse five to support their position of a post-Tribulation rapture. Yet, verses five and six are in contrast to verses twelve to thirteen, which supports the resurrection takes part in stages (cf. 1 Cor. 5:23). The same occurred following Christ's resurrection, whereas the sleeping saints followed (Matt. 27:52-53), which will also happen with the church; only next time the dead in Christ will rise first, and those still living will join them in the air (1 Thess. 4:13-18, 1 Cor. 15:51-52).

The next resurrection following the dead saints and rapture of the church will involve the two witnesses of the Tribulation (Rev. 11:3, 13). Followed again by the martyred saints of the great tribulation (Rev. 20:4), Those who share in the resurrection of the just are forever blessed (20:6);

those sharing in the resurrection of the unjust are eternally damned (Rev. 20:5, Dan. 12:2, Jn. 5:28-29, Acts 24:15).

In sum, the importance of the resurrection and judgement stages is further confirmed by the one-thousand-year gap, which is made clear by referencing it six times in chapter twenty alone (vv. 2, 3, 4, 5, 6, 7). The literal interpretation of the one thousand years is contextually supported through consistent referencing of specific periods (e.g., '42 months,' 11:2; 13:5; '1,260 days,' 11:3; 12:6).

At the beginning of the millennium, the nations are judged, the Tribulation saints are resurrected, and Satan is bound. At the end of the millennium, Satan is released for a short time to deceive the rebellious within the millennium; then he is defeated alongside his deceived army. Following, the nations are resurrected, judged, and cast into the lake of fire, alongside Satan, where the false prophet and the Antichrist have been for one thousand years, with not one less day to stay.

The following section of this work will address Satan's final defeat, which follows the one thousand years of Christ's rule and reign on the earth, otherwise known as the millennial dispensation and Messianic kingdom.

CHAPTER TWENTY

(vv. 7-10)
The Conquering Messianic King / The Defeat of Satan

Following verses one to six of chapter twenty, John starts his sentence of verse seven with the word 'and.' Here, like 'meta tauta,' (after this) the Greek implies a chronological continuation of the previous section leaving no argument for preterist ideology which separates chapters one to nineteen from chapters twenty to twenty-two. Again, from verses, one to seven, the mention of 'one thousand years' is referenced six times (vv. 2, 3, 4, 5, 6, 7). Verse seven picks up on the previous section, serving as a bookend. Verse two is the first to mention the one-thousand-year period, and verse seven is the last.

The millennium follows the second coming of Jesus Christ, where He then sets up His kingdom. During the one thousand years of His Messianic rule and reign on the earth, Satan is bound in chains, in the bottomless pit (vv. 2-3). The bottomless pit is only mentioned in the book of Revelation, yet referenced six times (9:1, 2, 11, 11:7, 17:8, 20:1). The words 'bottomless pit' comes from the Greek word (abyssos) often translated 'abyss,' also used by Luke (Lu. 8:31) and Paul (Rom. 10:7). Of course, nothing good comes out of the pit, and nothing good goes into it.

At the end of the millennium, after having spent one thousand years in the pit, Satan is released for a short time (v. 7). When he is released, he will once again go about deceiving the nations (v. 8). While the whole world is in Satan's scope, John gives specific reference to Gog and Magog (v. 8).

In the short time Satan is freed, he will amass a great army from Christ's Messianic kingdom (8b), which will be made up of the rebellious who refused to worship Jesus as the ruling King (Zech. 14:17-19). Even under seemingly perfect conditions (Isa. 65:18-25), where there is no tempter, where everyone will acknowledge God (Jer. 31:33-34), fallen humanity will still rebel against Jesus Christ. During the millennium, the millennials will not have glorified bodies, as the bride of Christ and the bride's friends do; however, they will still be subject to the sin nature. While all millennials will acknowledge Jesus, some will refuse to follow and worship Him, and Satan will quickly identify them. Here lies the doctrine of free will.

To summarise, the doctrine of free will states that humanity has a mind, and therefore the capacity to choose as free moral agents, choosing according to our inclinations, following our strongest desire. Free will was seen in the Garden, where Adam and Eve freely chose to sin (Gen. 3). They were without sin at the time, albeit they did have a tempter (Satan). The reverse will be true in the millennium, the millenniums will be without a tempter (Satan is bound in the pit), but they are not yet delivered of their Adamic sin nature (cf. Zech. 14:17-19, Rev 20:8-9).

For us (if in Christ), due to Christ's finished work on the cross, sin has lost its grip (power); and now, instead of being slaves to sin, we are to be slaves to righteousness (Rom. 6). Indeed, we are called to practice (perfect) righteousness, not sin (1 Jn. 3:7-9). Although we are saved sinners, in this world, we still struggle with the flesh (Rom. 7:15-24) and will continue to struggle in the flesh until we receive our glorified bodies, which occurs at the rapture (1 Cor. 15:35-58). For the glorified in Christ, in the millennial dispensation, sin will no longer be a problem. This side of the millennium, true converts of Christ will exercise their free will over sin, freely choosing to resist the desire to sin by submitting themselves to Jesus. This is the fruit of salvation, the evidence that someone is actually saved (Jn. 15:4, Phil. 1:9-11).

In sum, the true convert desires to please God moreover self by resisting sin, even though the desire to sin maybe still strong, and the tempter (Satan) still active. Whatever the heart wants most, sin or salvation (Jesus), the heart will have. Sinners sin freely, just as the saved remain free from sin by voluntarily choosing to serve and obey Jesus over sin. Those in Christ come to Him by calling on His name (Jn. 14:6, Acts 4:12, Rom. 10:8-13), then they remain in Him through obedience (Jn. 18:31, 14:10-15, 21, 23-24, 1 Jn. 2:3, 3:24, 5:3).

Remember, unless you first call on the name of Jesus Christ before, or at least on His return, you will not be invited to the marriage supper of the Lamb (Rev. 19:9); therefore you will not enter into the millennial kingdom. During the Tribulation, many Jews will come to faith in Jesus (Rev. 7, 14), bringing about a mass revival, converting multitudes from every nation, all tribes, peoples, and languages (Rev. 7:9). This Tribulation revival will be ongoing throughout the duration of seven years, concluding with Jesus' return. Even at this late point, leading right up to Jesus' return, people will still be able to repent due to God's extended grace and mercy. According to Zechariah, chapter twelve, and verse ten (Zech. 12:10), even up until the point when Jesus appears, seen with the naked eye, salvation is still on offer.

The appearance of Jesus is expanded on further in Revelation 1:7: "He is coming with the clouds, and every eye will see Him— even those who pierced Him. Moreover, all the tribes of the earth will mourn because of Him. So, shall it be! Amen." The word 'mourning' seen in Zechariah (12:10), and Revelation (1:7), is eschatological and in support of the phrase 'On that Day,' indicating, again, as to when this event takes place. The event takes place at the return of Jesus. The response seen in Zechariah (12:10) will be contrary to those of Revelation, chapter six (vv. 14-17), where they call for the rocks to fall on and hide them from the Lamb. The difference with Zechariah is, multitudes are collectively and individually saved, whereas in Revelation, chapter six, millions will be slaughtered. Through Zechariah's account, salvation is evident both individually and collectively by the words 'families' and 'wives,' and by 'themselves,' suggesting many will still come to faith in Jesus, through genuine repentance, even at His appearing (Zech. Chaps. 12-14).

Again, seen in Zechariah chapter twelve, verses ten to fourteen, at the appearance of Jesus (v. 10), an individual response is always required through genuine repentance and mourning. Such a response secures salvation, confirmed by chapter thirteen, verse one: "Where comes the cleansing of sin and uncleanness." Meaning, forgiveness is granted to repentant sinners, alone, due to God's grace and mercy, confirmed by Peter (2 Peter 3:9).

Remember, people who responded to Jesus before the commencement of the millennium are those who later rebel during the millennium. Here lies further evidence weighting against the doctrine of 'once saved always saved.' You can be in the kingdom of God but not of it, and therefore still lose your right to remain. The same applied to those within the churches, addressed in chapters two and three of the book of Revelation. Five of seven were once doing well, but when receiving their letters from Jesus, they had fallen and were subsequently in danger of the judgement by following in Israel's idolatrous footsteps.

Warnings of the coming judgement were announced by all the NT writers and were a common theme with the OT prophets as well. In the OT, the coming judgement is often referenced as 'The Day of the Lord,' or with words similar in effect. Zechariah pens these words sixteen times in all (12:3–4, 6, 8–9, 11; 13:1–2, 4; 14:4, 6, 8–9, 13, 20–21). Chapter fourteen, however, is of particular interest, which commences by saying, "A day is coming," followed by the phrase "On that Day," which is recorded seven times (vv. 4, 6, 8, 9, 13, 20, 21) serving as bookends within the chapter. The words "On that Day" refer to Jesus returning to judge the nations, otherwise known as Armageddon. Chapter twelve uses the term six more times, referring to Jesus' return, which coincides with the battle of Armageddon. Chapter thirteen uses the phrase three more times, stating when Jesus returns, He will cut off all idolatry and strike the failing shepherds who scattered the sheep. The remaining remnant will then go into the millennium where Jesus is the ruling King, where everyone will continually call upon His name.

Chapter fourteen of Zechariah is of particular interest due to providing a complete summary of the events unfolding at the close of the Tribulation, ushering in Jesus' return, followed by the millennial reign, concluding with judgement of the rebellious, and Satan, at the end of the one thousand years. The summary is as follows:

- Israel is in trouble during the tribulation (v. 2)
- The Lord fights against the nations at Megiddo (vv. 3, 12-15, cf. 13)
- Jesus returns (v. 4), followed by an earthquake (v. 5)

When Jesus died on the cross, there was a great earthquake (Matt. 27:54). When He was raised from the dead, another (Matt. 28:2), when He returns. His feet hit the ground at the Mount of Olives (Zech. 14:4a), the mount splits right down the middle (V. 4b), which is the great earthquake referenced in Revelation, chapter sixteen (v. 18).

- When Jesus returns, the religious are targeted (vv. 21-23)
- Those who survive go into the millennium (v. 16)
- There will be no atheist in the millennium (v. 16)
- All will be required to worship Jesus (vv. 17-19)
- The millennial remnant will be holy, worshipping God (v. 20)
- There will be no more traders in God's house, merchandising the gospel (v. 21)
- Jerusalem will dwell in peace and safety for the first time (vv. 9-11)
- Not just Jerusalem, but the whole world (v. 9)
- When Jesus returns, He restores (v. 6), and He revives (v. 8)
- Yet still, some will rebel (vv. 17-19)
- Satan will lead the rebels to make war against God and Jerusalem (Rev. 20:7-9)
- What took place with Armageddon (vv. 12-15), a thousand years earlier, is repeated

Adding to the above mentioned, Zechariah is an essential prophetic book to consider alongside the book of Revelation due to its chiastic structure. The chiastic structure of the book of Zechariah starts with a call to repentance (1:1-6) and ends with the restoration of Israel by their Messiah and King, Jesus (12:1-14:21). In-between, there are primary and secondary hinges. The primary hinge is The Messianic King-Priest (6:9-15). The secondary hinges are 1). The Messianic Priest and Lord of the earth (3:1-4:14); and 2). The Messianic King and Shephard (11:1-17). The chiastic structure of chapters nine to fourteen is also of particular interest when analysing chapter twenty of the book of Revelation. The chiastic arrangement of Zechariah, chapters nine to fourteen, is as below:

A God comes to protect and bless chapters 9—10
B The people reject God's shepherd 11:1-14
C The worthless shepherd hurts the flock 11:15-17
C' The nations come to destroy Jerusalem 12:1-9
B' The people repent and turn to God 12:10—13:6
A' God comes to protect and bless 13:7—14:21

As seen in the chiastic structure of the book of Zechariah, Jesus is Priest and King, and never man. Jesus is also the returning King who will deal with worthless shepherds and an idolatrous generation (including the lukewarm church – remember Laodicea means: People ruling).

In sum, Jesus will remove everything false, including worthless religion, self-serving shepherds, the false prophet, the Antichrist, and Satan, before setting up His Messianic kingdom. Then, for one thousand years, the God of Peace (Isa. 6:9, Zech. 9:10, cf. Rom. 16:20) will rule the world with an iron rod (Ps. 2:9, Rev. 2:27, 12:5, 19:15). However, and again, somewhere in-between, a rebellion will rise, where many millennials will reject Christ's rulership by refusing to worship Him (Zech. 14:18-19). These rebels will make up Satan's great millennial army, who gather from all corners of the globe and march against Jerusalem (Rev. 20:9).

When the nations rebel against Jesus, during the millennium, there is a specific reference to Gog and Magog in Revelation, chapter twenty (v. 8). Gog and Magog's connection is not a fulfilment of the Gog and Magog war mentioned in Ezekiel (38-39). Ezekiel's prophecy refers to armies of the north involving a handful of nations, whereas John's prophecy includes the whole world. The final battle against God, taking place at the end of the one thousand years, involving people from every nation, will come from all directions (NSEW) on the planet.

In the Ezekiel (38-39) prophecy, Gog was the ruler, and Magog represented the people, united in hating both God and Israel, which is allergically applied in the millennium. John did something similar in chapter eleven (v. 8) by writing, "And their (the two witnesses) dead bodies will lie in the street of the great city (Jerusalem) that symbolically is called Sodom and Egypt, where their Lord was crucified." In chapter eleven of John's revelation, Jerusalem was inhabited by everything evil, thereby called 'Egypt and Sodom.' Still, in the millennium, Jerusalem will be inhabited by the saints and by God (20:9). In the same way, Gog and Magog will march against Israel in the Tribulation (Ezek. 38-39), Satan (the ruler) and his people (the deceived) will march against the saints and Jesus in Jerusalem (v. 9).

In those days, Jerusalem will be the capital of the world (Isa. 2:1-5). Satan and his army will surround the beloved city, and God will respond with fire (v. 9). This final battle will have to be the shortest lasting in all of history, even shorter lasting than the battle of Armageddon (19:11-21).

The reference to fire coming down from heaven should be taken literally, as with the literal fulfilment of John's entire prophecy. Fire coming down from heaven is an act of divine judgement and is a regular occurrence in the OT (cf. Gen. 19:24; Ex. 9:23–24; Lev. 9:24; 10:2; Num. 11:1; 16:35; 26:10; 1 Kings 18:38; 2 Kings 1:10, 12, 14; 1 Chron. 21:26; 2 Chron. 7:1, 3; Ps. 11:6; etc.) re (cf. Gen. 19:24; Ex. 9:23–24; Lev. 9:24; 10:2; Num. 11:1; 16:35; 26:10; 1 Kings 18:38; 2 Kings 1:10, 12, 14; 1 Chron. 21:26; 2 Chron. 7:1, 3; Ps. 11:6; etc.). The same is true in the NT's closing book (Rev. 8:7-8, 9:17-18, 11:15, 16:8, 18:8, 20:9).

Following the defeat of Satan's army (20:9), Satan himself will be thrown into the lake of fire and sulphur where the beast and the false prophet are and have been for one thousand years (v. 10), with not one less day to stay. The Antichrist and the false prophet have been tormented every day and every night for a millennium; while Satan has been bound in the pit, putting an end to the false doctrine of annihilationism. All the while, the saints have been ruling and reigning with Jesus from Jerusalem.

The lake of fire is Satan's ultimate destination (Matt. 25:41), which will be shared by the Antichrist and the false prophet (19:20), and anyone else who follows them (14:9-11). Revelation, chapter twenty, verses eleven to fifteen, addresses those participating in Satan's judgement, which is unpacked in the next section: The Great White Throne Judgement.

Important note: Chapter twenty, verses seven to ten debunk a number of false doctrines:

- Amillennialism (No millennial dispensation)
- Reconstructionism (Seven Mountains, Kingdom Now theology)
- Annihilationism (Instant annihilation over everlasting torment)
- Universalism (Everyone ends up in the same place, eventually)
- Calvinism (Once saved always saved)
- Liberalism (Modern knowledge over doctrinal authority)

When studying the Bible contextually, in an expository format, and applying systematic theology, the reader is better equipped to handle God's word, mitigating error rightly. Remember, God did not say that those who 'read' His word will be able to handle it rightly, but rather those who 'study' it (2 Tim. 2:15). Many read the Bible, yet cannot handle it, evident by the increasing level of false doctrine taught by many standing behind pulpits.

CHAPTER TWENTY

Part Two
(vv. 11-15)
The Books Were Opened

As with the introduction for verses seven to ten, the word 'And' is used, supporting the chronological order and constancy of a literal timeframe; now verse eleven opens up with the word 'Then.' The word 'Then,' follows the yet to be fulfilled prophecy of the release and recapture of Satan. Following a short time where Satan is allowed for the last time to deceive the nation, he is then cast into the lake of fire where the false prophet and the Antichrist have been for one thousand years. Following Satan's final defeat and judgement, THEN everyone whose name is not written in the Lamb's Book of Life will be resurrected to face the great white throne judgement. This event is known as the resurrection of the unjust (Dan. 12:2, Jn. 5:28-29, Acts 24:15).

Important to note, is the great white throne judgement is not the same as the throne mentioned more than thirty times throughout the book of Revelation, beginning with chapter four (v. 2). Neither is it the same as the judgement seat of Jesus Christ, reserved for the just or redeemed (2 Cor.

5:10, cf. Rom. 14:12). Instead, the great white throne judgment is purposed to judge the dead/wicked (v. 12), not the living/righteous. The living will be found in the Lamb's book of life, whereas the dead will not be; therefore, they will be judged by their works under the Ten Commandments. Their works will be recorded in the books, not the book (of life). Their works recorded in the books will be wicked works (20:12) and breaches of the Ten Commandments. Wherever there is a single breach, the offender thereby becomes accountable to the full weight of the Law (Ja. 2:10). In fact, anyone relying on their 'good' works will be under a curse (Gal. 3:10-14). Only those redeemed from the Law (Gal. 3:13) through Christ will be found innocent and able to stand before the Lamb of God.

People relying on being a 'good' person will be judged by the Law, and, again, if you have fallen short in just one area, only once, then the whole weight of the Law will come against you (Ja. 2:10). The Law is as below:

The Law (Exodus 20)
(1) Don't have other gods before Me
(2) Don't make any idols
(3) Don't take My name in vain
(4) Remember the Sabbath
(5) Honour your mother and father
(6) Don't murder
(7) Don't commit adultery
(8) Don't steal
(9) Don't lie
(10) Don't covet

Contrary to false teaching, stating Jesus did away with the Law, He did not, but rather He fulfilled it (Matt. 5:17), which is a different thing entirely. If anything, Jesus increased the requirement of the Law (Matt. 5:21-22, 27-28), therefore any depending on their ability to keep it, are deeply deceived (Rom. 3:10, 12, 18, 23, 5:13). Once more, anyone outside of Christ, depending on their own 'good' works, will have their transgressions recorded in the 'books' (Rev. 20:12). Those in Christ will not have their deeds written in the books, for their sins have been blotted out (Ps. 51:1, 9, Isa. 43:25, Acts 3:19, Col. 2:14), but instead will have their name written in the 'book' of life.

The book of life is mentioned six times in the book of Revelation (3:5, 13:8, 17:8, 20:12, 15, 21:27) and one more time in Philippians (4:3). While the Philippians reference is positive, the references found in the book of Revelation are negative, serving as a warning of eternal damnation, starting with the church members of Sardis (3:5). The majority of the members of the church of Sardis had soiled their garments, having a reputation of being alive, but were dead (3:2), just like many today. They were dead and asleep spiritually speaking (v. 2), and unless they woke up before Jesus returns, He will come as a thief (v. 3), leaving them behind. For the few within Sardis who had not soiled their garments and continue to conquer by walking worthily (vv. 4-5), they, alone, would not have their names blotted out of the book of life (v. 5). The rest would have their names blotted out, implying that their names were once written in the book of life. Only the saved have their names written in the book of life (Rev. 17:8). The unsaved never did have (Rev. 13:8).

Anyone facing the great white throne of judgement does not have their name written in the book of life; therefore, they are unredeemable and eternally damned already. On that day, there will be nowhere to hide for the unsaved, whether great or small (20:12). The phrase 'great and small' is also referenced in chapter thirteen (v. 16), in reverse, being 'small and great' speaking of those who received the mark (666). Other references that should be considered are found in chapter six (vv. 15-16) and in chapter nineteen (vv. 17-19), where none are spared at the battle of Armageddon. While some escape natural punishment in this life through death, none will escape eternal death, which is everlasting, unending torment.

Following the one thousand years of peace on earth, even the sea will give up the unjust, as will Hades (20:13). There are two more references using the phrase 'small and great,' found in the book of Revelation, but contrary to referring to sinners, they refer to the saints, who feared God (11:18, 19:5). Only those who fear God will be saved (11:11, 18, 14:7, 19:5).

Here lies the problem with the majority of churches today.

They do not fear God, therefore they worship as they please, producing false worship, which is idolatry. False worship was the central problem for five of the seven churches addressed in chapters two and three. Unless repentance came first and fast, judgement would fall. Without repentance, natural judgement would then be followed by eternal judgement. Remember, the words of Peter, "For it is time for judgement to begin with the family of God; and if it begins with us, what will the outcome be for those who disobey the gospel of God?" And "If it is hard for the righteous to be saved, what will become of the ungodly and the sinner?" (1 Pet 4:17-18). The disobedience and the ungodly are destined to Hades, where they will await their final judgement.

The statement "Hades gave up the dead" (20:13) refers to the sleeping (but not the resting) unsaved, who are resurrected and reunited with their physical bodies for the purpose of everlasting torment (Matt. 5:29-30, 10:28, Mk. 9:43-48, Rom. 2:6). The immortal body of the unsaved is, in fact, the everlasting food for the worm and the eternal fuel for the fire in the everlasting place of torment (Mk. 9:48). Contrary to the false teaching that states Hell is not a physical place of torment, the scriptures say otherwise. In Hell, there is no relief, and there is no rest (Rev. 14:9-11, 20:10), despite the false claims of 'grace' preachers who subscribe to annihilationism. Grace preachers formed the doctrine of annihilationism due to having a flawed understanding of the nature and character of God. While they major on grace and mercy, they overlook that God is also just and severe (Rom. 11:22). God is kind to those who obey Him (the just), but severe to those who do not (the unjust).

Running in a different direction to annihilationism, Grace preachers are also guilty of teaching universalism, which suggests that 'everyone will end up in heaven eventually.' Revelation, chapter twenty could not make it any clearer; the unjust will never see heaven, but be cast into the eternal lake of fire.

The resurrection of the just and the unjust is mentioned by Daniel (12:2), John (5:28-29), and Luke (Acts 24:15). Again, the phrase 'the resurrection of the unjust' refers to the dead in Hades who are awaiting their final judgement. Hades is a place of torment in itself (Lu. 16:19-30), but the last and eternal degree of suffering is yet to be announced. In the final judgement, there will be different levels or degrees of punishment. The worst degree is reserved for those who led others astray when given the responsibility to teach scripture (Matt. 23:14, Ja. 3:1). The next degree is for the servants of Christ who knew His will but disobeyed (Lu. 12:47-48). The next degree is for those who received the gospel yet fell away (2 Pet. 2:20-22), and also for those who heard and saw the power of the gospel and did not respond (Lu. 10:14-15). Evidently, going by the aforementioned, the great white throne judgement will be the experience for most (Matt. 7:13-14, Lu. 13:23-34), including confessing Christians (Matt. 7:21-23). However, regardless of the degree of suffering in the lake of fire, all who face the great white throne judgement end up in the same place.

The lake of fire (vs. 14–15) referred to as "the fiery lake of burning sulphur" (19:20) is the same as Gehenna (cf. Matt. 5:22, 29–30; 10:28; 18:9; 23:15, 33; Mark 9:43, 45, 47; Luke 12:5; James 3:6), which is also translated, Hell. The topic of Hell has disappeared from neo-Christianity, despite Jesus speaking on the subject more than any other. Today, many have replaced Hell with grace teaching, and thereby ignore a good portion of the Bible which describes Hell in great detail, as summarised below:

- Hell is the realm of the dead (Ps. 9:17, Prov. 15:24, Act 2:27)
- It is the second death (Rev. 2:11, 20:6, 14, 21:8)
- It is a place of eternal abandonment (Ps. 16:10)
- It is a place for both the body and the soul (Matt. 10:28, Mk. 9:43)
- It is a place of eternal punishment (Matt. 25:46, 2 Thess. 1:9, Jude 1:7)
- It is a place of everlasting destruction (2 Thess. 1:9)
- It is a place of eternal fire (Matt. 18:8, 24:41, Ja. 3:6)
- It is a place of unquenchable fire (Matt. 3:12, Mk. 9:43, Lu. 3:17, Heb. 10:26-31)
- It is a fiery lake burning with sulphur (Rev. 19:20, 20:13-14)
- It is a place of weeping and gnashing of teeth (Matt. 8:12, 13:42, 50, 22:13, 24:51, 25:30, Lu. 13:28)
- It is a place of eternal torment (Lu. 16:19-21)
- It is a place where there is no rest day or night (Rev. 14:11, 20:10)
- It is a place of darkness (Matt. 8:12, 23:13, 25:30, 2 Pet. 2:4, Jude 1:13)
- It is a place of eternal separation from God (2 Thess. 1:9)
- It is a place where God's wrath is stored up (Jn. 3:36, Rom. 2:5)
- In Hell, the damned are entirely and eternally conscious (Lu. 16:19-21)

Much more could be said about Hell; needless to say, none will want to be there, although most will be. Following the judgement of the unjust (20:5), Death and Hades are thrown into the lake of fire (20:14), which is the second death (20:6). "Blessed and holy is the one who shares in the first resurrection" (20:6). The first resurrection takes place in stages, as mentioned previously, and only refers to the saved. The second resurrection only applies to the unsaved.

Regardless of the degree of suffering awaiting the unsaved, even to stand before the great white throne in itself will be terrifying. Think back to when John saw Jesus in His returning state to judge the nations (Rev. 1:17). So startling was the image of Christ, John fell to the ground. The Greek implies that John 'fell to the ground as a man dead.' In other words, John was terrified to death and could not stand. The writer of Hebrews picks up on something similar, stating, "It is a fearful thing to fall into the hands of a living God (Heb. 10:31).

Again, important to note, when penning the warning above, the writer of the book of Hebrews was not addressing the unbelievers but rather confessing believers. The author is thereby warning churchgoers, which is made very clear with statements like "Don't Drift Away!" And "Pay Attention," also "Fear, Strive, Hold Fast, and Draw Near." Chapter two, verse one is the first of five warnings found within the book of Hebrews. The others are found in chapters three to four, five to six (5:11-6:20), and chapter ten (vv. 19-39), and twelve. Chapter six (vv. 6-8) supports the context of the verse as mentioned earlier (v. 31), contextually interpreted from chapter ten (vv. 26-39). In chapter nine, the warning is given again, "Just as it is appointed for man to die once, and after that comes judgement" (v. 27), and also in chapter twelve, "For God is a consuming fire" (v. 29). The warnings issued by the writer of the book of Hebrews are also supported by the words of Paul, who said, "Therefore, my beloved, just as you have always obeyed, not only in my presence but now even more in my absence, continue to work out your salvation with fear and trembling" (Phil 2:12). The warning to work out salvation with fear and trembling is also seen in the words of Jesus (Lu. 12:5), who later rebuked five of seven churches addressed in the book of Revelation, all of which were in danger of judgement (chap. 2-3).

Knowing the terror of the day coming, Luke (Acts 10:42) and Paul (2 Cor. 5:11), among others, urge the redeemed to preach the gospel of repentance (Acts 2:38, 3:19, 11:18, 17:30, 20:21, 26:20), warning of the dangers to come (Col. 1:28). Similarly, God told Ezekiel if he did not warn of judgement, affording Israel an opportunity to repent, then their blood would be in his hands (3:18, 33:8). God desires to deliver, not to destroy. Peter said, "God will have none perish, but all come to repentance" (2 Pet. 3:8-10).

The word 'repent' is found in ten verses throughout the book of Revelation (2:4, 16, 21, 22, 3:3, 3:19, 9:20, 21, 16:9, 16:11), with six references given to the churches (2:4, 16, 21, 22, 3:3, 3:19), and the remaining four addressing those in the Tribulation (9:20, 21, 16:9, 16:11). Again, the five churches in need of repentance practiced false worship, which included an allowance for sin. When sin is not addressed, the doctrine of eternal judgement (Hell) is also ignored. Thereby those guilty have taken away from scripture (Deut. 4:2, Rev. 22:19) and consequently subjected themselves to the plagues of the book; the worst of which is Hell.

In closing, Revelation, chapter, twenty and verse eleven should remind us of chapter six, verse fourteen, with the closing question: "Who can stand the great day of the Lord?" The answer is that none unless sealed by the Holy Spirit due to being in Christ Jesus. Only the redeemed can stand before the Lamb of God. The rest, who do not have their names written in the book of life, will go before the great white throne judgement, where they will receive their eternal 'reward' (Rom. 2:6, Rev. 20:13). While standing before the great white throne, their works will be examined in accordance with the Law. All standing before the great white throne shall be found guilty, falling short of God's standard of perfection (Matt. 5:20). Following judgement, they will then be cast into the eternal lake of fire where the false prophet and the Antichrist have been for one thousand years. Satan has also been recently thrown into the lake of fire, suffering, not ruling, as some suggest.

Remember, Hell was created for the devil and his angels (Matt. 24:41), not for humanity. But, if humanity continues to reject Jesus, they then, by default, follow Satan and will end up in the same place that he does, which is the eternal lake of fire.

CHAPTER TWENTY-ONE

(vv. 1-8)
The New Heaven, Earth, and Jerusalem

Following the unjust being cast into the lake of fire for all eternity, 'then' (21:1) John saw the eternal new heaven and a new earth, for the first heaven and the first earth have passed away. What John describes, Peter also saw and writes about this event in his second letter, chapter three, stating that after the millennial dispensation, the earth is cleansed with fire (2 Pet. 3:10). Peter's prophecy is also supported by Isaiah (34:4). Peter and Isaiah agree the earth is refurbished with fire; similarly, it was also once cleansed by the Flood (Gen. 9:11). When the earth was cleansed with the Flood, it was not done away with, but rather the earth was purged of people. The same will be repeated after the millennium; the earth will be renewed and even reborn, and anyone not born again will be removed. Only those who are born again will inherit the new earth (21:7). Furthermore, the earth will be cleansed and set free from everything corrupt (21:8, 27) which will also be the fulfilment of Paul's prophecy, in his letter to the Romans, chapter eight (vv. 21-22).

In sum, the earth will be delivered but never destroyed. Solomon confirmed this fact when writing in Ecclesiastes (1:4), "The earth abides forever" (see also Ps. 148:4-6). On the grounds of what is written above, the phrase, 'the old has passed away' refers to being burned up, thus refurbished with fire, not replaced. This will take place 'after' the great white throne of judgement (20:11-15). First, the unjust are burned in the fire, and then the earth will be.

As written above, the opening word in verse one, 'then,' supports the chronological order of the prophecy, which is picked up again in verse nine, and in chapter twenty-two, verse one. Following the millennial reign, coming down from the new heaven to the new earth, John saw the holy city, the new Jerusalem (v. 2). Although little is written about the new earth, in verse twenty-two, John adds what is missing, is the temple (v. 22). God has replaced the temple. Also missing is the sea (v. 1), the sun, and the moon (v. 23). The sun and moon are no longer needed because, in that day, the glory of God will give light; therefore, the stars may also be missing, possibly due to being dissolved (2 Pet. 3:10-12). Again, something else that will be missing is anyone whose names were not written in the book of life, for they are being tormented in Hell (14:9-11, 20:11-15, 21:8, 27).

Adding to those mentioned above, another thing missing from John's description of the things to come is how big the new earth will be and what it will look like. John's description is, needless to say, very vague, and scripture as a whole is also almost silent on the new heaven and the new earth. Although there are a few other brief mentions of it from Isaiah (65:17, 66:22) and Peter (2 Pet. 3:10-13), still no detailed information is provided. As for the millennium, the scripture is much more descriptive, yet the millennial dispensation is often confused with the eighth day, comprising of the new heaven and the new earth.

An example of where and how readers are becoming confused is with Isaiah chapter sixty-five, which addressed both the millennium and the eighth day. From verses seventeen to nineteen, Isaiah refers to the new heaven and the new earth, and from verses twenty to twenty-five, he is referring to the millennium. Ezekiel (47:8-20, 48:28) also clearly makes a distinction of the millennium from the new earth referencing the sea, as does Isaiah, elsewhere (11:9), and Zechariah (9:10, 14:8). Simply put, the sea is missing from the eighth day onwards, albeit there will be at least one river (Rev. 22:1-2).

Regarding dispensationalism, the millennium is the seventh day, following the pattern of creation provided in Genesis (1-2). The seventh day is a day of rest, and the eighth day is everything made new, which is yet to be revealed. Peter concurs with the following statement, "And by that same word, the present heavens and earth are reserved for fire, being kept for the Day of Judgment and destruction of ungodly men. Beloved, do not let this one thing escape your notice: With the Lord, a day is like a thousand years, and a thousand years are like a day. The Lord is not slow in keeping His promise as some understand slowness, but is patient with you, not wanting anyone to perish but everyone to come to repentance" (2 Pet. 3:7-9).

In sum, each creation day represents one thousand years, which is where we get the doctrine of dispensationalism. While some have an issue with the doctrine of dispensationalism, Paul does not, using the term four times:

> 1 Corinthians 9:17
> For if I do this thing willingly, I have a reward: but if against my will, a dispensation of the gospel is committed unto me.

Ephesians 1:10
That is the dispensation of the fullness of times he might gather together in one all things in Christ, both which are in heaven, and which are on earth; even in him.

Ephesians 3:2
"If ye have heard of the dispensation of the grace of God which is given me to you-ward."

Colossians 1:25
"Whereof I am made a minister, according to the dispensation of God, which is given to me for you, to fulfil the word of God."

We are currently at the end of the sixth dispensation, which is the dispensation of grace and the church age. We are also at the close of that sixth thousandth year, where Jesus returns to commence the seventh. The seventh thousandth year is the millennial dispensation of rest, which is the next, but not the last, on the biblical calendar. The seventh period of one thousand years will be followed by the eighth dispensation, or the eighth day, which is eternal.

The Six Ages, as formulated by Augustine of Hippo, are defined in De catechizandis rudibus (On the catechizing of the uninstructed), Chapter 22:

- The First Age "is from the beginning of the human race, that is, from Adam, who was the first man who was made, down to Noah, who constructed the ark at the time of the flood", i.e., the Antediluvian period.
- The Second Age "extends from that period on to Abraham, who was called the father indeed of all nations."
- The Third Age "extends from Abraham on to David, the king."

- The Fourth Age is "from David on to that captivity whereby the people of God passed over into Babylonia."
- The Fifth Age is "from that transmigration down to the advent of our Lord Jesus Christ."
- The Sixth Age: "With His [Jesus Christ's] coming, the sixth age has entered on its process."

The Ages reflect the seven days of creation, of which the last day is the rest of Sabbath, illustrating the human journey to find eternal rest with God, a common Christian belief.

When interpreting scripture according to the understanding of a literal creation day, which also represents one-thousand-year periods (2 Pet. 3:8), it contests the theory of an old earth. The earth is seven-thousand-years-old, not millions or billions of years old. The current, near, seven-thousand-year-old earth will expire on its eighth birthday, giving way to a new, refurbished, one, albeit little is known about the new earth, and John seems to be less interested in it than he is with the new city.

I would argue that John is not interested, or at least not descriptive, about the new heaven and the new earth - this is due to being consumed and even overwhelmed by the new Jerusalem (v. 2). The new Jerusalem is unlike the old, for the old was symbolically called 'Sodom' (11:8), and the new is called 'Holy' (21:2). The new Jerusalem will be Holy due to being the City of God (3:13).

Both the millennial Jerusalem and the new Jerusalem on the new earth will be holy. However, I would reason there is a difference between the new Jerusalem in the millennium and the one on the new earth. In the millennium the new Jerusalem is above the earth (Zech. 14:10), whereas in the new earth, the new Jerusalem is on the earth, and comes down from heaven (Rev. 21:2). From Zechariah's prophecy (14:10, 16), we learn that

Jerusalem is 'aloft' and those coming to worship the King (Jesus) during the millennium 'go up' year after year. The word 'aloft' in Hebrew is 'rā-'ăm,' which means, 'rise up high.' The words for 'go up' in Hebrew is 'ā-lā(h)' which translates 'go up, be lifted up, and ascend (like with the rapture).' Something similar is seen in Ezekiel's prophecy when speaking of the millennial temple. He writes, "The Spirit lifted me up and brought me into the inner court; and behold, the glory of the LORD filled the temple" (34:5). Ezekiel's vision could also be compared to Paul's account, where he writes, "I know a man in Christ who fourteen years ago was caught up to the third heaven—whether in the body or out of the body I do not know, God knows. And I know that this man was caught up into paradise—whether in the body or out of the body I do not know, God knows— and he heard things that cannot be told, which man may not utter" (2 Cor. 12:2-4).

Paul describes his heavenly experience, twice using the word 'caught up' (vv. 2-3), which is the same word for 'rapture' (harpazo). It was used again in Paul's letter to the Thessalonians, "Then we who are alive, who are left, will be caught up (raptured) together with them in the clouds to meet the Lord in the air, and so we will always be with the Lord" (1 Thess. 4:17).

For the reasons mentioned above, I am arguing that the millennial city will be suspended in the air; it will not be on the ground, and I am not alone in saying so. The suggestion has been made before, where Dwight Pentecost states, "If the New Jerusalem is in existence during the millennial reign of Christ, it may have been suspended in the heavens as a dwelling place for resurrected and translated saints, who nevertheless would have immediate access to the earth to carry on their functions of ruling with Christ." Pentecost continues, quoting F.C. Jennings, William Kelly, and Walter Scott, in support of the concept of the new Jerusalem as a satellite city during the Millennium (Things to Come. Grand Rapids: Zondervan Publishing House, 1958. pp. 577–79). Dwight concludes, "In the Millennium the new Jerusalem clearly does not rest on the earth, for there is an earthly Jerusalem and an earthly temple (Ezek. 40–48)."

Perhaps the reason the millennial city is suspended above the earth is to prevent sinners from entering in. Support for this statement is seen with the angels guarding the new Jerusalem's entry to keep sinners out (Rev. 21:12, 27; 22:14-15). Thus, the city must be close enough to the earth for this to matter, but not on it. Angels will guard the millennial Jerusalem in the same way they guarded the entrance to Eden after Adam sinned (Gen. 3:22-24).

Another interesting observation with the new Jerusalem is that it is compared to the bride of Christ (v. 2). The church is the bride (2 Cor. 11:2); however, the city is not the bride but is beautiful and holy like the bride (Eph 5:26-27). Still, the city and the bride are very much connected (v. 9).

Unlike the corrupt Jerusalem of today, in the new Jerusalem, God will dwell with men, they will be His people, and He will be with them as their God (v. 3). After the millennial dispensation, never again will humanity be separated from their God; never again will they suffer death or pain (v. 4). John described something of the same for those delivered from the Tribulation through death (7:9-17). Isaiah picks up on something similar also (25:8).

In sum, the things to come will be a case of 'out with the old and in with the new' (21:5), former things have passed away (v. 4), and nothing will be the same again. God will make everything brand new (v. 5).

So important is the topic of the things to come. What John saw, he was instructed to write down, serving as a permanent record of being trustworthy and true (21:5). The concept of the new earth is as trustworthy and true as Christ's return (22:6). What John saw is as good as done (21:6) as far as God is concerned. Isaiah supports that statement by writing, "Remember what happened long ago, for I am God, and there is no other;

I am God, and there is none like Me. I declare the end from the beginning and ancient times from what is still to come. I say, 'My purpose will stand, and all My good pleasure I will accomplish'" (46:9-10).

The proclamation is further confirmed by the words of Jesus regarding Himself. Jesus said that He is the Alpha and the Omega, the Beginning and the End (Rev. 1:18, 21:6, 22:13). The announcement implies that not only are the things to come already done, but the partakers of the things to come are also already named in the same way the rest are not spoken of. (13:8, 17:8). Everything, and everyone included in the eighth day, from the beginning to the end, has already been written and was so before the foundation of the world (Jer. 1:5, Rom. 8:28, Eph 4:1).

Although everyone has been given an invitation to respond, few do, only the thirsty drink from the spring of the water of life, without payment. Isaiah (55:1) said the same thing; in fact, four times Isaiah says 'Come' in verse one. Isaiah, chapters fifty-five and fifty-six should be read together, and in the context of Christ being presented in chapters fifty-two and fifty-three, establishing an everlasting covenant (chapter 54), then inviting all to respond (chapters 55-56). The closing verses of Isaiah fifty six (vv. 9-12) speak of Israel's corrupt state (and the church), especially its rulers, which is the start of a new message in chapter fifty-seven. In chapter fifty-seven, God deals with Israel's idolatry (as He will the church), paralleling Revelation, chapters eighteen and nineteen.

Despite the idolatry of Israel and the church, Jesus continues to extend His invitation to 'Come,' as seen in Revelation, chapter twenty-two (v. 17). Here, the reader should also be reminded of the letter to the church of Laodicea (3:14-22), where Jesus warned its lukewarm members to repent (stop buying from the world) and instead, 'buy from Him.' The word 'buy' means to 'obtain,' and in this case, the thirsty (for God) obtain without cost. While buying from the world it will come at a price, both naturally now and eternally then, obtaining from Jesus is free. Albeit free, the one obtaining must first forsake the world.

In sum, while salvation is free (21:6), it will cost you everything worldly, for unless you renounce this world, you cannot share in the next. Only those who conquer (overcome) the things of this world are found in the following (21:7).

Conquering results in inheriting eternal life. So important is this message that Jesus ended all seven of His letters to the churches with the same instruction (2:7, 11, 17, 26, 3:5, 12, 21). The one who conquers will likewise have this heritage, "I will be his God, and he will be my son" (21:7). The one who does not, will not (21:8, 27). Therefore, alongside the promise, it is essential to note it is conditional, reserved alone 'for those who conquer.' Paul provides similar warnings (Rom 8:17, 11:22, 2 Tim. 2:12), which quickly quash the false doctrine of universalism. Only those remaining will inherit the promises of God.

The call to conquer and the reward of conquering is seen nine times throughout the book of Revelation. Following the letters to the churches (chapters 2-3), chapter five (v. 5) describes Jesus as the one who conquered. Following, chapter twelve (v. 12) describes the followers of Jesus who conquered, and in doing so, lost their natural lives. The same enduring saints are mentioned again in chapter fifteen (v. 2). Chapters six (v. 2), eleven (v. 7), and thirteen (v. 7) speak of the beast (Antichrist) who conquers the saints during the Tribulation, and who is later conquered by Jesus (17:14) when He returns (19:20). Those who failed to conquer (overcome), and or remain overcomers, are disqualified (cf. 1 Cor. 9:27, 2 Tim. 3:8) from the promised heritage (21:7), and instead, will find their portion (reward) in the lake that burns with fire and sulphur (21:8). Anyone who fails to repent, or fails to repent and endure, by instead practicing sin, will suffer the second death due to not having their names written in the book of life (21:8, 27, 22:15).

Again, this was the same message given to the seven churches (Rev. 2-3) and is the message in need of most today. Sadly, it is missing from most pulpits, replaced by worldly promises of here and now prosperity. In sum, the message to the churches then is the same message to the church now: Come, return, repent and remain, or else! (Rev. 2-3).

CHAPTERS TWENTY-ONE AND TWENTY-TWO

(21:9-27 – 22:1-5) The New and Eternal City of Jerusalem

As with the previous sections, John commenced the next passage with the word 'then,' leaving no room for an error in mistaking the prophecy's chronological order, supporting a futuristic view. Again the chronological order provides the means to interpret correctly. Adding to the chronological order is the heptadic arrangement seen through chapters twenty-one and twenty-two of the seven new things:

- New heaven (Rev. 21:1)
- New earth (Rev. 21:1)
- New Jerusalem (Rev. 21:2)
- New things (Rev. 21:5)
- New paradise (Rev. 22:1–5)

- New place for God's throne (Rev. 22:3)
- New source of light (Rev. 22:5)

As mentioned in my first book, 'The Revelation the Revival,' the events that occur at the close of the millennial dispensation will ultimately deal with anything and anyone less than perfect, specifically, those who have not become new (John 3:3–8). Nothing new will enter into the eighth day, where everything becomes firsthand. Everything new is only promised to the bride of Christ.

On this, the Beatitudes (Matt. 5:2–12) claim the same, literally stating that the kingdom of God will be inherited by the blessed and the blessed alone. The blessed are those who are approved by God. This theme is echoed throughout scripture, and the book of Revelation makes no exception: "He that conquers shall inherit all things, and I shall be his God, and he shall be My son" (Rev. 21:7). The conqueror (overcomer) is the one who obtains and holds a victory over sin through Christ Jesus; hence, he or she alone is the approved of God.

Further support for this is found in the twenty-second chapter: "Blessed are they that do His commandments that they may have the right to the tree of life and may enter in through the gates into the city" (Rev. 22:14). It is by no coincidence that both of these verses (Rev. 21:7 and 22:14) are followed by a warning that describes the fate of those who do not partake of the promise. Those rejecting and or forsaking Christ forfeit the future and eternal inheritance described in chapters twenty and twenty-one. The forsakers who are forsaken, are the same unrepentant people who will be subject to the plagues during the tribulation.

Following the introduction to the new heaven and the new earth, John sees a familiar angel, seen previously in chapter sixteen. In chapter sixteen, there were seven bowl carrying angels (16:1) who poured out on the earth, the wrath of God (v. 2). During the Tribulation, the seven angels will repay the left-behind population for their evil deeds (v. 6), namely their rejection of Jesus Christ. Even then, and at that late stage of the Tribulation, they will remain in a non-repentant state (vv. 8, 11).

The sixth of seven angels is interesting because it will be the one who dries up the river Euphrates preparing for the kings of the East to crossover (v. 12). There is a parallel between the event of the sixth angel and the closing event in the millennium, revealing the deceived rebellious will be led to march against Christ (Rev. 20:8-9). Similarly, the Revelation, chapter sixteen event reveals that the kings of the East lead the two-hundred million mounted troops seen in chapter nine, who were released by the sixth trumpet-blowing angel (9:14).

The massive army of two-hundred million is also deceived by demons performing signs and wonders that came out of the mouth of the Antichrist and the false prophet (16:13-14). These demons are not only leading and deceiving the kings of the East, but the kings of the whole world to assemble for the battle of Armageddon (vv. 14-15). Their campaign will lead them towards Jerusalem, specifically, Megiddo, where the battle of Armageddon takes place. There, the cup Jesus drank from (Matt. 26:39) is poured out on the warring nations (Jer. 10:25, Rev. 16:1), which leads us to the seventh bowl carrying angel.

The seventh bowl-carrying angel (16:17) completes the wrath of God with the announcement 'It is done,' which is repeated by the angel accompanying John (21:6). The wrath of God was completed only after making the nations drain the cup of the wine of the fury of His wrath (v. 19), and then God stoned the blaspheming population with one-hundred-pound hailstones. The Tribulation population will respond by cursing God all the more (v. 21).

Chapter sixteen presents seven angels carrying a wrath-filled bowl each, which is to be poured out on the remaining, and depleted population. Yet chapter twenty-one speaks of one of the same angels 'who had the seven bowls full of the seven last plagues.' Which one of the seven John is referring to, we do not know; however, what we do know is, the angel's task is very different this time around from what it was in chapter sixteen.

In chapter twenty-one, the angel shows John the bride, the Lamb's (Jesus) wife. The bride of Christ was previously referenced in verse two. The bride is seen in the new city, the bride and the new city are connected, but they are not the same.

Chapter twenty-one of the book of Revelation is the first time the bride (church) is mentioned since chapters two and three of John's prophecy. In chapters two and three, there are seven churches addressed by Jesus, representing the collective church. The church today, as a whole, shares the same qualities, both good and bad, of the collective seven. Of the seven addressed Churches, five were in trouble, requiring repentance, representing a failure ratio of seventy percent.

The church's final reference is seen in chapter four, verse one, which is symbolic of the rapture and will take place before the Tribulation commences. Following the church's rapture, chapters four and five reveal the events that will be taking place in heaven, and then, from chapter six, John describes the events taking place on the earth. Chapter six is the commencement of the Tribulation, starting with the opening of the seven seals, which also reveals the release of the Antichrist (6:2) The Antichrist is not revealed until after the church is removed (2 Thess. 2:1-12). Again, after chapters two and three of John's prophecy, the church is not mentioned at any point, outside of being in heaven, until chapter twenty (v. 9). In chapter twenty, the church (bride of Christ) is then seen as eternally established on the earth, where God will dwell (v. 3).

The new city of Jerusalem is the focus of the remainder of chapter twenty-one. The city comes down from heaven (vs. 2, 10) and is presented like a rare jewel (v. 11). In the previous section, I argued that the millennial temple will be suspended in the air; therefore, it will be above the earth, not being on the earth. In the new earth, the new city will be on the earth. While John's description lacks any details of the new heaven and the new earth, John is particular about the new city, providing facts and precise measurements. John is also careful to include the exact number of gates, angels, tribes (v. 12), foundations, names, apostles (v. 14), pearls (v. 21), months, and kinds of fruit (22:2), being twelve. Twelve of everything!

The city's precise measurements include 12,000 stadia (1380 miles), with length and height being equal (v. 16). The city walls were 144 cubits. The measurements are by both human standard and angel (v. 17). While most state the city is square, or a cube, it could also be a pyramid. There is an argument for the city being a pyramid based on the pyramids of Egypt. Evidence states that it would have been impossible for humans to have built the pyramids; therefore, aliens must have been involved. The biblical explanation is that those 'aliens' were, in fact, fallen angles. The fallen angel's explanation suggests that the fallen who followed Satan after his expulsion for heaven then re-created something of the same on the earth that what was in heaven, were the pyramids.

Therefore, it is argued, the new Jerusalem is a pyramid, not a square, or a cube. Adding to the description above, the city is also surrounded by a wall 216 feet thick (vv. 17-18) built of jasper. The city was pure gold (v. 18), and the streets were pure gold (v. 21); so pure is the gold that it will be transparent and decorated with every kind of jewel (v. 19).

The twelve tribes of Israel (v. 12) and the twelve apostles (v. 14) are inscribed on the city gates and walls, supporting that Israel and the church are separate entities, debunking replacement theology. The church has not replaced Israel, as reconstructionism suggests, and it never will do. The distinction between Israel and the church is maintained throughout the eighth day.

Similarly, as the church replaced the OT temple in the dispensation of grace; God will replace the millennial temple on the eight-day (v. 22). The glory of God will also replace the need for the sun and the moon (v. 23); there will be no night (v. 25). There will be no other kind of darkness as the 'unclean' will not be permitted entry or access (v. 27). Only those who fear and worship God, who walk in His ways (vv. 24, 26), will be found in the new Jerusalem (v. 26). Only those whose names are written in the Lamb's book of life will inherit the new and eternal city (v. 27, 21:8, 22:15).

After the angel showed John the bride of Christ (21:9) and the holy city of Jerusalem (v. 10), then the angel showed him the river of the water of life (22:1). The river of life is both literal and symbolic; its symbolic nature is purity and holiness, flowing from the throne of God and the Lamb (v. 2). The river of life will flow from the throne of God through the city of God. The river of life is not the same as the millennial river mentioned in Ezekiel (47:1, 12) and Zechariah (14:8). The eighth-day account is more like a stream than a river, flowing through the middle of the street (Rev. 22:2), which feeds the tree of life.

The tree of life is not found in the millennial kingdom but is only now reintroduced. The tree of life is the same mentioned in the book of Genesis (2.9). Having access to the tree of life was promised to the church of Ephesus (2:7) on the condition they repent and return to their first love (v 5).

The evidence against the false doctrine of 'once saved always saved' is seen in the conditional promise granted to those who conquer (alone) to eat from the tree, thereby entering paradise. Only those having an ear to hear will partake of the promise (2:7). Most, however, will not inherit, having only itching ears to hear what they want to hear, not what they need to hear (2 Tim. 4:3). Remember, both Jesus' and Paul's address and warning are to the church! John adds further support to that statement by later saying, "Blessed are those who wash their robes, so that they may have the right to the tree of life and that they may enter the city by the gates" (Rev. 22:14). This is backed up by Jesus in verses eighteen and nineteen, "I warn everyone who hears the words of the prophecy of this book: if anyone adds to them, God will add to him the plagues described in this book, and if anyone takes away from the words of the book of this prophecy, God will take away his share in the tree of life and in the holy city, which are described in this book." As mentioned, those dismissing and twisting the scriptures are subject to the book's plagues, the worst of which is Hell.

On either side of the river, the tree of life bears twelves types of fruits, twelve months of the year (22:2), and produces healing leaves. The word 'healing' in Greek is 'therapeian,' which is translated, 'health-giving.' The English translation from Greek is 'therapeutic.' The fruit and the leaves from the tree sustain eternal life, which is why none can access it before the eighth day. Following Adam and Eve's transgression, God appointed an angel with a flaming sword to guard the tree of life (Gen. 3:24). The tree will not be accessible until after the millennial dispensation and will only be accessible for the non-accursed (Rev. 22:3), which says, 'no curse' will have access to eternal healing and eternal life. Neither will anything cursed see the face of God, and neither will it bear His name (v. 4). Only those consecrated to God will take His name (2:17; 3:12; 7:3; 14:1). Those given access to paradise will be the opposite of those expelled (Gen. 3:22). The same inherited sin-nature of those expelled will be seen in those eternally rejected (Rev. 21:27, 22:15).

Until humanity is 'healed' (through repentance and forgiveness), through Christ alone, they cannot see the face of God and live (Ex. 33:20);

they will not be able to abide in the same place. God and the new city on the new earth are united, alongside its population.

In the new city, where God dwells, are the ruling and reigning saints, under the kingship of Jesus for all eternity (v. 5). As previously mentioned, God's people are not ruling and reigning on the earth here and now and will not be until Jesus returns (Rev. 20:6b). When Jesus sets up His millennium kingdom, the saints commence their rule, which lasts for one thousand years. After that, on the eighth day, the rule of Christ and the saints is eternal. Further evidence for this statement is seen in chapter five (v. 10) and chapter eleven (v. 15), debunking the idea that chapter one (v. 5) applies to the current dispensation. It does not!

As dealt with in the previous sections of this work, alongside presenting everything new, chapters twenty-one and twenty-two debunk several false doctrines:

- Preterist theology (historic view over futuristic view)
- Replacement theology (the church has replaced Israel)
- Universalism (everyone ends up in the same place, eventually)
- Calvinism (once saved, always saved)
- Liberalism (cultural norms over scriptural authority)
- Seven Mountains (Kingdom Now) Reconstructionism

CHAPTER TWENTY-TWO

(vv. 6-21)
I Am Coming Soon

"These words are trustworthy and true" (Rev. 21:5, 22:6). Twice in the closing chapters of the book of Revelation, Jesus says, "These words are trustworthy and true," which is the same as when He said, "I am telling you the truth" (Jn. 8:45-46), albeit the religious leaders at the time did not believe Him. The religious leaders did not believe the words of Jesus when He was on the earth the first time, and they still do not believe the words of Jesus regarding His second coming (2 Pet. 3:3, Jude 1:18). Specifically, they do not believe that the book of Revelation is relevant, or at least urgent for the church, to be reading and heeding in preparation for the things that must soon take place (Rev. 1:1, 22:6).

Standing in good company with Jesus is Paul, who also experienced the same treatment of rejection and resistance, this time, from those calling themselves Christians. In the same way, the words of Jesus were rejected, Paul's were also, and like Jesus, he too was considered an enemy for speaking the truth (Gal. 4:16). The same is seen when reading the seven letters to the churches in chapters two and three of John's prophecy, where only two of seven were in good standing, Smyrna and Philadelphia.

Both Smyrna and Philadelphia's churches were attacked by the religious, who called themselves Jews (Rev. 2:9, 3:9). These two faithful churches were poor (2:9) and weak (3:7), yet they worshipped God without compromise or corruption. The same is true today; only a remnant is remaining faithful and is faithfully telling the truth, which comes at a high cost. Most would instead fulfil scripture by having their ears tickled and be comforted with a lie (2 Tim. 4:3).

The reason Jesus had to reinforce the message with the words, "These words are trustworthy and true" is because so many have difficulty hearing and believing His words, which is why, while on the earth, He repeatedly said after teaching, "He who has ears to hear" (Matt. 11:15, Mk. 4:9, Lu 8:8, 14:35). Similarly, concluding the seven letters, Jesus said seven times, once to each church, "He who has an ear let him hear what the Spirit is saying to the churches" (Rev. 2-3). The statement is to all the churches, not the single church being addressed at the time, indicating it was a message for all time to every church through the ages.

Further evidence of the above statement is where Jesus both opens and closes the book of Revelation with this address to the churches (Rev. 2-3, 22:16). Regarding Jesus' first proclamation, "These words are trustworthy and true" (21:5), He stated everything would be made new; in fact, it is already done! This is reinforced by announcing He is the Omega (1:8, 21:6, 22:13), the beginning and the end (1:4, 8, 17, 2:8, 21:6, 22:13), emphasising He is not restricted in any way, including time itself. Jesus is just as much at the beginning of time as He is at the end of time. Humanity is bound by time, But God is not, which is to say, what will happen already has happened.

Again, the proclamation is to the church, promising, any who thirst for God (21:6) and conquer this world (21:7), are already secure in the things to come; the things that must soon take place (1:1, 22:6). The second occasion Jesus made the proclamation relates to His second coming (22:6). As sure as His first arrival came to pass, the second will also, in fact, it is already as good as done (21:6).

Prophecies regarding Jesus' first arrival number around three hundred and fifty, and one hundred percent of them were fulfilled with literal, historic, and pinpoint accuracy. Also prophecies concerning Jesus' second coming number around three hundred and fifty. Suppose the first group came to pass, being one hundred percent fulfilled, literally, historically, and to pinpoint accuracy. What do you think the chances of the second group being fulfilled in the same way will be? One hundred percent! The mathematical odds for just fourteen of three hundred and fifty prophecies from the first group to be fulfiled is so great that you would have more chance of winning the gold lotto fourteen times back-to-back. Again, not just fourteen prophecies were fulfilled, but all of them.

The fulfilment of the first group of prophecies alone should be enough to convince you that the words of Jesus are trustworthy and true. Yet still, Jesus adds further weight with the assurance of who He is (22:16) and what He is about to do, "Behold, I am coming soon!" (cf. 1:7; 22:12, 20). The same announcement was made to the seven churches. The promise to the members of the church of Thyatira, providing they repent (conquer) and remain (endure), until the end (2:26), was that they would receive the morning star (2:28).

Jesus is the morning star (22:16); therefore, the promise relates to receiving Jesus. Contrary to false teaching, suggesting that when you come to Jesus, you get health, wealth, and happiness; when you come to Jesus, you get Jesus, and that is enough. Jesus is the testimony and the prophecy of the book (19:10b).

Those failing to respond to the prophecy through repentance and then remain until the end will not inherit the morning star. The promise and the warnings are clear, as seen in so many parables relating to the same.

In sum, the warning serves the believer, affirming we are to be looking for and living for the return of Jesus. From the opening chapter of the book of Revelation to the closing chapter, Jesus makes the same announcement; that there is a blessing for the one who reads, hears, and keeps the prophecy (1:3), "Blessed is the one who keeps these words" (22:7). To keep the prophecy or 'these words' is to keep Jesus' commandments, thereby keep (hold on to) Jesus (Rev. 12:17, 14:12, cf. Lu. 6:46).

The announcement and vision of Christ's return and the re-establishment of the new heaven and the new earth were so incredible, so overwhelming that John fell down and worshipped the accompanying angel, resulting in a rebuke (Rev. 22:8). It is the second time an angel commanded John not to worship him (19:10).

Today, angel worship and the worship of dead saints are practiced by the Catholics and some Charismatics, particularly members of the New Apostolic Reformation (NAR). For example, some within The NAR are known for practicing 'angel card readings,' which is no different from reading tarot cards. Others welcome 'healing angels,' while seeking, accepting, and celebrating falling angel feathers, gold dust, and jewels, apparently deposited by angels, during church services. Some practice 'grave soaking,' claiming (receiving) the mantel (anointing) of a dead saint for themselves. A well-known faith-healer did this, claiming Kathryn Kuhlman's anointing, forbidden by God in scripture (Lev. 19:31, 20;6, 27, Deut. 18:9-12, 2 Kgs. 21:6, 2 Chron. 33:6, Isa. 8:19); these occultic practices are from the devil.

Another prominent American NAR church and Bible college have built a reputation on such practices, placing a priority on angels. Angels are at the forefront of their ministry, evident by angel card readings and angelic prophecy paintings, which is a common occurrence. The Charismatics performing such things are nothing less than 'Christian' clairvoyants practicing necromancy (cf. 1 Sam. 28). The danger in seeking angels is that the angel often engaged with is a fallen angel, or demon, masquerading as an angel of light. 'Ministers' promoting such practices are as fallen as the demons empowering them (2 Cor. 11:13-15).

Needless to say, seeking angels is a dangerous practice, and angel worship is deadly. The very thing Satan desires most is to be worshipped (Isa. 14:15, Matt. 4:1-11), which is why the angel rebuked John for worshipping him. God's angels always direct worship back to God and will never receive it for themselves, unlike many 'ministers' today. The closer we get to the return of Jesus, the more we will see these devilish deeds and doctrines (1 Tim 4:1), which have crept into the church, mostly unnoticed. This reality is undoubtedly why John was instructed to keep the book of Revelation open, for the time is near (Rev. 22:10).

When Daniel received a similar vision to that of John, he was told to "Seal (the book) until the time of the end" (Dan. 8:26, 12:4, 9). Sadly today, most confessing Christians know very little about the book of Revelation, or the Bible for that matter, hence they forfeit the blessing (Rev. 1:3) and also risk not being ready for the return of Christ. Few people today open the book up, and even fewer keep it open, despite the book's command. This command will undoubtedly be highlighted for many, especially preterists, on the day of judgement, who deceived their followers into believing the book of Revelation is historical and not futuristic, therefore not relevant.

The primary danger of preterist teaching is that it takes away the urgency and relevance of the message, stating that it is not for us today, and instead, was for those being addressed, being the seven churches (Ephesus, Smyrna, Pergamum, Thyatira, Sardis, Philadelphia, and Laodicea). Jesus foreknew this would happen, therefore, warned - that any who leads others astray, who adds and takes away from this prophecy, will severely pay, in the same way as those rejecting Jesus by remaining in their sin (22:11).

The prophecy's point and purpose are to urgently warn and keep those who have ears to hear away from sin; however, many will not read or take heed of the warning (1:3, 22:7). Failing to read and heed, those without ears to hear, will continue to do evil, and they will continue to be filthy, thereby they will remain cursed (22:11) and will forever be (22:15). On the other hand, the one who does read and heed to the prophecy, will do right and remain holy (22:11b).

Again, the two churches without charge (Smyrna and Philadelphia) exemplify the remnant 'doing right' where 'the holy still be holy.' As for the rest, those failing to have ears to hear, corresponding with repentance, and judgement will soon and swiftly fall.

The closing verses of the passage and the book comes with a repeat reminder; confirmation or condemnation (22:11) of those either remaining in Christ or remaining in sin, with a sense of urgency, "I am coming soon" (22:12). Jesus is coming soon, and He will bring His recompense with Him, to repay each one for what they have done." Three times, Jesus reminds the reader that He is coming soon (22:6, 12, 20), and when He does, He will repay. The same warning was given to the church of Thyatira where Jesus said, "All the churches will know that I am the one that searches the mind and heart, and I will give to each according to your works" (2:23).

Despite the false teachings from the 'grace camp' maintaining Jesus will never judge the church, His own words say differently. Paul also confirms the words of Jesus in his letter to the church of Corinth (2 Cor. 5:10), going on to say, "Therefore, knowing the fear of the Lord, we persuade others" (5:11). It is followed up with, "We appeal to you not to receive the grace of God in vain" (6:1). Paul's messages, like Jesus', also gives a sense of urgency, "Behold, now is the favourable time; behold now is the day of salvation" (6:2).

Like Jesus, Paul places urgency on the gospel, with the requirement to respond while you still can. Contrary to the false teaching stating, 'while there is breath, there is still hope,' which implies, as long as you are alive, you can call on the name of Jesus, Paul says otherwise. In his letter to the Romans, Paul made it clear where chapter one makes the point - God will lift His hand entirely if you continue in sin.

The promise of eternal life is reserved for those who respond, while they still can, by washing their robes, they (only) have access to the New Jerusalem and its tree of life (Rev. 22:14, cf. v. 19). Those inheriting are the 'blessed.' Again, there are seven references to the blessed in the book of Revelation, known as the beatitudes of Revelation (1:3; 14:13; 16:15; 19:9; 20:6; 22:7, 14).

On the other hand, the 'dogs' (22:15, cf. Phil. 3:2) who fail to respond are damned already (Rev. 13:8, 17:8, 20:15) and will be shut out of the kingdom forever. Amongst them are those who practice magic. Interestingly, sorcerers are referenced three times throughout the book of Revelation (9:21; 18:23; 21:8), indicating an increase of satanic activity in the church in the last days.

As pointed out earlier, there are church leaders and members of the NAR who are engaged in the occult, directly, and indirectly; therefore they are subsequently in danger of qualifying as spiritual 'dogs.' Dogs are eternally shut out of the kingdom – no dogs allowed! Those who have washed their robes in the blood of Jesus may have at some time been guilty of sorcery, but they are not now. So, they are no longer guilty of this and other sins preventing them from accessing paradise; they are now clean, having their names written in the book of life (cf. 21:27).

In conclusion, despite so many today failing to read and keep the book of Revelation open, thereby failing to obey its commandments, the entire prophecy and the warning is for the church (2:7, 11, 29, 3:6, 13, 22, 22:16). The book commences by addressing the churches and closes by readdressing the church. The church is to hear and take heed of the invitation, and the warning contained.

The church also has a responsibility to share this prophecy with others (22:17). In the same way, Jesus invited the worst of the churches - Laodicea, to 'buy from Him' (3:18). Now the church is to proclaim and extend that same message to the lukewarm, and the world, 'Come, buy without price' (22:17). But the condition to come is for those who do come to Christ must first repent (overcome) and then remain (endure) unto the end.

Come, Lord Jesus! (22:20).

www.ingramcontent.com/pod-product-compliance
Lightning Source LLC
Chambersburg PA
CBHW071303110426
42743CB00042B/1155